The Attack

story
LOÏC DAUVILLIER

art & color
GLEN CHAPRON

adapted from the novel by
YASMINA KHADRA

FIREFLY BOOKS

A FIREFLY BOOK

Published by Firefly Books Ltd. 2016

Adapted from the novel *L'attentat* © 2005 Editions Julliard, Paris
Original French publication copyright © 2012 Glénat
This translation copyright © 2016 Firefly Books

First printing

Publisher Cataloging-in-Publication Data (U.S.)

Names: Dauvillier, Loïc, 1971- , author | Chapron, Glen, 1982-, illustrator | Hahnenberger, Ivanka, translator.
Title: Attack / Loïc Dauvillier ; illustrator, Glen Chapron.
Description: Richmond Hill, Ontario, Canada : Firefly Books, 2016. | Previously published by Glenat Publishing, Grenoble, France, 2005 as "L'attentat". | Summary: "A translation of Yasmina Khadra's novel "L'attentat," adapted into a graphic novel by Loïc Dauvillier and illustrated by Glen Chapron. It tells the story of Amin Jaafari, an Arab-Israeli surgeon in Tel Aviv living with his wife. After a deadly attack in the city, Israeli police inform Amin that the suicide bomber was his wife. Amin is left searching for answers and must come to terms with the warning signs that he had not recognized" — Provided by publisher.
Identifiers: ISBN 978-1-77085-761-2 (hardcover)
Subjects: LCSH: Suicide bombers – Comic books, strips, etc. | Terrorism – Comic books, strips, etc. | Graphic novels.
Classification: LCC PN6790.D388Att | DDC 741.5944 – dc23

Library and Archives Canada Cataloguing in Publication

Dauvillier, Loïc, 1971-
[Attentat. English]
    Attack / Loïc Dauvillier ; adapted from Yasmina Khadra ; illustrator, Glen Chapron.
Translation of Yasmina Khadra's novel, L'Attentat, adapted into a graphic novel.
Translator: Ivanka Hahnenberger.
ISBN 978-1-77085-761-2 (hardback)
    1. Graphic novels. I. Hahnenberger, Ivanka, translator II. Chapron, Glen, 1982-, illustrator III. Title.
IV. Title: Attentat. English
PN6747.D37A8813 2016   741.5'944   C2016-900893-2

Published in the United States by
Firefly Books (U.S.) Inc.
P.O. Box 1338, Ellicott Station
Buffalo, New York 14205

Published in Canada by
Firefly Books Ltd.
50 Staples Avenue, Unit 1
Richmond Hill, Ontario L4B 0A7

Printed in China

This book is for Monia.

Thanks to those who were by my side and helped me through this time full of shadows:
My parents, Muriel and Olivier, Gaël, Delphine and Christophe, Hellen and Bernard, Marie-Luz and Pascal, my great friend Alain, Geneviève and Arnaud, Sylvie and Marc, Valérie, Baptiste, Virginie, Jérôme, Thibault, Amandine, Benoît, Julien, Greg, Servane, Frédérique, Nancy, Abdelhak, Sandrine and Myriam, Sophie and Anne-Marie, the Charrette family, the 6 pieds family, my Picards friends, the Lombard team and, very obviously, Glen...
... And especially, especially, especially, thanks to my extraordinary big girl, Laurene ... And her mother, Céline.
        Loïc

A big thank you to my team of colorists:
Nikol, Vincent, Mathieu, Arnaud, Sarah, Yoko, Clément, Yann, Ellen and Axel.
Thanks also to Maud and Mathieu for having supported me at the studio.
And thanks to Julia.
        Glen

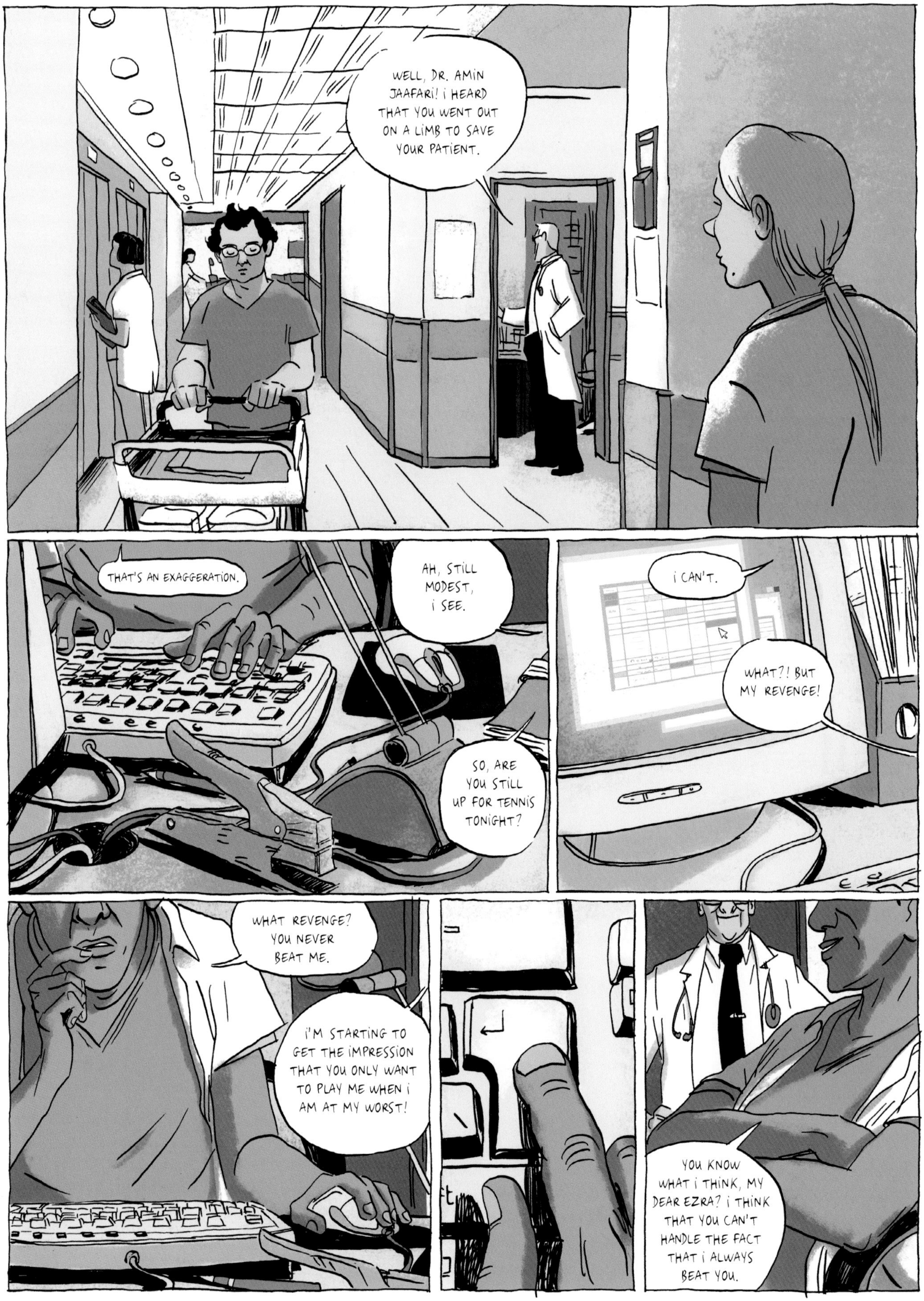
WELL, DR. AMIN JAAFARI! I HEARD THAT YOU WENT OUT ON A LIMB TO SAVE YOUR PATIENT.
THAT'S AN EXAGGERATION.
AH, STILL MODEST, I SEE.
SO, ARE YOU STILL UP FOR TENNIS TONIGHT?
I CAN'T.
WHAT?! BUT MY REVENGE!
WHAT REVENGE? YOU NEVER BEAT ME.
I'M STARTING TO GET THE IMPRESSION THAT YOU ONLY WANT TO PLAY ME WHEN I AM AT MY WORST!
YOU KNOW WHAT I THINK, MY DEAR EZRA? I THINK THAT YOU CAN'T HANDLE THE FACT THAT I ALWAYS BEAT YOU.

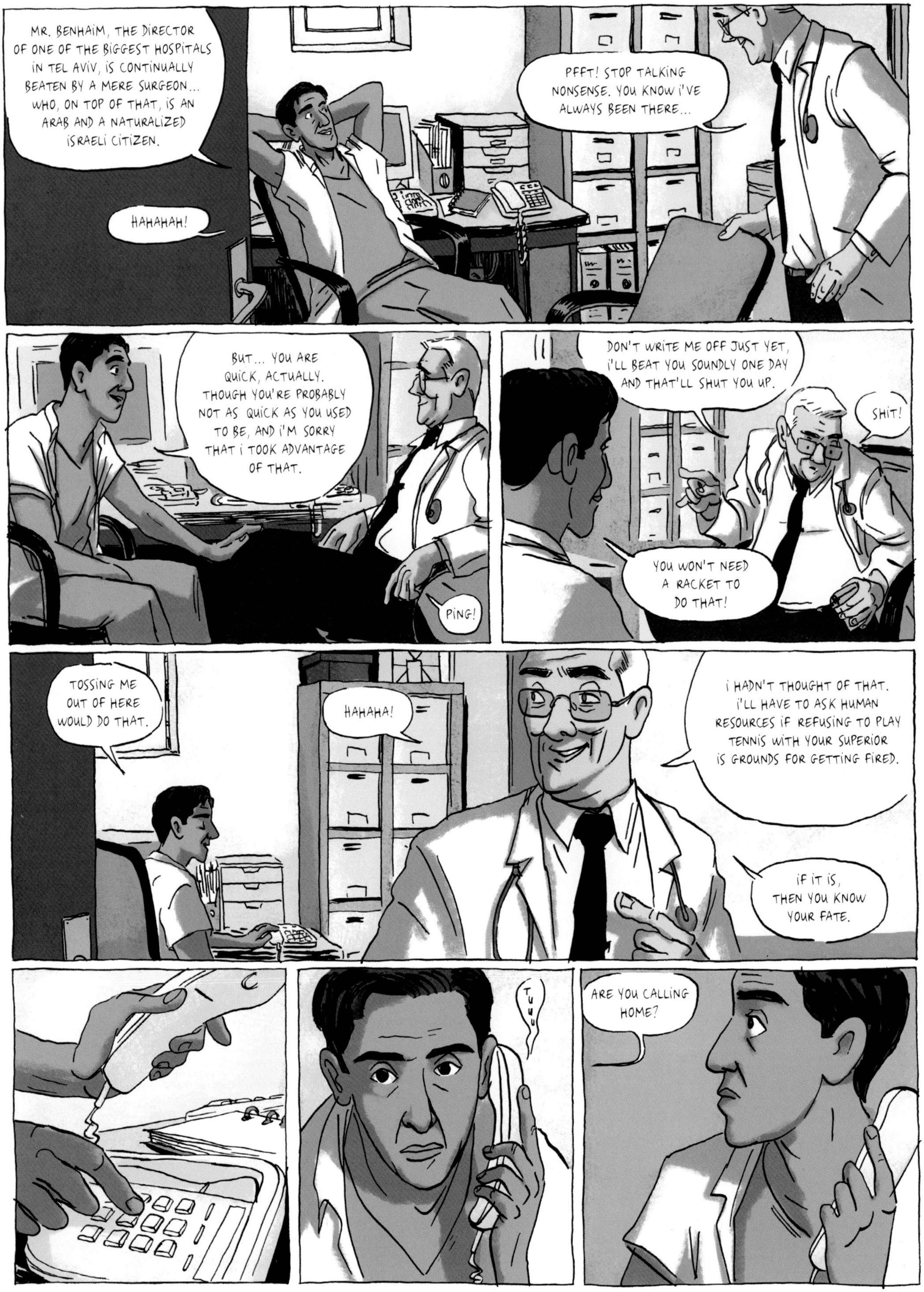
MR. BENHAIM, THE DIRECTOR OF ONE OF THE BIGGEST HOSPITALS IN TEL AVIV, IS CONTINUALLY BEATEN BY A MERE SURGEON... WHO, ON TOP OF THAT, IS AN ARAB AND A NATURALIZED ISRAELI CITIZEN.
HAHAHAH!
PFFT! STOP TALKING NONSENSE. YOU KNOW I'VE ALWAYS BEEN THERE...
BUT... YOU ARE QUICK, ACTUALLY. THOUGH YOU'RE PROBABLY NOT AS QUICK AS YOU USED TO BE, AND I'M SORRY THAT I TOOK ADVANTAGE OF THAT.
PING!
DON'T WRITE ME OFF JUST YET, I'LL BEAT YOU SOUNDLY ONE DAY AND THAT'LL SHUT YOU UP.
SHIT!
YOU WON'T NEED A RACKET TO DO THAT!
TOSSING ME OUT OF HERE WOULD DO THAT.
HAHAHA!
I HADN'T THOUGHT OF THAT. I'LL HAVE TO ASK HUMAN RESOURCES IF REFUSING TO PLAY TENNIS WITH YOUR SUPERIOR IS GROUNDS FOR GETTING FIRED.
IF IT IS, THEN YOU KNOW YOUR FATE.
TUUU
ARE YOU CALLING HOME?

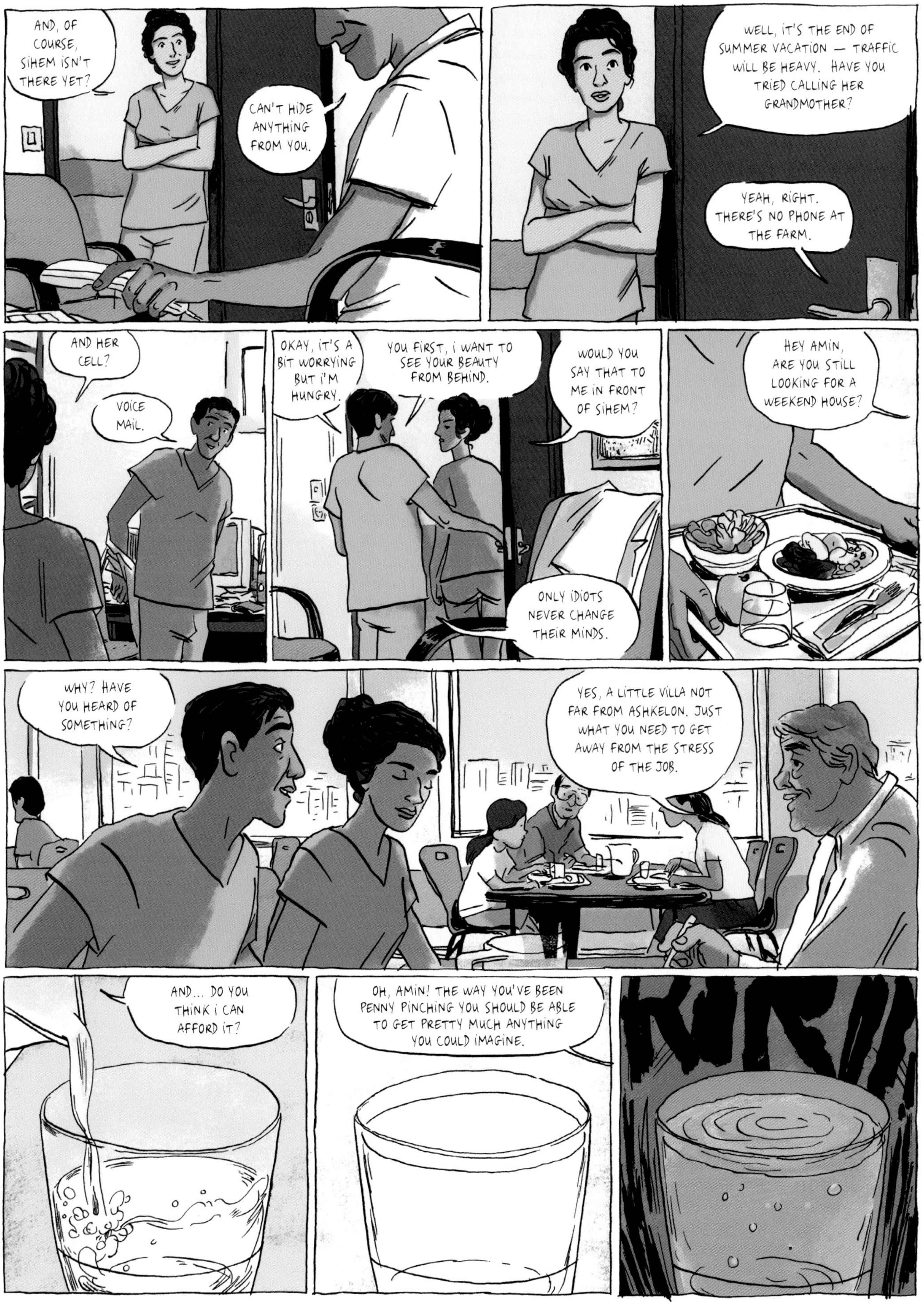
AND, OF COURSE, SIHEM ISN'T THERE YET?
CAN'T HIDE ANYTHING FROM YOU.
WELL, IT'S THE END OF SUMMER VACATION — TRAFFIC WILL BE HEAVY. HAVE YOU TRIED CALLING HER GRANDMOTHER?
YEAH, RIGHT. THERE'S NO PHONE AT THE FARM.
AND HER CELL?
VOICE MAIL.
OKAY, IT'S A BIT WORRYING BUT I'M HUNGRY.
YOU FIRST, I WANT TO SEE YOUR BEAUTY FROM BEHIND.
WOULD YOU SAY THAT TO ME IN FRONT OF SIHEM?
ONLY IDIOTS NEVER CHANGE THEIR MINDS.
HEY AMIN, ARE YOU STILL LOOKING FOR A WEEKEND HOUSE?
WHY? HAVE YOU HEARD OF SOMETHING?
YES, A LITTLE VILLA NOT FAR FROM ASHKELON. JUST WHAT YOU NEED TO GET AWAY FROM THE STRESS OF THE JOB.
AND... DO YOU THINK I CAN AFFORD IT?
OH, AMIN! THE WAY YOU'VE BEEN PENNY PINCHING YOU SHOULD BE ABLE TO GET PRETTY MUCH ANYTHING YOU COULD IMAGINE.

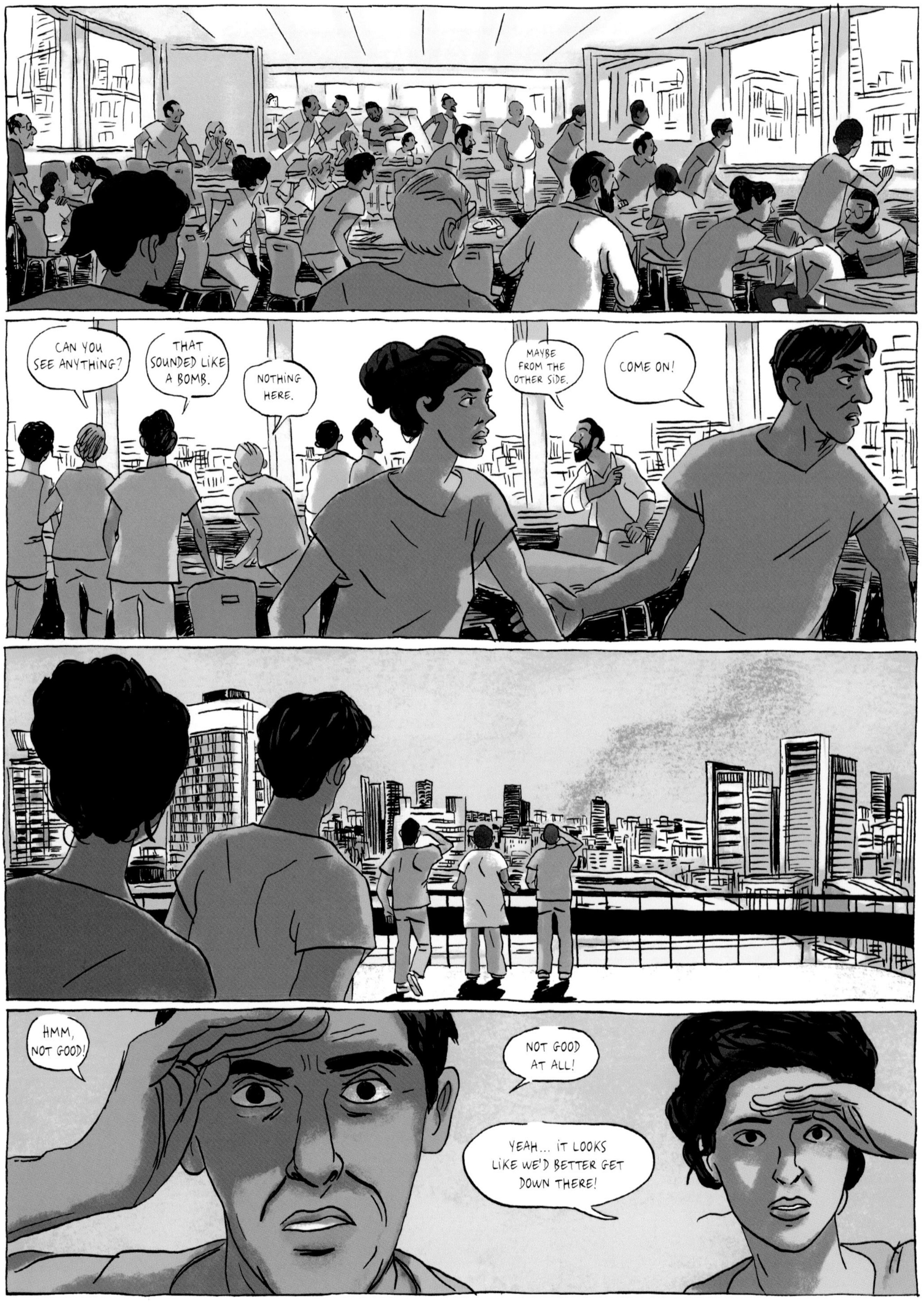
CAN YOU SEE ANYTHING?
THAT SOUNDED LIKE A BOMB.
NOTHING HERE.
MAYBE FROM THE OTHER SIDE.
COME ON!
HMM, NOT GOOD!
NOT GOOD AT ALL!
YEAH... IT LOOKS LIKE WE'D BETTER GET DOWN THERE!

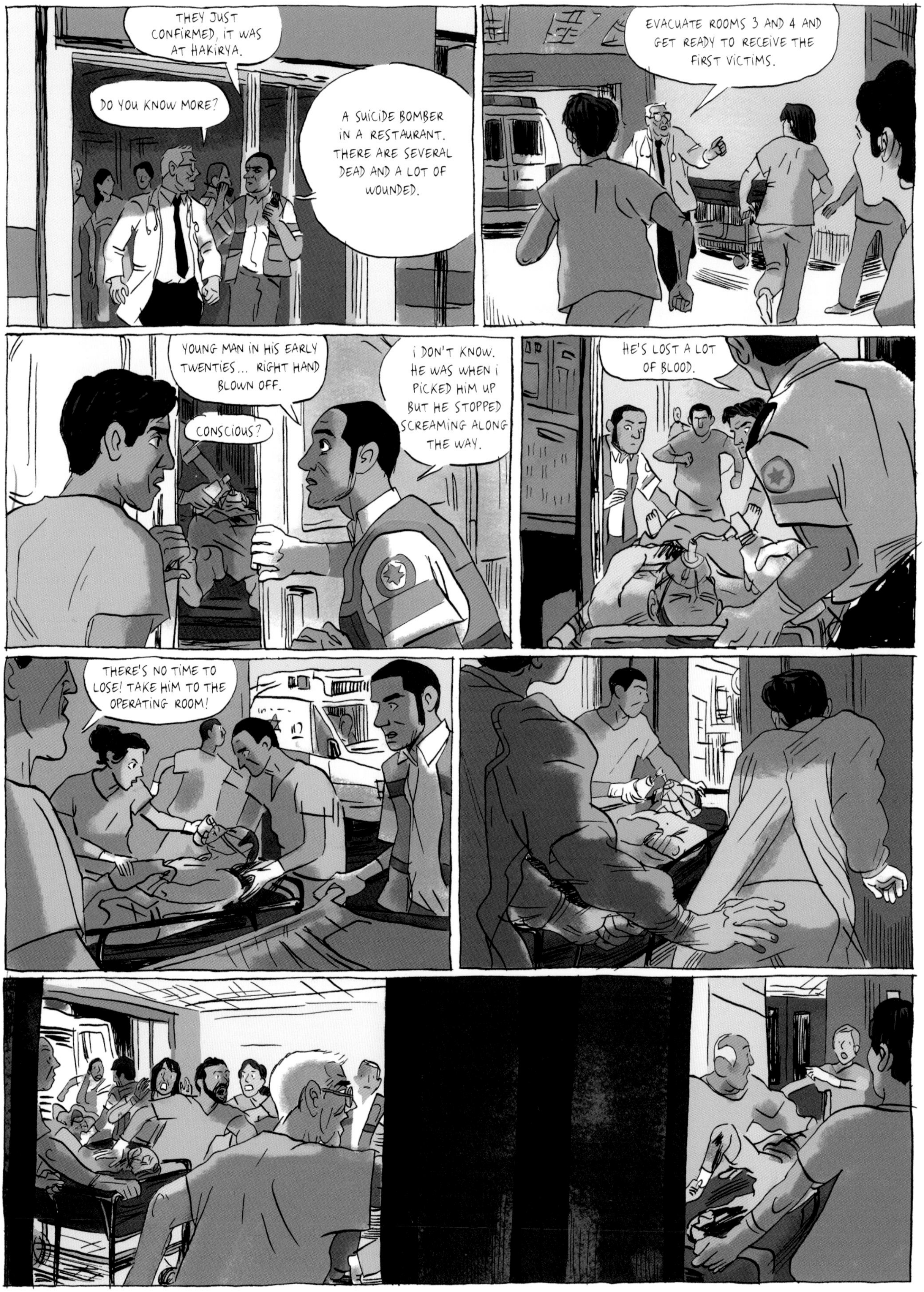

THEY JUST CONFIRMED, IT WAS AT HAKIRYA.
DO YOU KNOW MORE?
A SUICIDE BOMBER IN A RESTAURANT. THERE ARE SEVERAL DEAD AND A LOT OF WOUNDED.
EVACUATE ROOMS 3 AND 4 AND GET READY TO RECEIVE THE FIRST VICTIMS.
YOUNG MAN IN HIS EARLY TWENTIES... RIGHT HAND BLOWN OFF.
CONSCIOUS?
I DON'T KNOW. HE WAS WHEN I PICKED HIM UP BUT HE STOPPED SCREAMING ALONG THE WAY.
HE'S LOST A LOT OF BLOOD.
THERE'S NO TIME TO LOSE! TAKE HIM TO THE OPERATING ROOM!

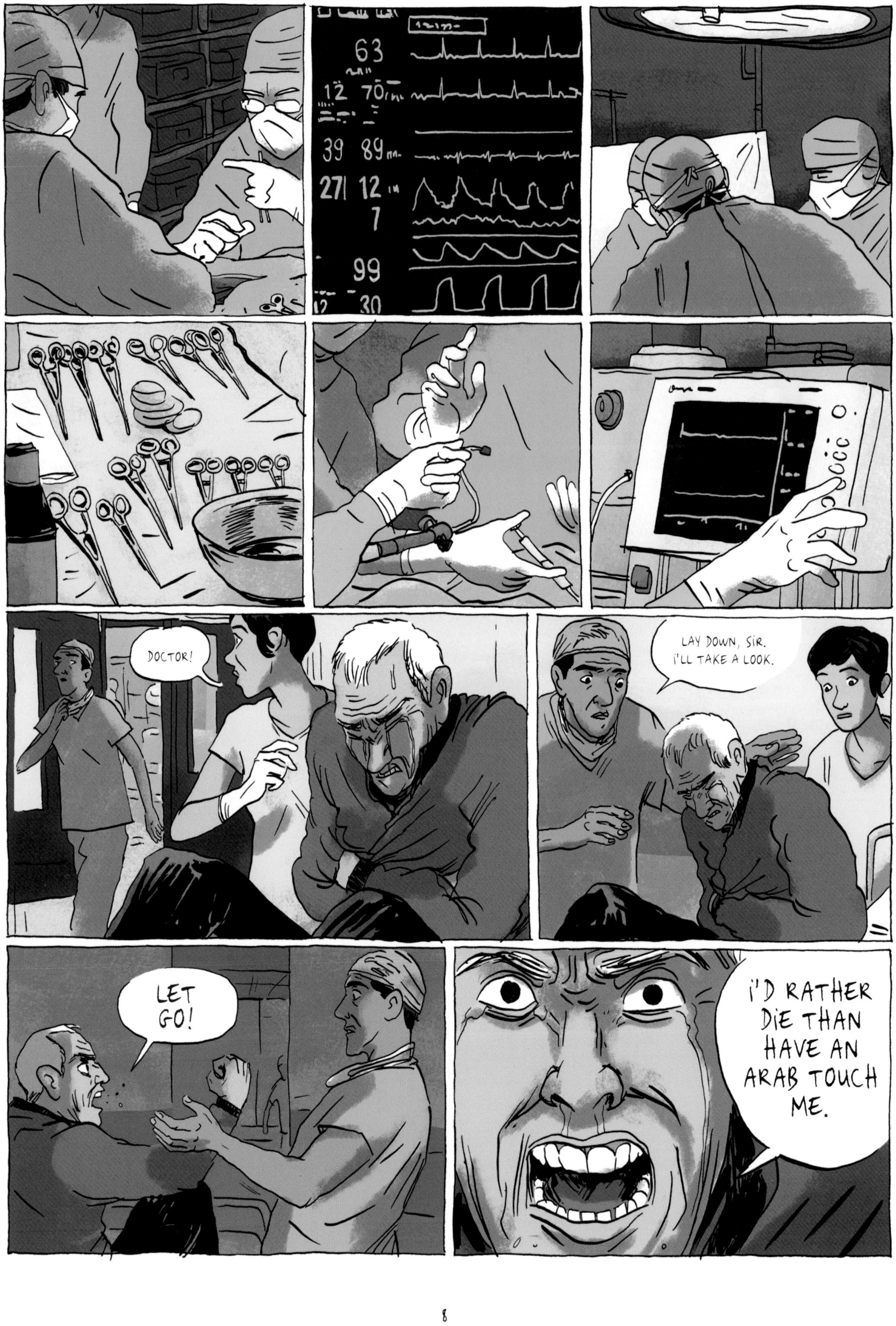
63
12 70
39 89
271 12
7
99
30
DOCTOR!
LAY DOWN, SIR. I'LL TAKE A LOOK.
LET GO!
I'D RATHER DIE THAN HAVE AN ARAB TOUCH ME.

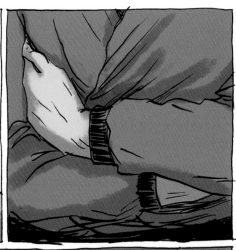

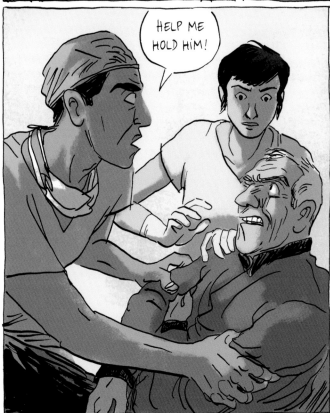

HELP ME
HOLD HIM!

?!?

TAKE HIM TO
THE OPERATING ROOM!
HE TAKES PRIORITY OVER
THE OTHERS. PREP HIM, AND
I'LL BE RIGHT THERE.

I DON'T KNOW HOW MANY
I OPERATED ON.

EVERY TIME I FINISHED ONE, I SAW
ANOTHER GURNEY ARRIVE.

I HAD NO IDEA HOW I WAS
STILL STANDING.

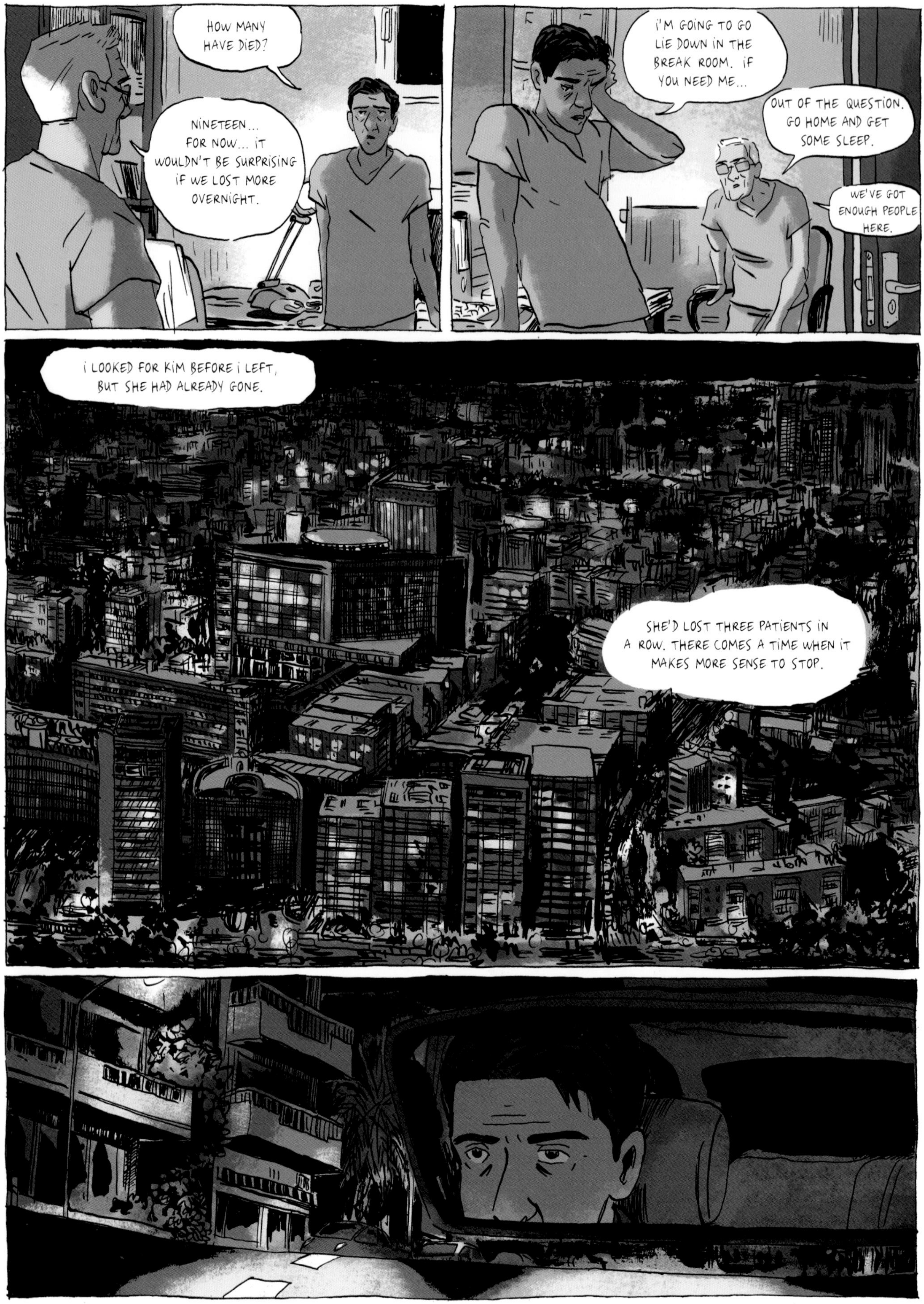
HOW MANY HAVE DIED?
NINETEEN... FOR NOW... IT WOULDN'T BE SURPRISING IF WE LOST MORE OVERNIGHT.
I'M GOING TO GO LIE DOWN IN THE BREAK ROOM. IF YOU NEED ME...
OUT OF THE QUESTION. GO HOME AND GET SOME SLEEP.
WE'VE GOT ENOUGH PEOPLE HERE.
I LOOKED FOR KIM BEFORE I LEFT, BUT SHE HAD ALREADY GONE.
SHE'D LOST THREE PATIENTS IN A ROW. THERE COMES A TIME WHEN IT MAKES MORE SENSE TO STOP.

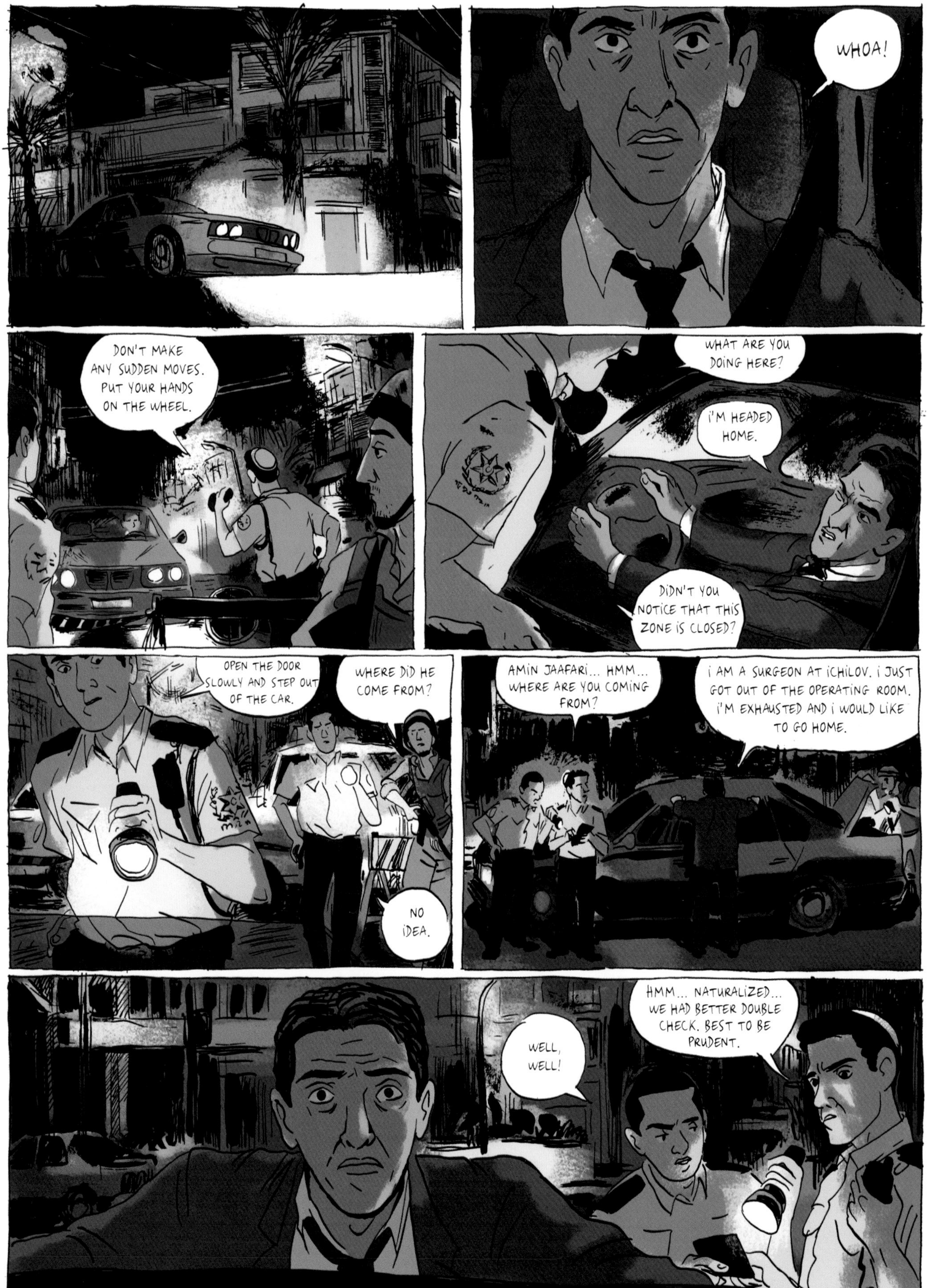
WHOA!
DON'T MAKE ANY SUDDEN MOVES. PUT YOUR HANDS ON THE WHEEL.
WHAT ARE YOU DOING HERE?
I'M HEADED HOME.
DIDN'T YOU NOTICE THAT THIS ZONE IS CLOSED?
OPEN THE DOOR SLOWLY AND STEP OUT OF THE CAR.
WHERE DID HE COME FROM?
NO IDEA.
AMIN JAAFARI... HMM... WHERE ARE YOU COMING FROM?
I AM A SURGEON AT ICHILOV. I JUST GOT OUT OF THE OPERATING ROOM. I'M EXHAUSTED AND I WOULD LIKE TO GO HOME.
WELL, WELL!
HMM... NATURALIZED... WE HAD BETTER DOUBLE CHECK. BEST TO BE PRUDENT.

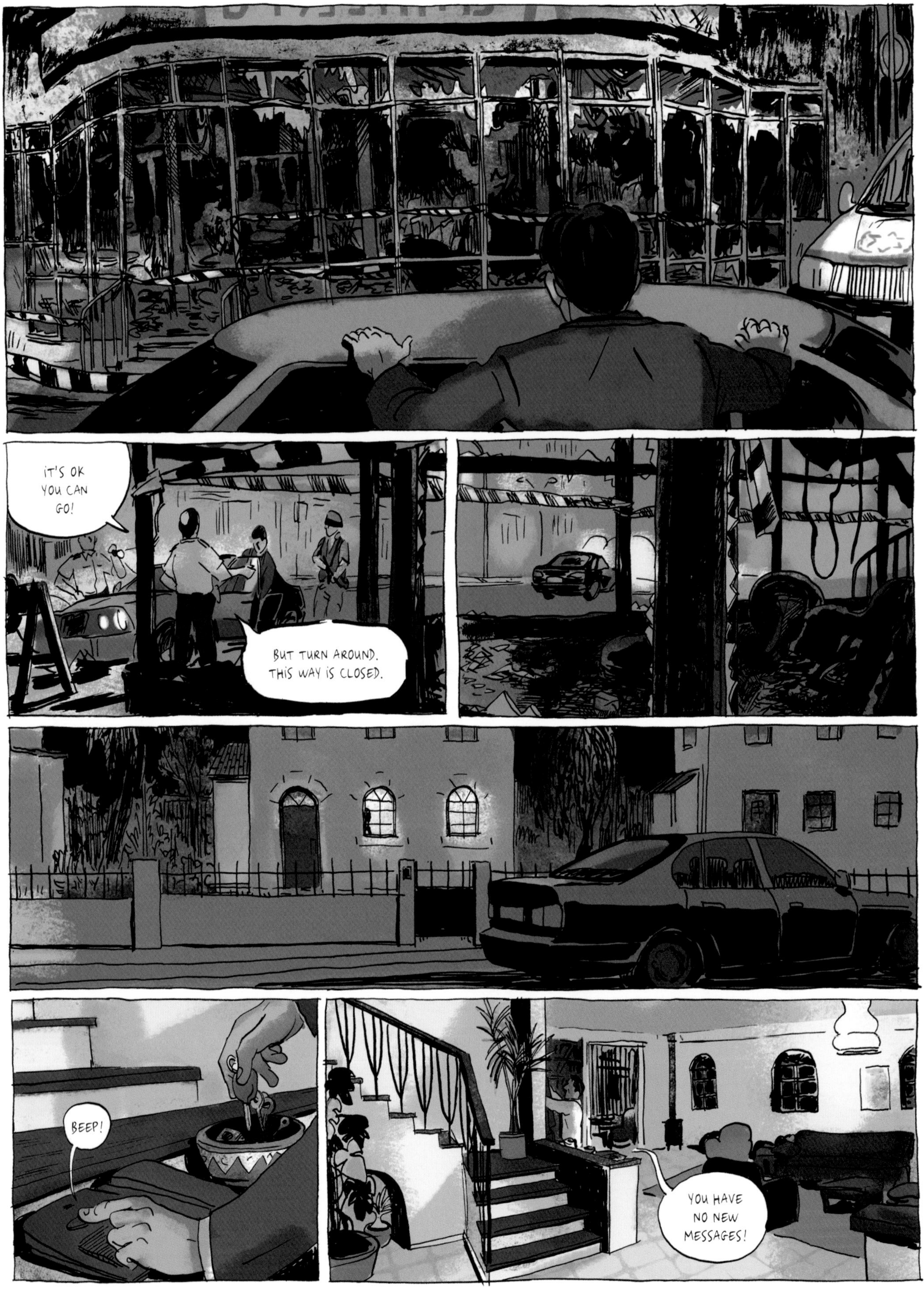
IT'S OK YOU CAN GO!
BUT TURN AROUND. THIS WAY IS CLOSED.
BEEP!
YOU HAVE NO NEW MESSAGES!

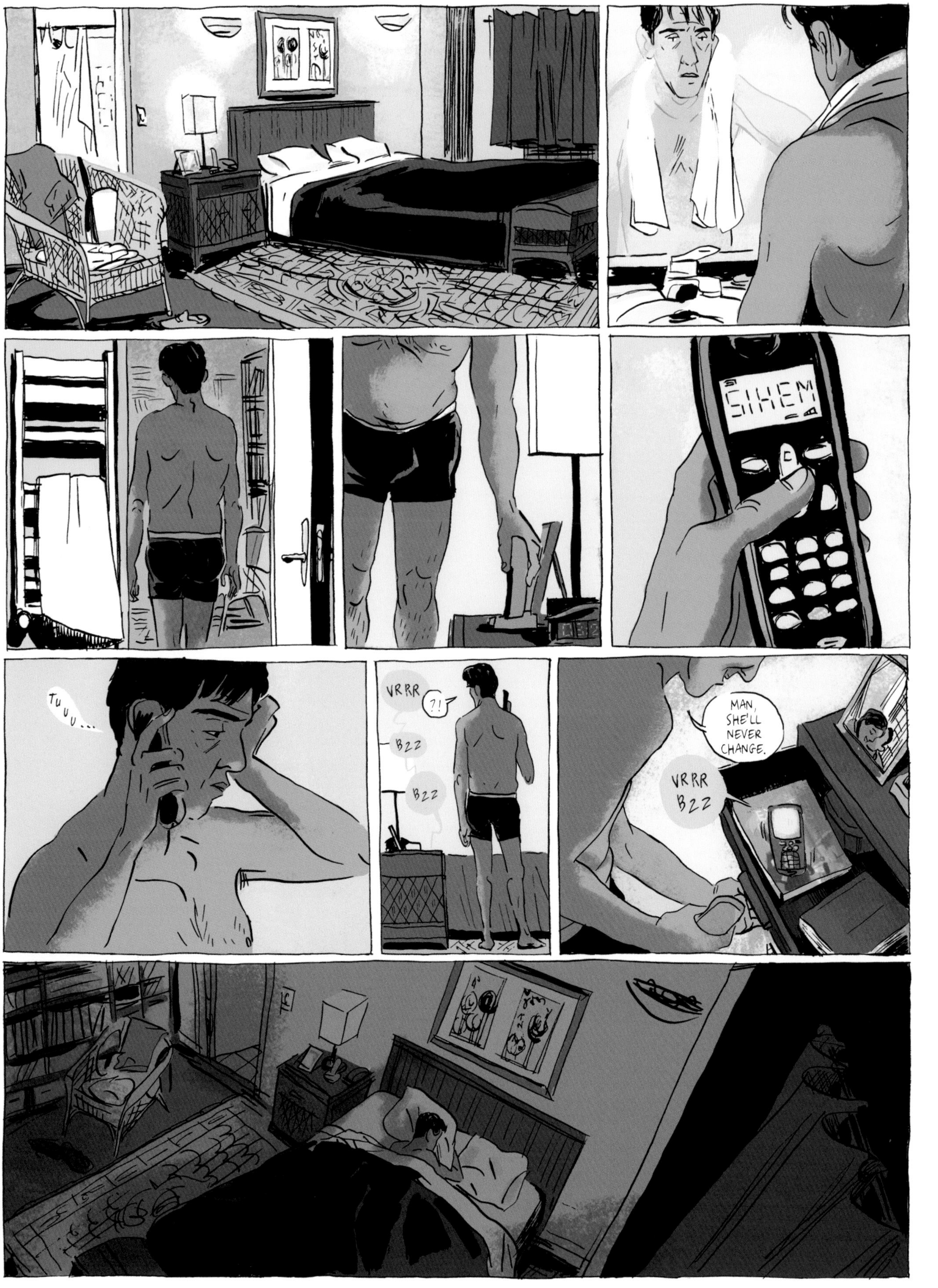
SIHEM
TUUU...
VRRR
?!
BZZ
BZZ
MAN, SHE'LL NEVER CHANGE.
VRRR BZZ

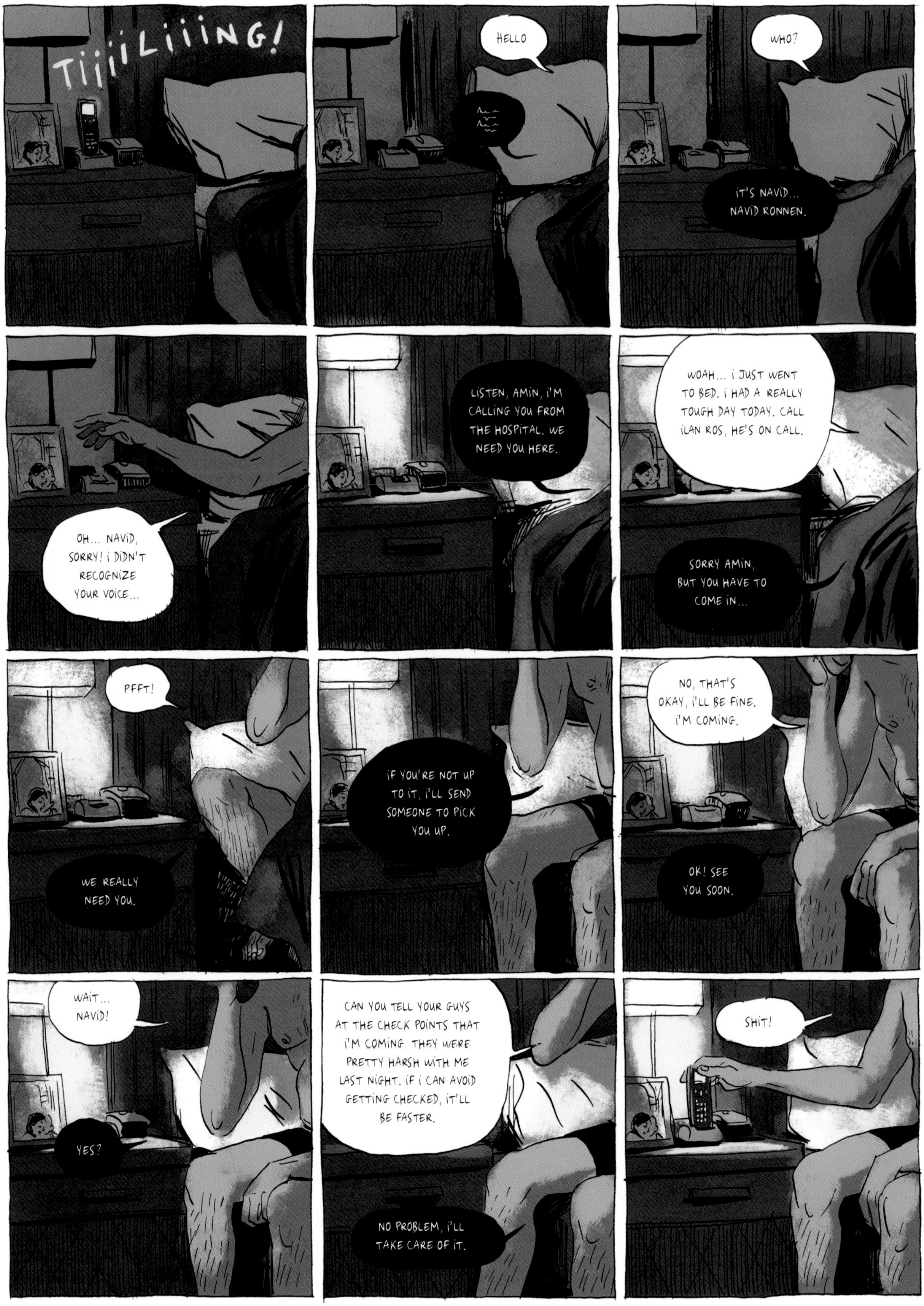
TiiiiLiiiNG!
HELLO
WHO?
iT'S NAViD... NAViD RONNEN.
OH... NAViD, SORRY! i DiDN'T RECOGNiZE YOUR VOiCE...
LiSTEN, AMiN, i'M CALLiNG YOU FROM THE HOSPiTAL. WE NEED YOU HERE.
WOAH... i JUST WENT TO BED. i HAD A REALLY TOUGH DAY TODAY. CALL iLAN ROS, HE'S ON CALL.
SORRY AMiN, BUT YOU HAVE TO COME iN...
PFFT!
WE REALLY NEED YOU.
iF YOU'RE NOT UP TO iT, i'LL SEND SOMEONE TO PiCK YOU UP.
NO, THAT'S OKAY, i'LL BE FiNE. i'M COMiNG.
OK! SEE YOU SOON.
WAiT... NAViD!
YES?
CAN YOU TELL YOUR GUYS AT THE CHECK POINTS THAT i'M COMiNG. THEY WERE PRETTY HARSH WITH ME LAST NiGHT. iF i CAN AVOiD GETTiNG CHECKED, iT'LL BE FASTER.
NO PROBLEM, i'LL TAKE CARE OF iT.
SHiT!

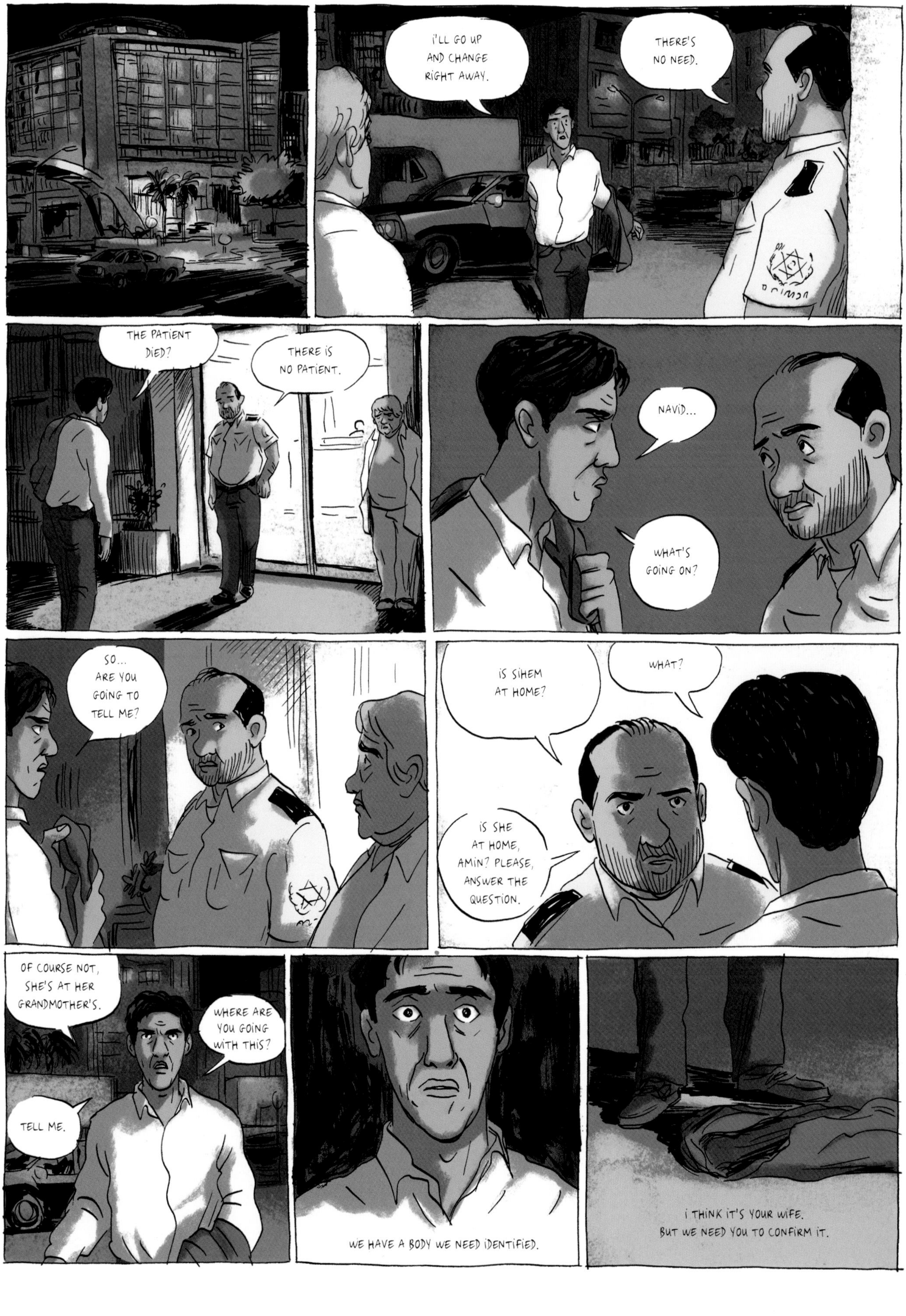
I'LL GO UP AND CHANGE RIGHT AWAY.
THERE'S NO NEED.
THE PATIENT DIED?
THERE IS NO PATIENT.
NAVID...
WHAT'S GOING ON?
SO... ARE YOU GOING TO TELL ME?
IS SIHEM AT HOME?
WHAT?
IS SHE AT HOME, AMIN? PLEASE, ANSWER THE QUESTION.
OF COURSE NOT, SHE'S AT HER GRANDMOTHER'S.
WHERE ARE YOU GOING WITH THIS?
TELL ME.
WE HAVE A BODY WE NEED IDENTIFIED.
I THINK IT'S YOUR WIFE. BUT WE NEED YOU TO CONFIRM IT.

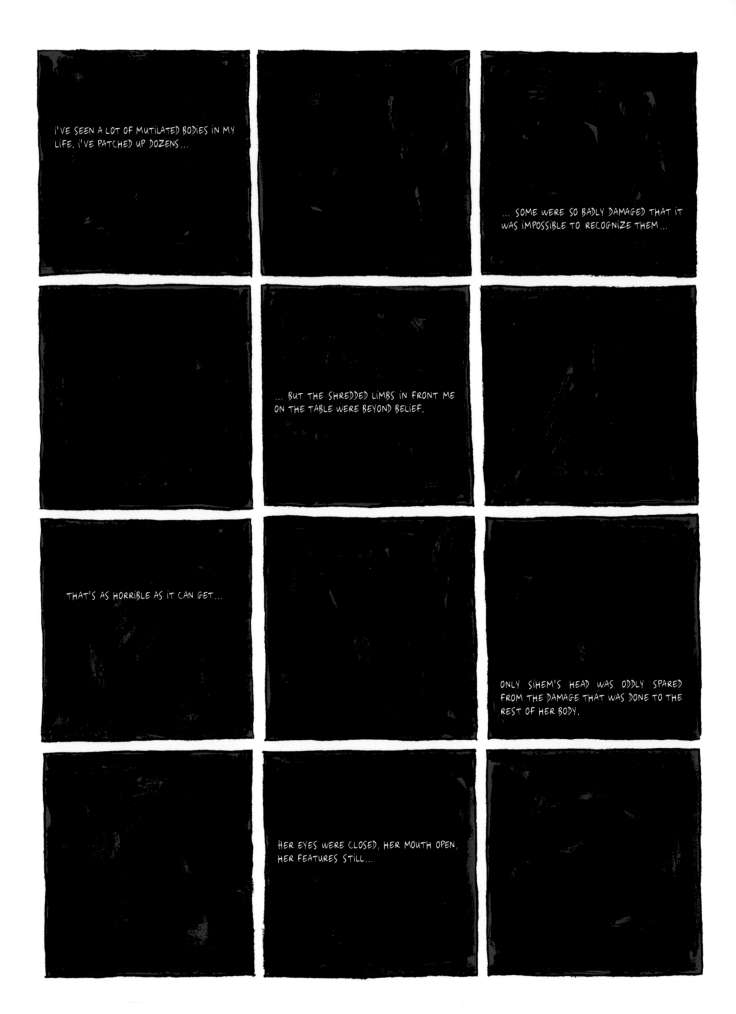

I'VE SEEN A LOT OF MUTILATED BODIES IN MY LIFE. I'VE PATCHED UP DOZENS...

... SOME WERE SO BADLY DAMAGED THAT IT WAS IMPOSSIBLE TO RECOGNIZE THEM...

... BUT THE SHREDDED LIMBS IN FRONT ME ON THE TABLE WERE BEYOND BELIEF.

THAT'S AS HORRIBLE AS IT CAN GET...

ONLY SIHEM'S HEAD WAS ODDLY SPARED FROM THE DAMAGE THAT WAS DONE TO THE REST OF HER BODY.

HER EYES WERE CLOSED, HER MOUTH OPEN, HER FEATURES STILL...

16

AS THOUGH RELIEVED
OF THEIR FEARS.

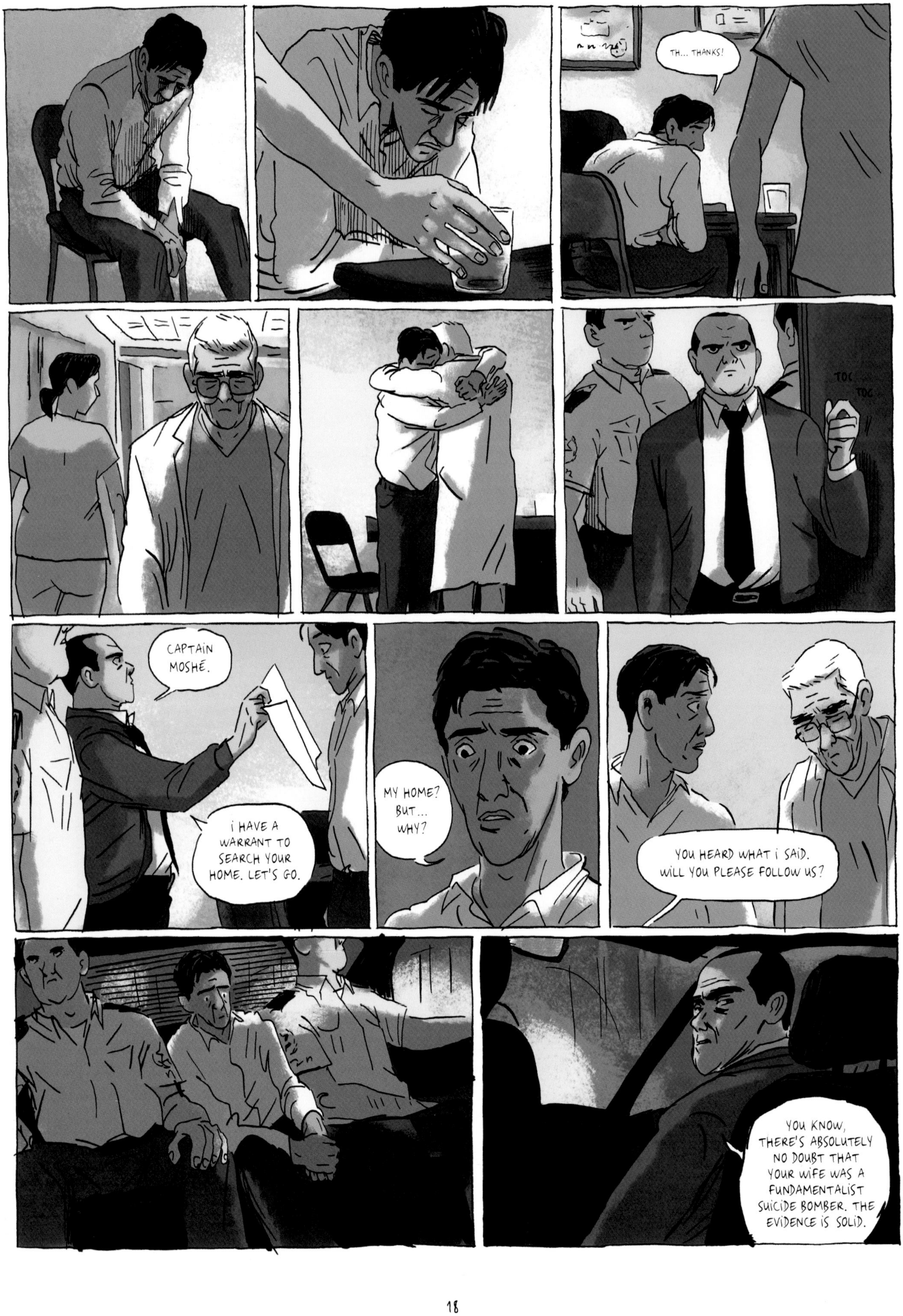
TH... THANKS!
TOC... TOC...
CAPTAIN MOSHÉ.
I HAVE A WARRANT TO SEARCH YOUR HOME. LET'S GO.
MY HOME? BUT... WHY?
YOU HEARD WHAT I SAID. WILL YOU PLEASE FOLLOW US?
YOU KNOW, THERE'S ABSOLUTELY NO DOUBT THAT YOUR WIFE WAS A FUNDAMENTALIST SUICIDE BOMBER. THE EVIDENCE IS SOLID.

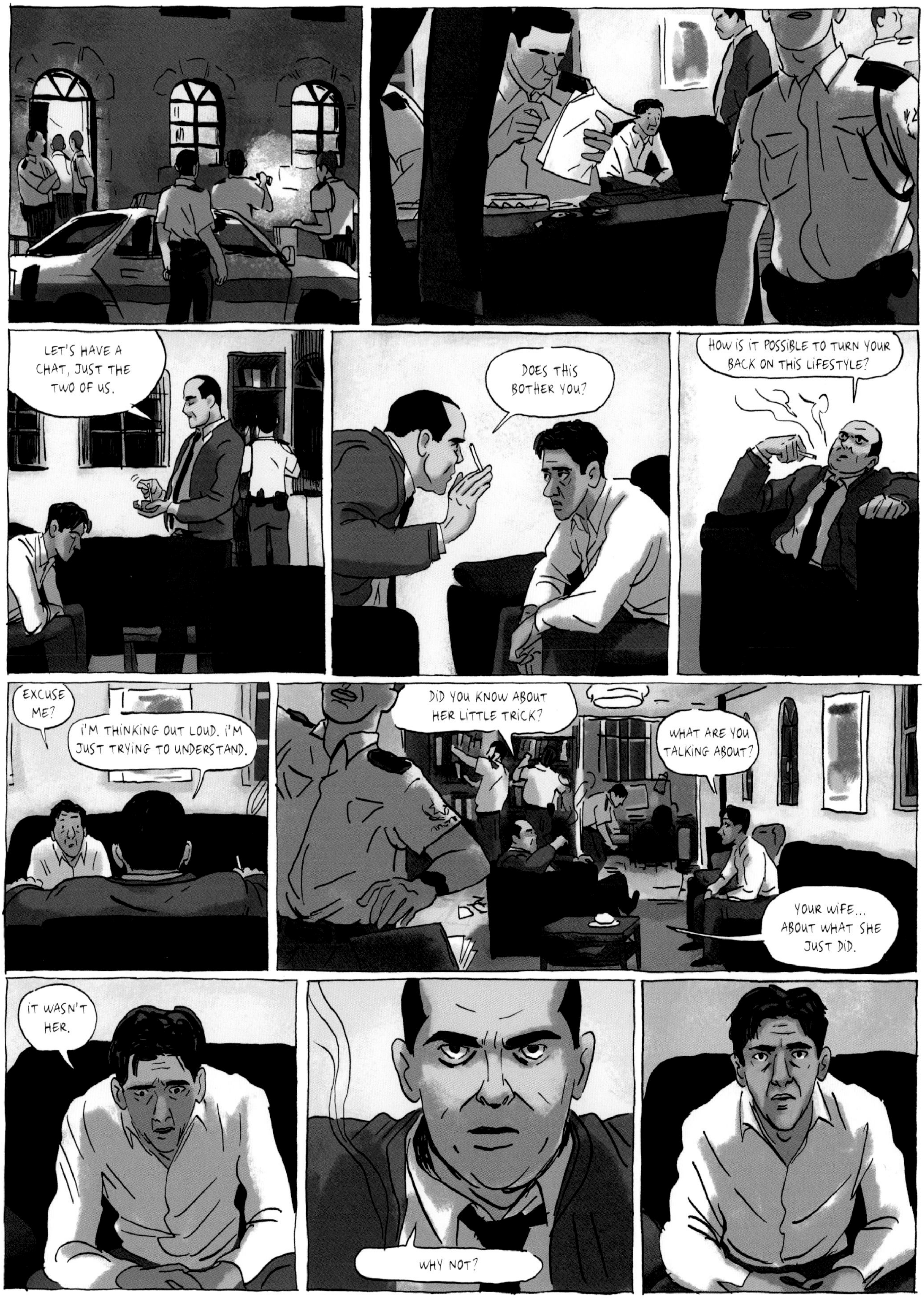
LET'S HAVE A CHAT, JUST THE TWO OF US.
DOES THIS BOTHER YOU?
HOW IS IT POSSIBLE TO TURN YOUR BACK ON THIS LIFESTYLE?
EXCUSE ME?
I'M THINKING OUT LOUD. I'M JUST TRYING TO UNDERSTAND.
DID YOU KNOW ABOUT HER LITTLE TRICK?
WHAT ARE YOU TALKING ABOUT?
YOUR WIFE... ABOUT WHAT SHE JUST DID.
IT WASN'T HER.
WHY NOT?

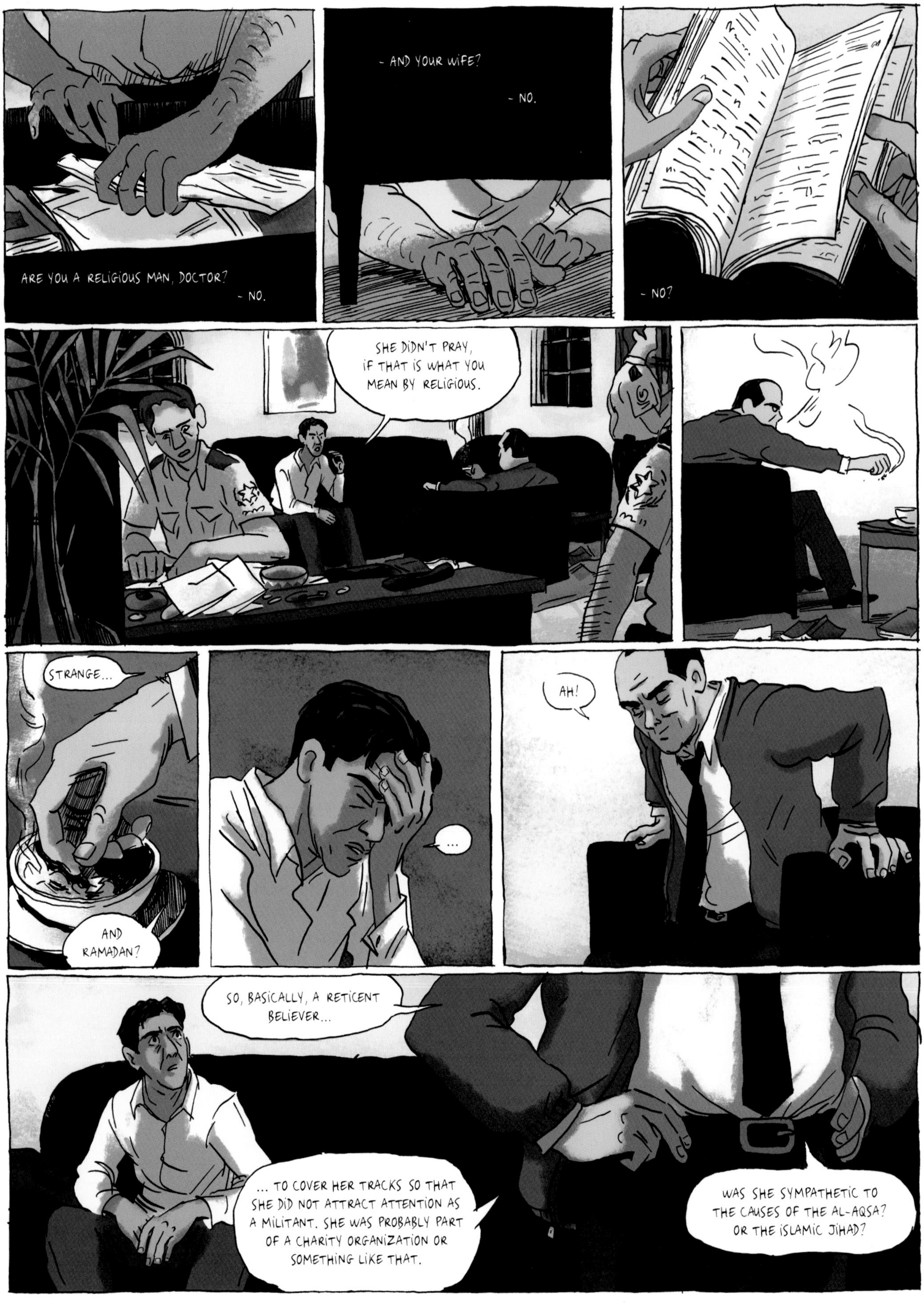
ARE YOU A RELIGIOUS MAN, DOCTOR?
- NO.
- AND YOUR WIFE?
- NO.
- NO?
SHE DIDN'T PRAY, IF THAT IS WHAT YOU MEAN BY RELIGIOUS.
STRANGE...
AND RAMADAN?
...
AH!
SO, BASICALLY, A RETICENT BELIEVER...
... TO COVER HER TRACKS SO THAT SHE DID NOT ATTRACT ATTENTION AS A MILITANT. SHE WAS PROBABLY PART OF A CHARITY ORGANIZATION OR SOMETHING LIKE THAT.
WAS SHE SYMPATHETIC TO THE CAUSES OF THE AL-AQSA? OR THE ISLAMIC JIHAD?

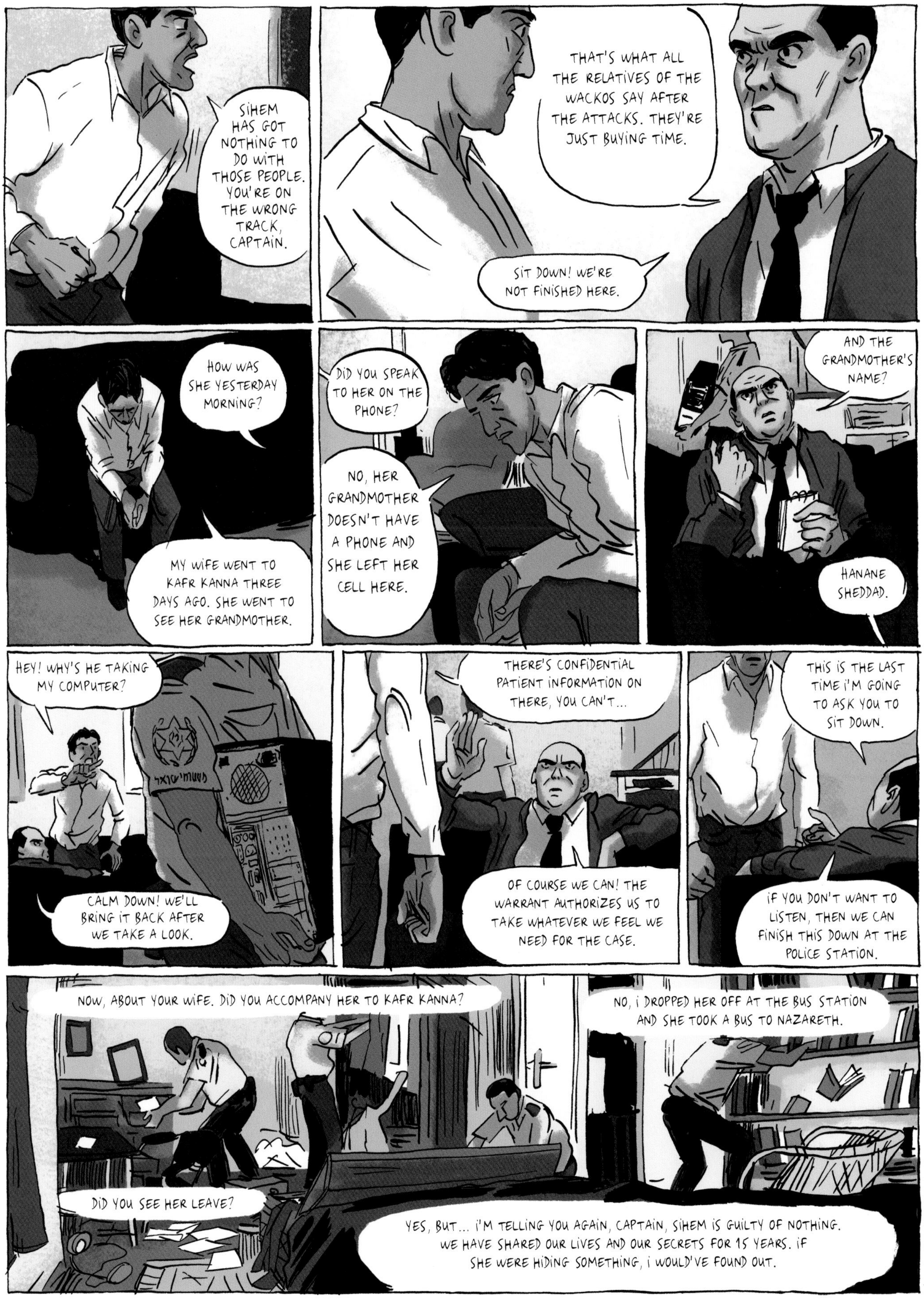
SIHEM HAS GOT NOTHING TO DO WITH THOSE PEOPLE. YOU'RE ON THE WRONG TRACK, CAPTAIN.
THAT'S WHAT ALL THE RELATIVES OF THE WACKOS SAY AFTER THE ATTACKS. THEY'RE JUST BUYING TIME.
SIT DOWN! WE'RE NOT FINISHED HERE.
HOW WAS SHE YESTERDAY MORNING?
MY WIFE WENT TO KAFR KANNA THREE DAYS AGO. SHE WENT TO SEE HER GRANDMOTHER.
DID YOU SPEAK TO HER ON THE PHONE?
NO, HER GRANDMOTHER DOESN'T HAVE A PHONE AND SHE LEFT HER CELL HERE.
AND THE GRANDMOTHER'S NAME?
HANANE SHEDDAD.
HEY! WHY'S HE TAKING MY COMPUTER?
CALM DOWN! WE'LL BRING IT BACK AFTER WE TAKE A LOOK.
THERE'S CONFIDENTIAL PATIENT INFORMATION ON THERE, YOU CAN'T...
OF COURSE WE CAN! THE WARRANT AUTHORIZES US TO TAKE WHATEVER WE FEEL WE NEED FOR THE CASE.
THIS IS THE LAST TIME I'M GOING TO ASK YOU TO SIT DOWN.
IF YOU DON'T WANT TO LISTEN, THEN WE CAN FINISH THIS DOWN AT THE POLICE STATION.
NOW, ABOUT YOUR WIFE. DID YOU ACCOMPANY HER TO KAFR KANNA?
NO, I DROPPED HER OFF AT THE BUS STATION AND SHE TOOK A BUS TO NAZARETH.
DID YOU SEE HER LEAVE?
YES, BUT... I'M TELLING YOU AGAIN, CAPTAIN, SIHEM IS GUILTY OF NOTHING. WE HAVE SHARED OUR LIVES AND OUR SECRETS FOR 15 YEARS. IF SHE WERE HIDING SOMETHING, I WOULD'VE FOUND OUT.

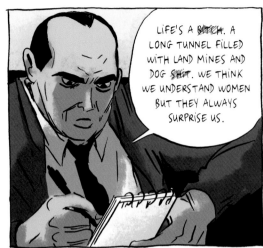

LIFE'S A BITCH. A LONG TUNNEL FILLED WITH LAND MINES AND DOG SHIT. WE THINK WE UNDERSTAND WOMEN BUT THEY ALWAYS SURPRISE US.

THAT'S ENOUGH!

IT'S HARDLY BEEN AN HOUR SINCE I FOUND OUT THAT MY WIFE WAS KILLED IN AN EXPLOSION...

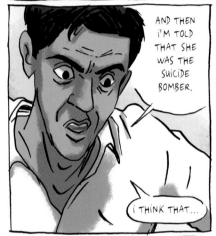

AND THEN I'M TOLD THAT SHE WAS THE SUICIDE BOMBER.

I THINK THAT...

EASY, JAAFARI!

DON'T TOUCH ME!

AND I FORBID YOU FROM SULLYING MY WIFE'S NAME.

THAT BOMB WAS NOT ON HER. YOU'RE WRONG. SHE MUST HAVE BEEN RIGHT NEXT TO THE BOMBER. THAT'S WHY SHE LOOKS LIKE THAT.

NOW JUST CALM DOWN THERE A BIT, OK? IT'S BETTER FOR EVERYONE.

IT WASN'T MY WIFE. IT WASN'T HER...

I KNOW HER. IT WASN'T HER...

OKAY! TAKE HIM AWAY. AND HOPEFULLY WHEN HE WAKES UP HE'LL BE A BIT MORE TALKATIVE.

YO! YO! YO! STAY WITH US PAL. WE'RE NOT DONE YET.

HERE!

THIS'LL HELP YOU STAY AWAKE.

SO NOW...

ABOUT 10 MILES FROM THE BUS STATION YOUR WIFE GOT OFF THE BUS SAYING IT WAS URGENT. SHE GOT INTO A CREAM-COLORED MERCEDES. MEAN ANYTHING TO YOU?

WHOEVER TOLD YOU THAT IS FULL OF IT.

WE'LL SEE.

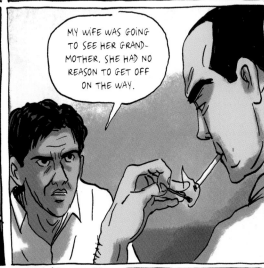

MY WIFE WAS GOING TO SEE HER GRAND-MOTHER. SHE HAD NO REASON TO GET OFF ON THE WAY.

HANANE SHEDDAD... THAT'S YOUR WIFE'S GRANDMOTHER'S NAME.

YES.

GOOD THING, BECAUSE WE WENT TO SEE HER.

SHE AND HER NEPHEW HAVE NOT SEEN YOUR WIFE IN OVER 9 MONTHS.

I'LL LET YOU THINK ABOUT THAT FOR A WHILE, UNLESS MY COLLEAGUE HAS SOME QUESTIONS.

SO, DOCTOR, TELL ME ABOUT YOUR RELATIONSHIP WITH YOUR WIFE...

DIFFICULT?

YOU CAN SAY THAT AGAIN.

GO TAKE A BREAK, I'LL TAKE OVER.

MY WIFE DID NOT HAVE A LOVER...

NONE THAT YOU KNEW OF, ANYWAY.

GOOD! NOW LET'S START OVER FROM THE BEGINNING...

YOU'RE NOT GOING TO TRY AND CONVINCE ME THAT YOU DIDN'T NOTICE ANYTHING ODD IN YOUR WIFE'S BEHAVIOR RECENTLY?

YOU'LL NEVER FORCE ME TO SAY WHAT YOU WANT TO HEAR.

THEY'RE PUTTING HIM UNDER THE SHOWER. HE SHOULD BREAK SOON, AFTER TWO DAYS WITHOUT SLEEP.

AND ANYWAY, HE DOESN'T HAVE A CHOICE.

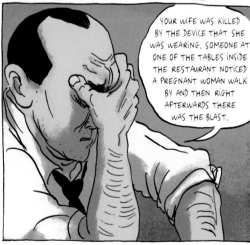

YOUR WIFE WAS KILLED BY THE DEVICE THAT SHE WAS WEARING. SOMEONE AT ONE OF THE TABLES INSIDE THE RESTAURANT NOTICED A PREGNANT WOMAN WALK BY AND THEN RIGHT AFTERWARDS THERE WAS THE BLAST.

WE SHOWED HIM PHOTOS OF HER, AND WITHOUT ANY HESITATION HE RECOGNIZED YOUR WIFE.

YOU SEE WHAT I'M SAYING?

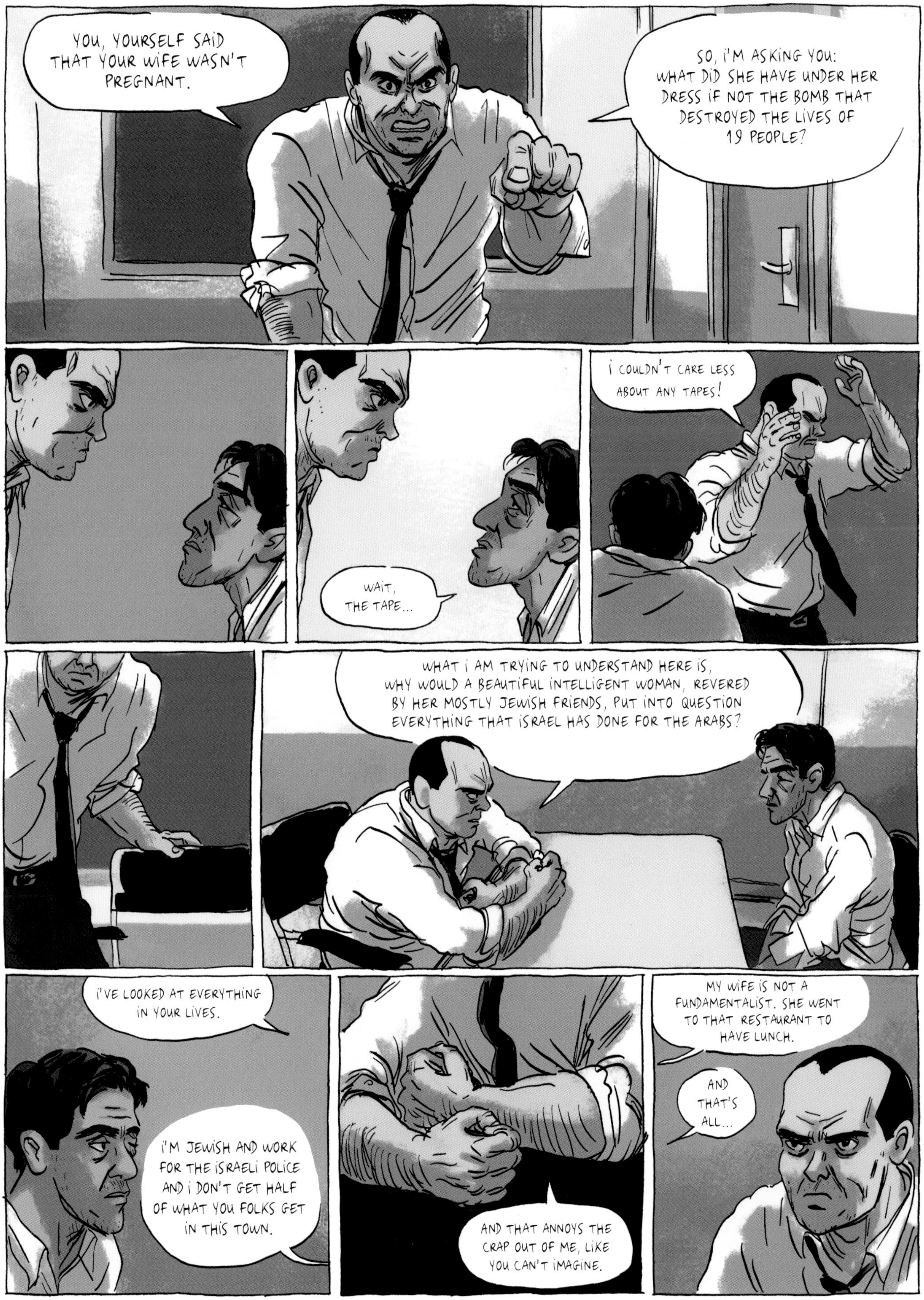
YOU, YOURSELF SAID THAT YOUR WIFE WASN'T PREGNANT.
SO, I'M ASKING YOU: WHAT DID SHE HAVE UNDER HER DRESS IF NOT THE BOMB THAT DESTROYED THE LIVES OF 19 PEOPLE?
WAIT, THE TAPE...
I COULDN'T CARE LESS ABOUT ANY TAPES!
WHAT I AM TRYING TO UNDERSTAND HERE IS, WHY WOULD A BEAUTIFUL INTELLIGENT WOMAN, REVERED BY HER MOSTLY JEWISH FRIENDS, PUT INTO QUESTION EVERYTHING THAT ISRAEL HAS DONE FOR THE ARABS?
I'VE LOOKED AT EVERYTHING IN YOUR LIVES.
I'M JEWISH AND WORK FOR THE ISRAELI POLICE AND I DON'T GET HALF OF WHAT YOU FOLKS GET IN THIS TOWN.
AND THAT ANNOYS THE CRAP OUT OF ME, LIKE YOU CAN'T IMAGINE.
MY WIFE IS NOT A FUNDAMENTALIST. SHE WENT TO THAT RESTAURANT TO HAVE LUNCH.
AND THAT'S ALL...

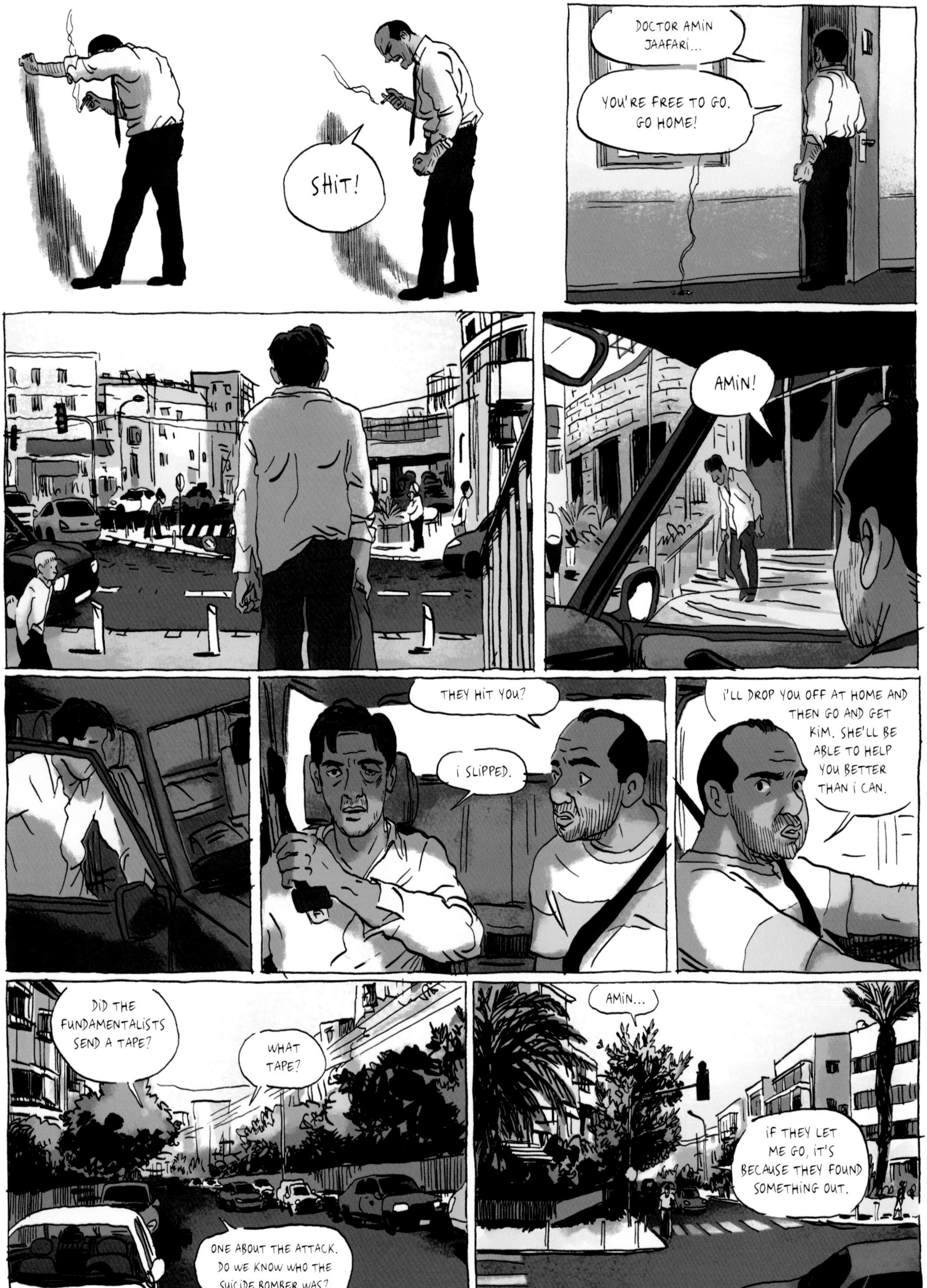
SHIT!
DOCTOR AMIN JAAFARI...
YOU'RE FREE TO GO. GO HOME!
AMIN!
THEY HIT YOU?
I SLIPPED.
I'LL DROP YOU OFF AT HOME AND THEN GO AND GET KIM. SHE'LL BE ABLE TO HELP YOU BETTER THAN I CAN.
DID THE FUNDAMENTALISTS SEND A TAPE?
WHAT TAPE?
ONE ABOUT THE ATTACK. DO WE KNOW WHO THE SUICIDE BOMBER WAS?
AMIN...
IF THEY LET ME GO, IT'S BECAUSE THEY FOUND SOMETHING OUT.

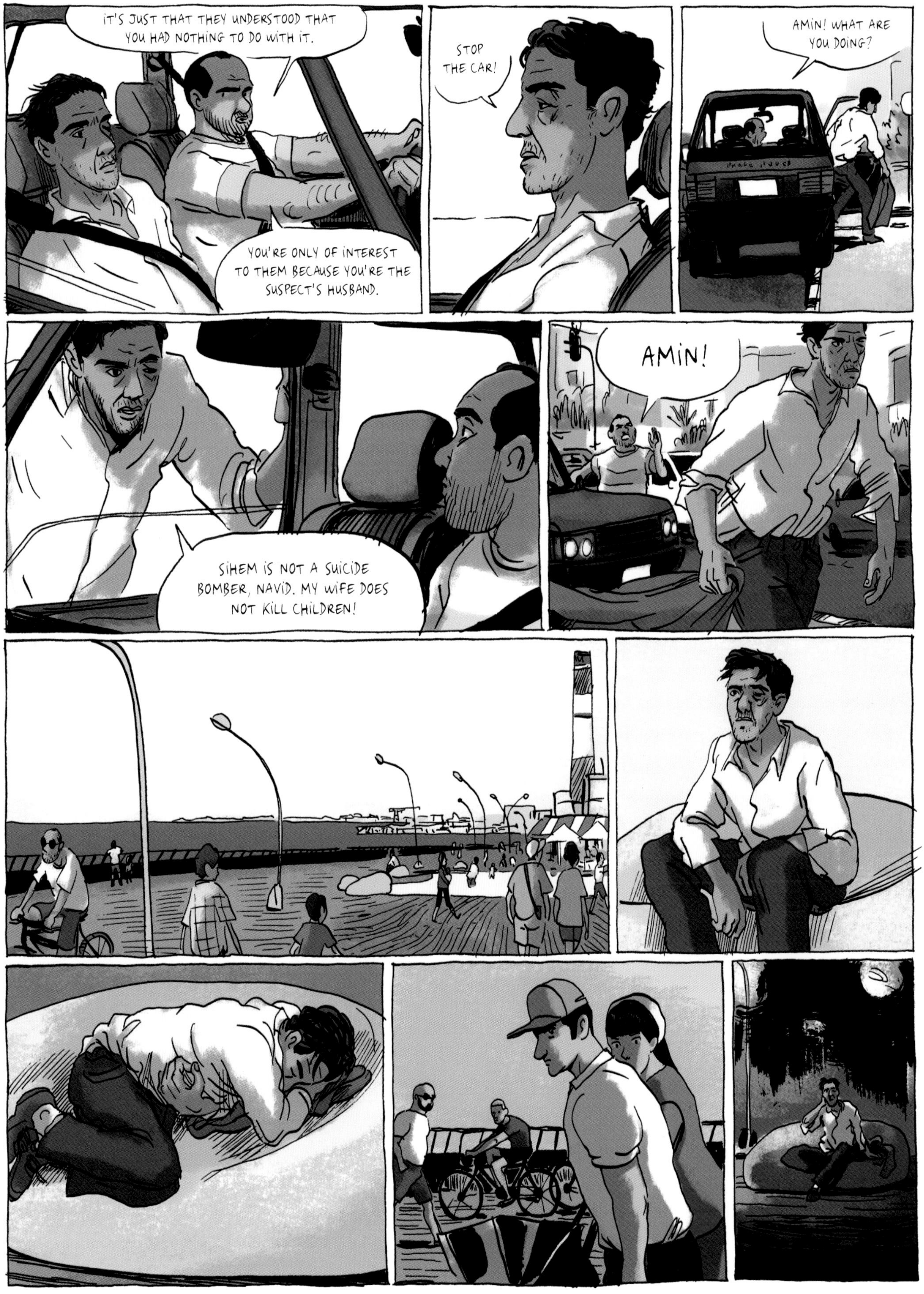
IT'S JUST THAT THEY UNDERSTOOD THAT YOU HAD NOTHING TO DO WITH IT.
YOU'RE ONLY OF INTEREST TO THEM BECAUSE YOU'RE THE SUSPECT'S HUSBAND.
STOP THE CAR!
AMIN! WHAT ARE YOU DOING?
SIHEM IS NOT A SUICIDE BOMBER, NAVID. MY WIFE DOES NOT KILL CHILDREN!
AMIN!

THE VILE BEAST IS AMONG US

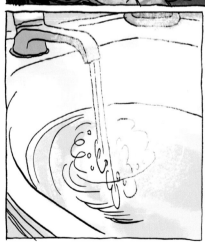

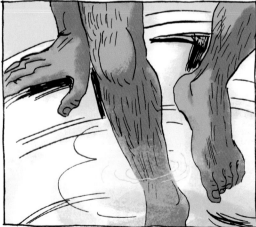

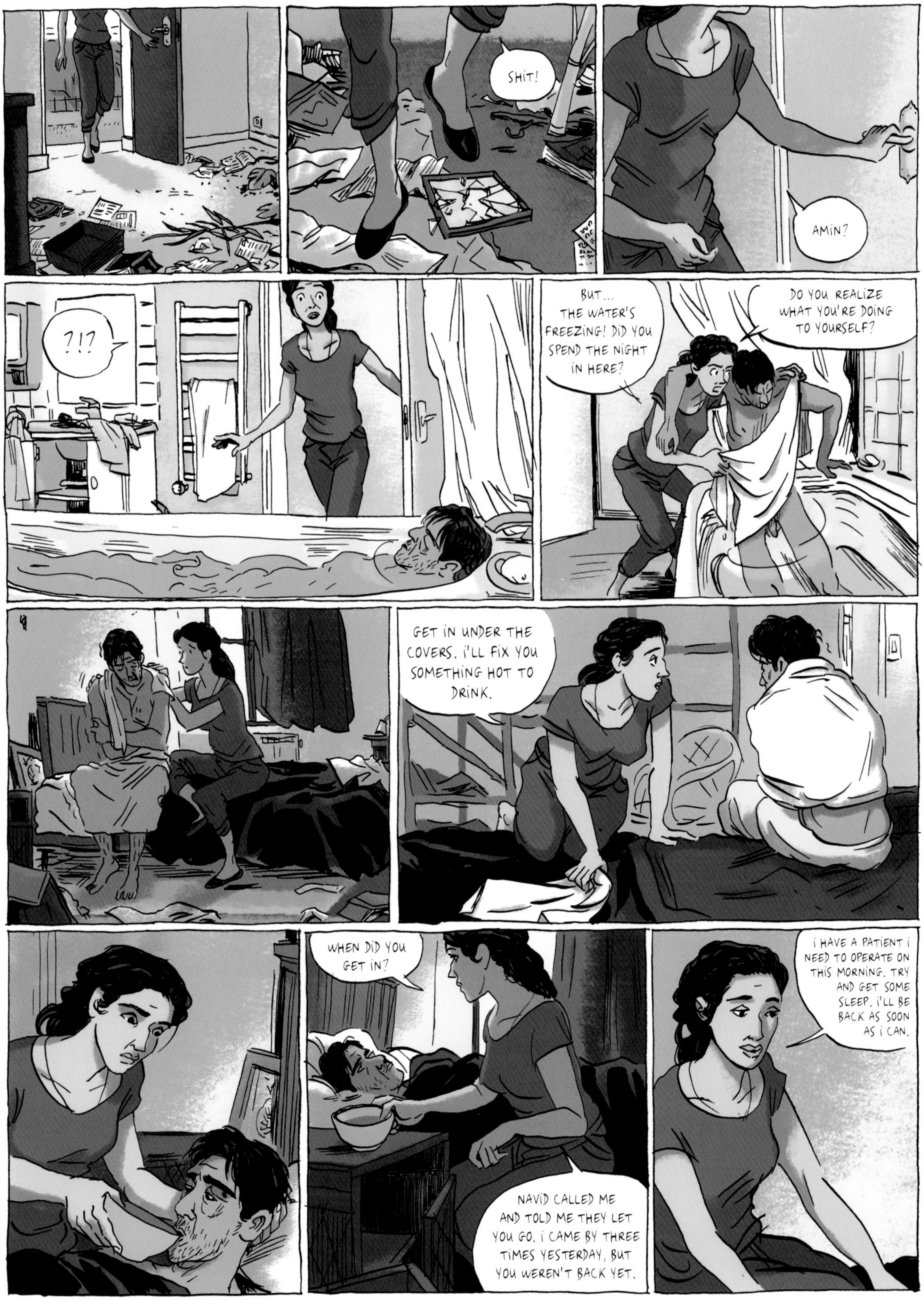
SHIT!
AMIN?
?!?
BUT... THE WATER'S FREEZING! DID YOU SPEND THE NIGHT IN HERE?
DO YOU REALIZE WHAT YOU'RE DOING TO YOURSELF?
GET IN UNDER THE COVERS. I'LL FIX YOU SOMETHING HOT TO DRINK.
WHEN DID YOU GET IN?
NAVID CALLED ME AND TOLD ME THEY LET YOU GO. I CAME BY THREE TIMES YESTERDAY, BUT YOU WEREN'T BACK YET.
I HAVE A PATIENT I NEED TO OPERATE ON THIS MORNING. TRY AND GET SOME SLEEP. I'LL BE BACK AS SOON AS I CAN.

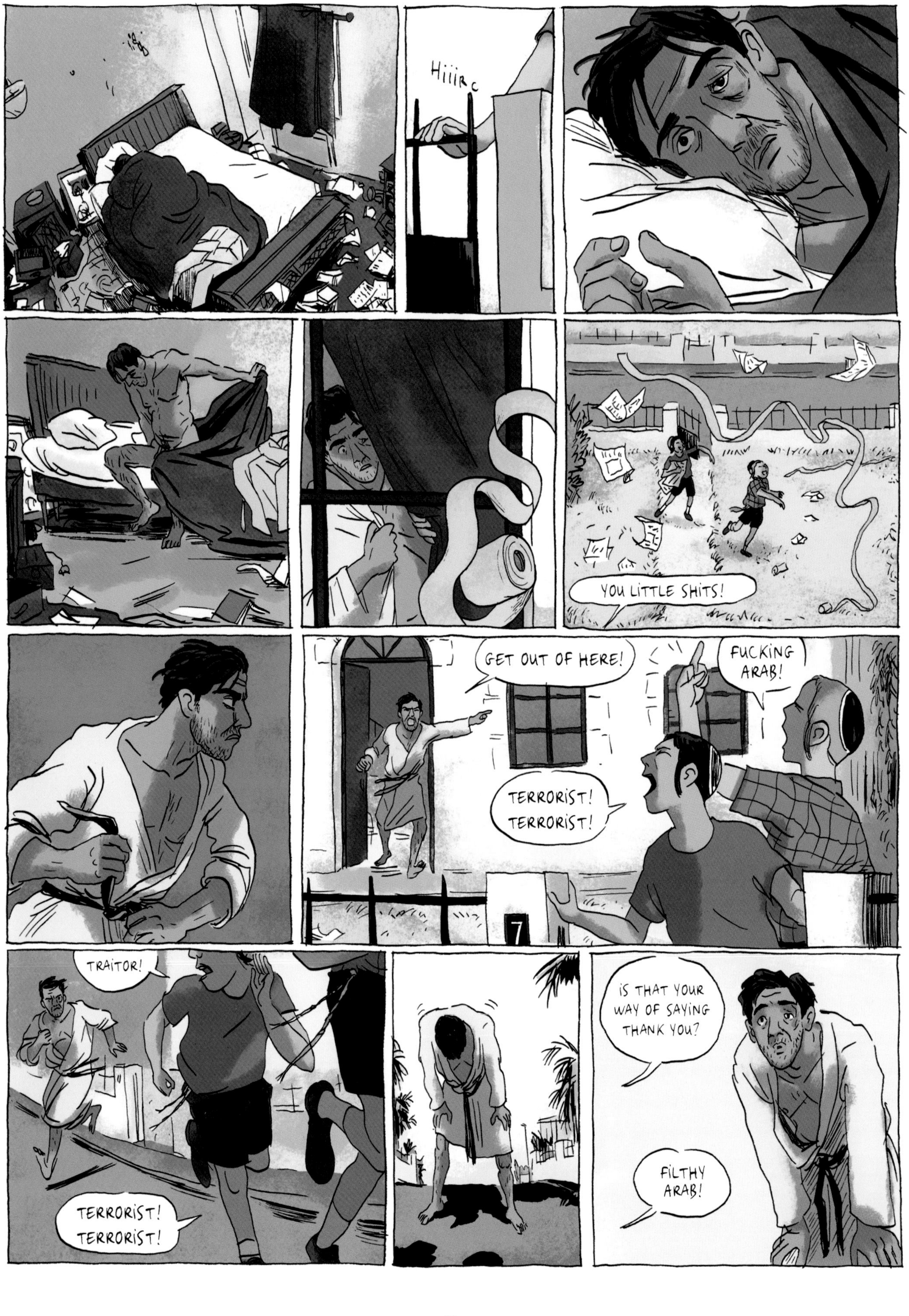
Hiiirc
YOU LITTLE SHITS!
GET OUT OF HERE!
FUCKING ARAB!
TERRORIST! TERRORIST!
TRAITOR!
TERRORIST! TERRORIST!
IS THAT YOUR WAY OF SAYING THANK YOU?
FILTHY ARAB!

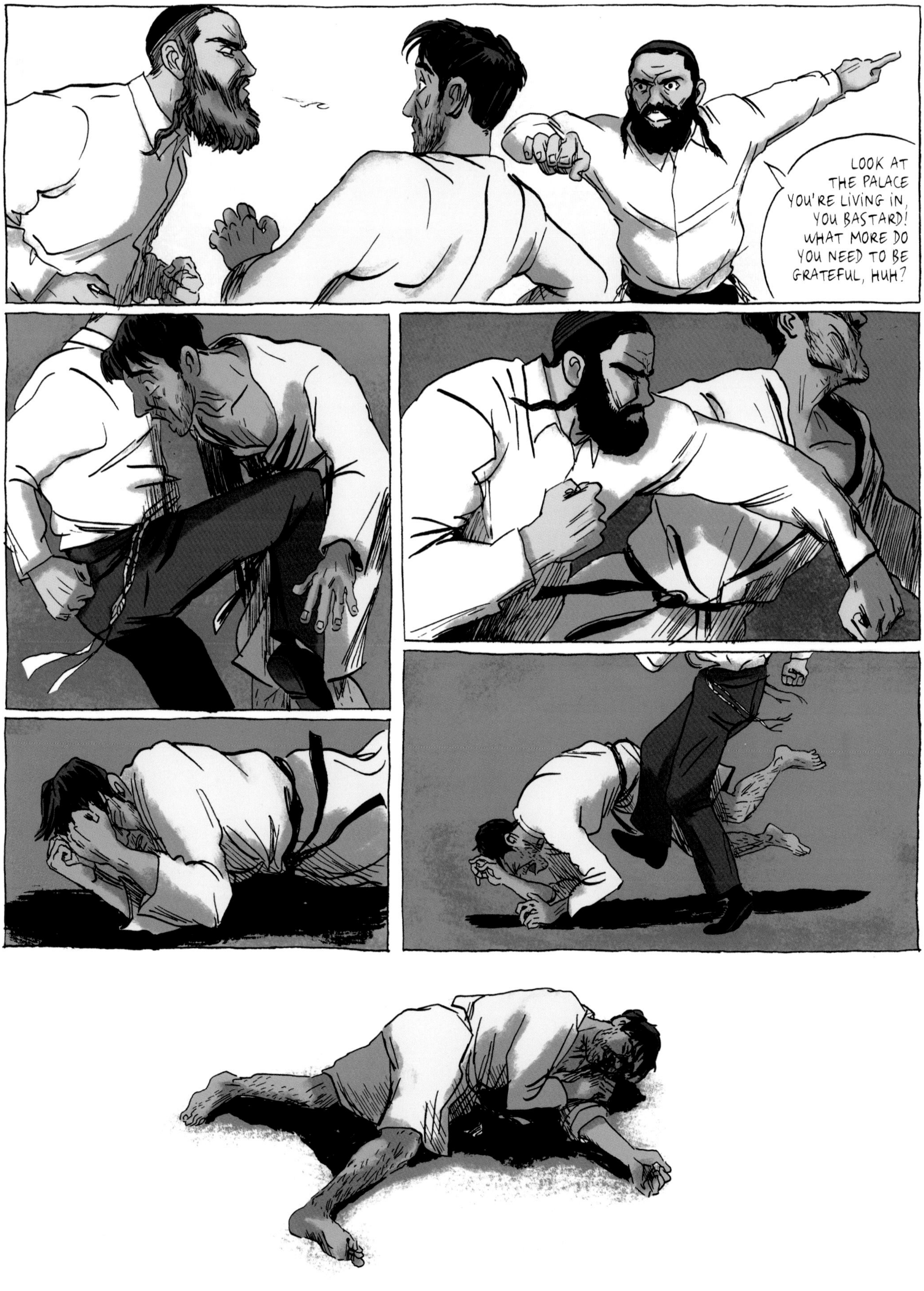
LOOK AT THE PALACE YOU'RE LIVING IN, YOU BASTARD! WHAT MORE DO YOU NEED TO BE GRATEFUL, HUH?

NO SKULL FRACTURE. BUT PRETTY SEVERE DAMAGE TO THE RIGHT WRIST AND KNEE.

THEY'RE GOING TO BE SORE FOR SEVERAL DAYS.

THERE'S NO WAY YOU'RE GOING BACK TO YOUR PLACE. NEXT TIME THEY'LL KILL YOU.

HANG ON, I'LL HELP YOU.

LEAVE IT! I KNOW HOW TO TAKE CARE OF MYSELF.

WELCOME!

I SPOKE TO NAVID. HE'S GOING TO STOP BY YOUR PLACE AND PICK UP SOME THINGS.

MAKE YOURSELF AT HOME!

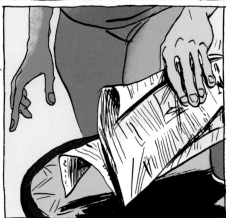

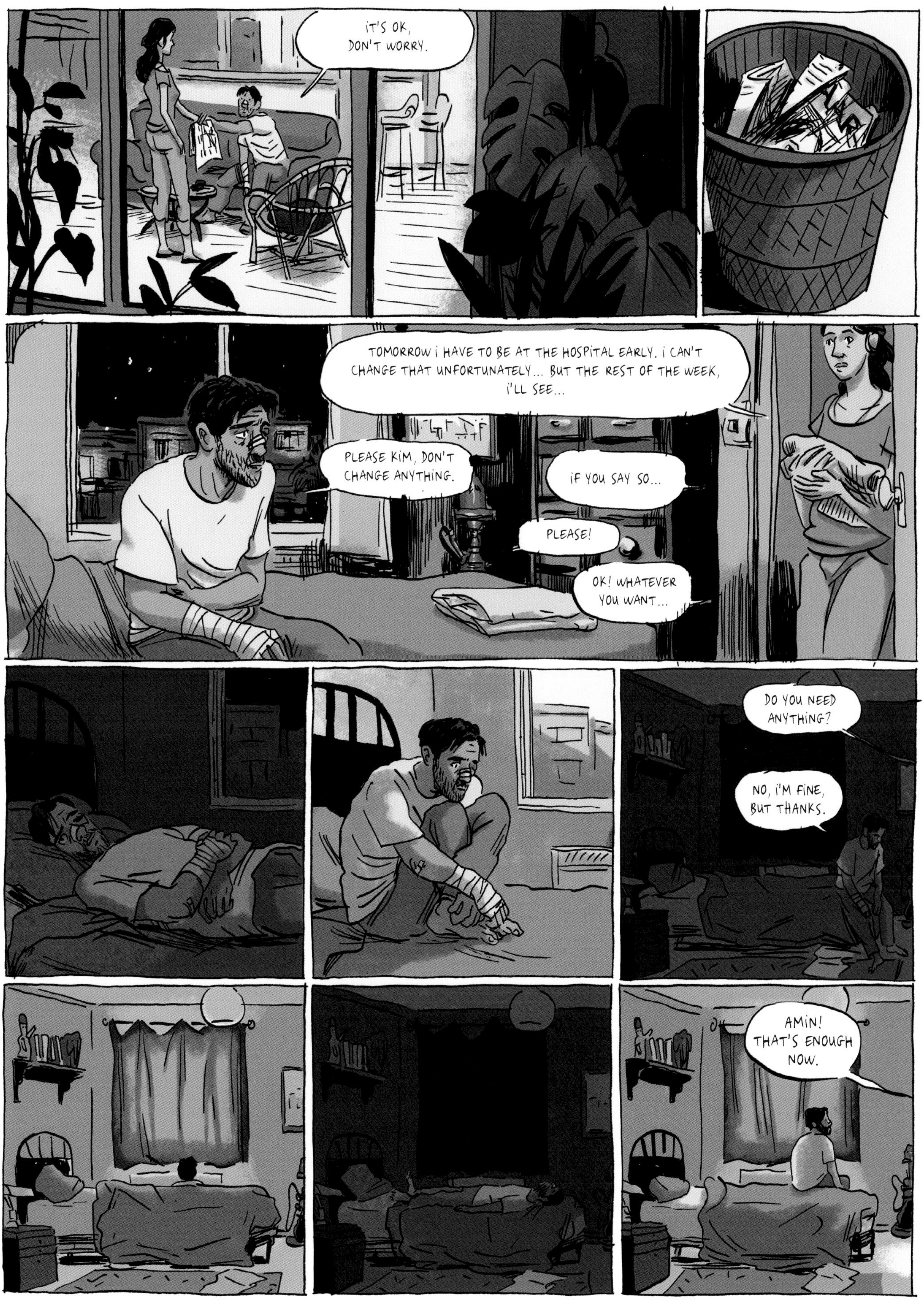
IT'S OK, DON'T WORRY.
TOMORROW I HAVE TO BE AT THE HOSPITAL EARLY. I CAN'T CHANGE THAT UNFORTUNATELY... BUT THE REST OF THE WEEK, I'LL SEE...
PLEASE KIM, DON'T CHANGE ANYTHING.
IF YOU SAY SO...
PLEASE!
OK! WHATEVER YOU WANT...
DO YOU NEED ANYTHING?
NO, I'M FINE, BUT THANKS.
AMIN! THAT'S ENOUGH NOW.

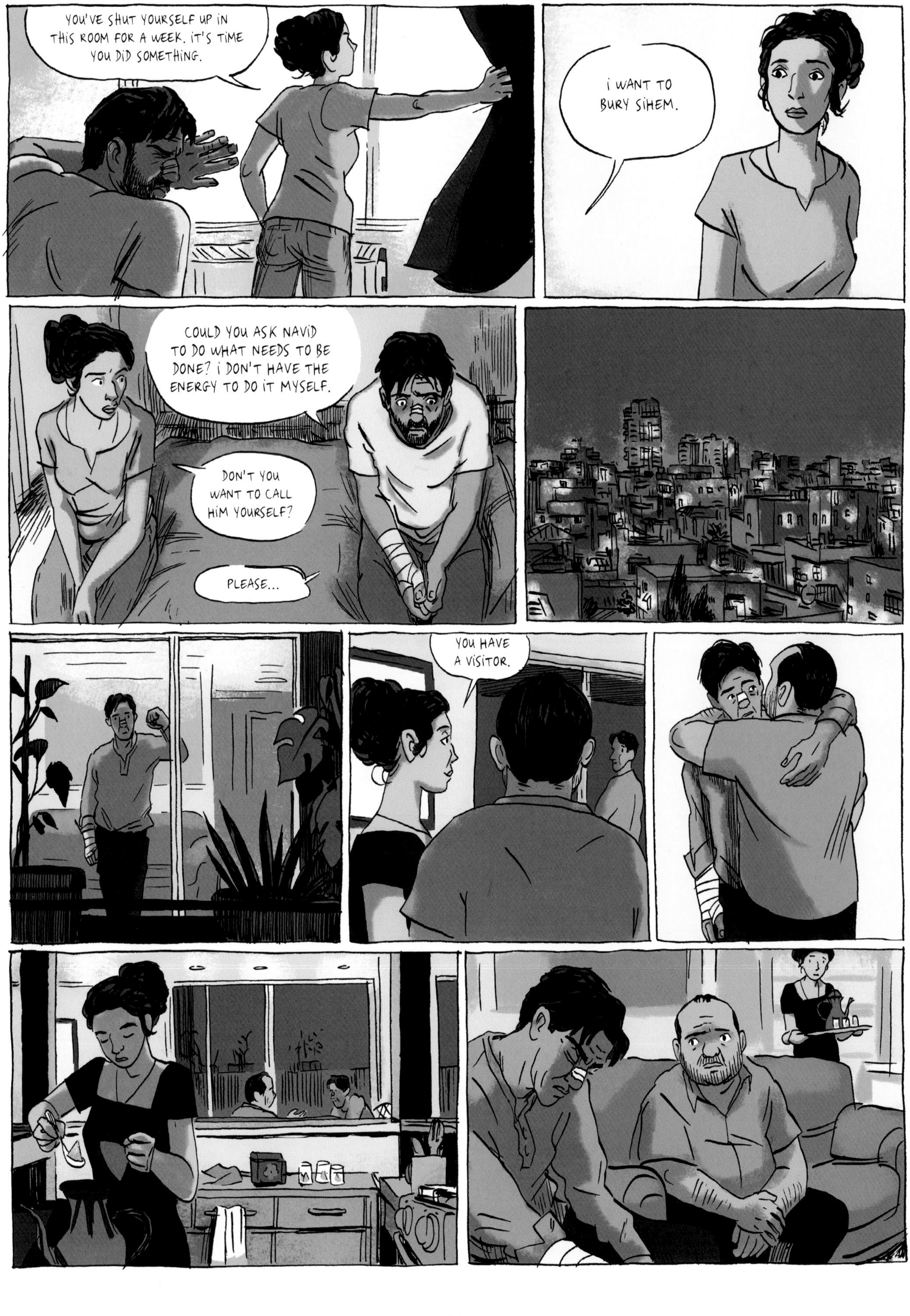
YOU'VE SHUT YOURSELF UP IN THIS ROOM FOR A WEEK. IT'S TIME YOU DID SOMETHING.
I WANT TO BURY SIHEM.
COULD YOU ASK NAVID TO DO WHAT NEEDS TO BE DONE? I DON'T HAVE THE ENERGY TO DO IT MYSELF.
DON'T YOU WANT TO CALL HIM YOURSELF?
PLEASE...
YOU HAVE A VISITOR.

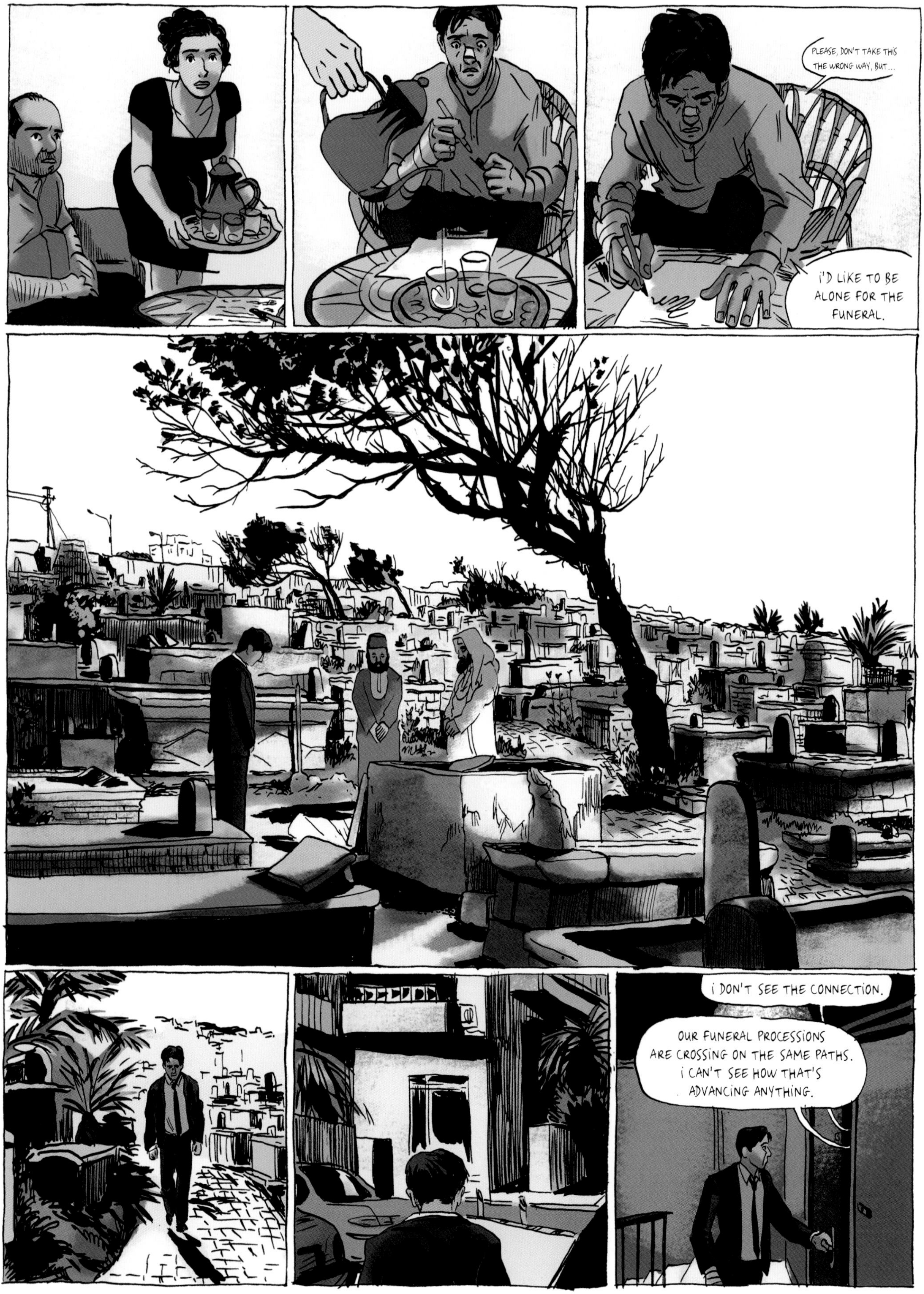
PLEASE, DON'T TAKE THIS THE WRONG WAY, BUT...
I'D LIKE TO BE ALONE FOR THE FUNERAL.
I DON'T SEE THE CONNECTION.
OUR FUNERAL PROCESSIONS ARE CROSSING ON THE SAME PATHS. I CAN'T SEE HOW THAT'S ADVANCING ANYTHING.

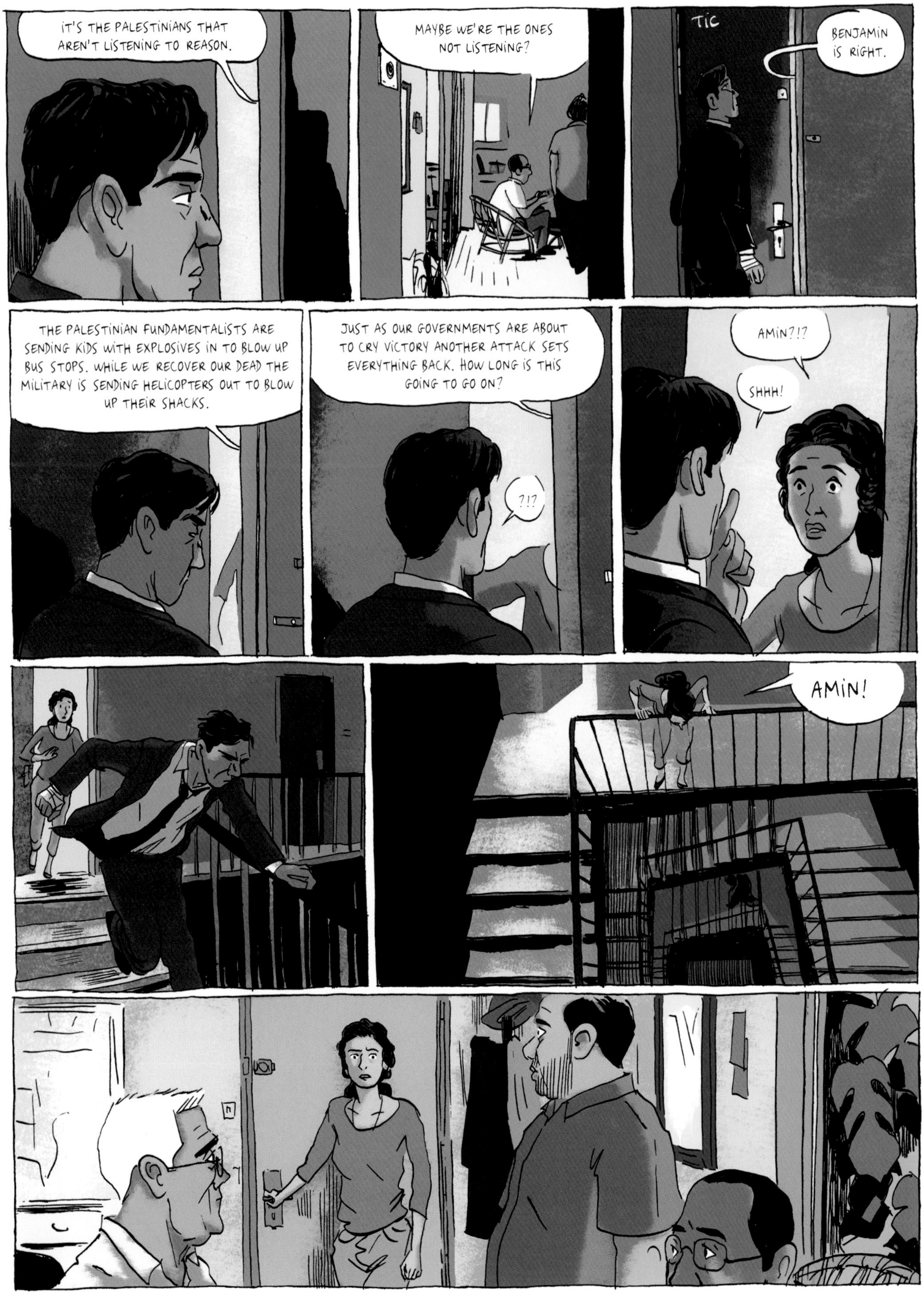
IT'S THE PALESTINIANS THAT AREN'T LISTENING TO REASON.
MAYBE WE'RE THE ONES NOT LISTENING?
TIC
BENJAMIN IS RIGHT.
THE PALESTINIAN FUNDAMENTALISTS ARE SENDING KIDS WITH EXPLOSIVES IN TO BLOW UP BUS STOPS. WHILE WE RECOVER OUR DEAD THE MILITARY IS SENDING HELICOPTERS OUT TO BLOW UP THEIR SHACKS.
JUST AS OUR GOVERNMENTS ARE ABOUT TO CRY VICTORY ANOTHER ATTACK SETS EVERYTHING BACK. HOW LONG IS THIS GOING TO GO ON?
?!?
AMIN?!?
SHHH!
AMIN!

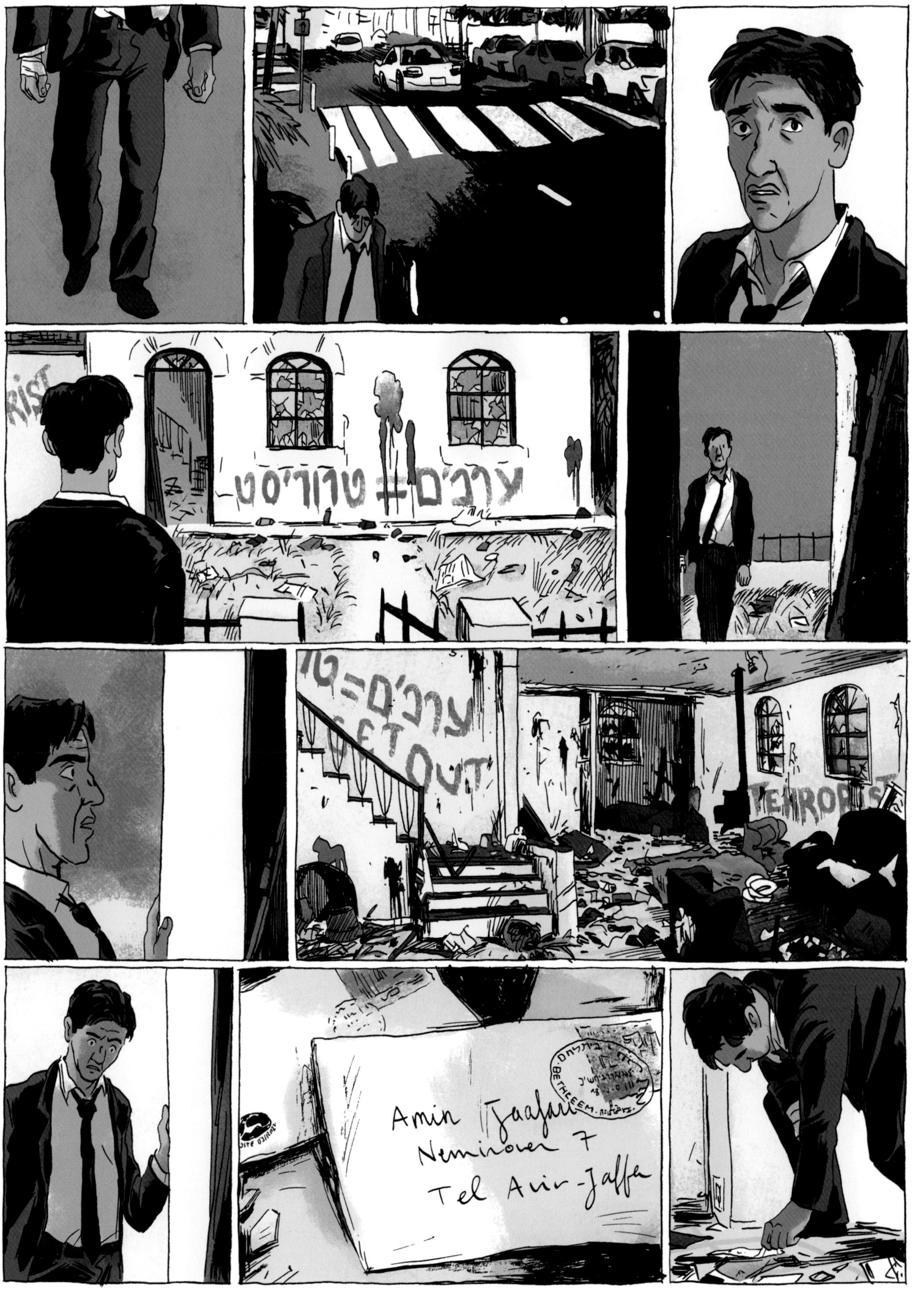
RIST
ערבים = טרוריסט
GET OUT
TERRORIST
Amin Jaafari
Nemirover 7
Tel Aviv-Jaffa

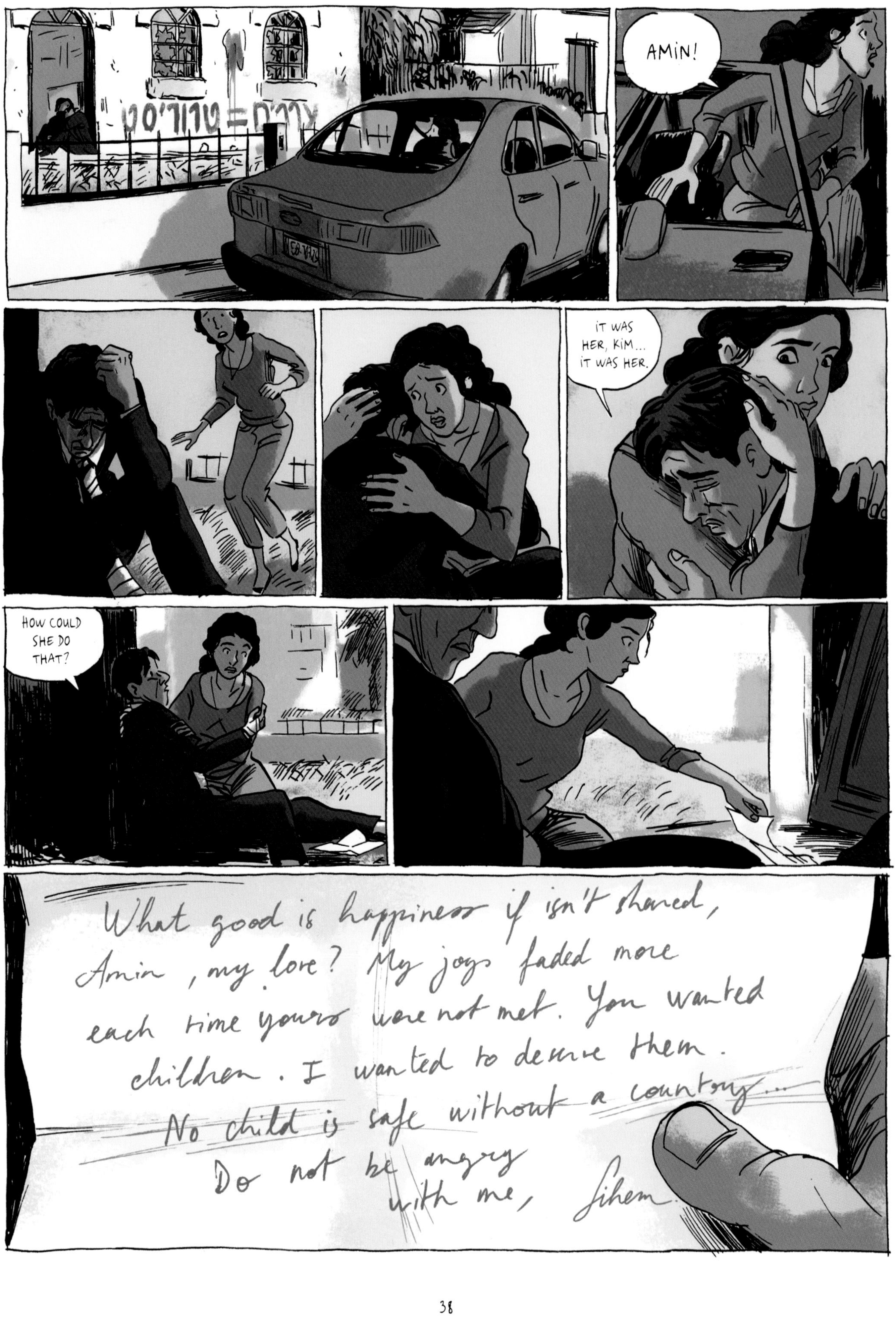
AMIN!
IT WAS HER, KIM... IT WAS HER.
HOW COULD SHE DO THAT?
What good is happiness if isn't shared, Amin, my love? My joys faded more each time yours were not met. You wanted children. I wanted to deserve them.
No child is safe without a country...
Do not be angry with me, Sihem.

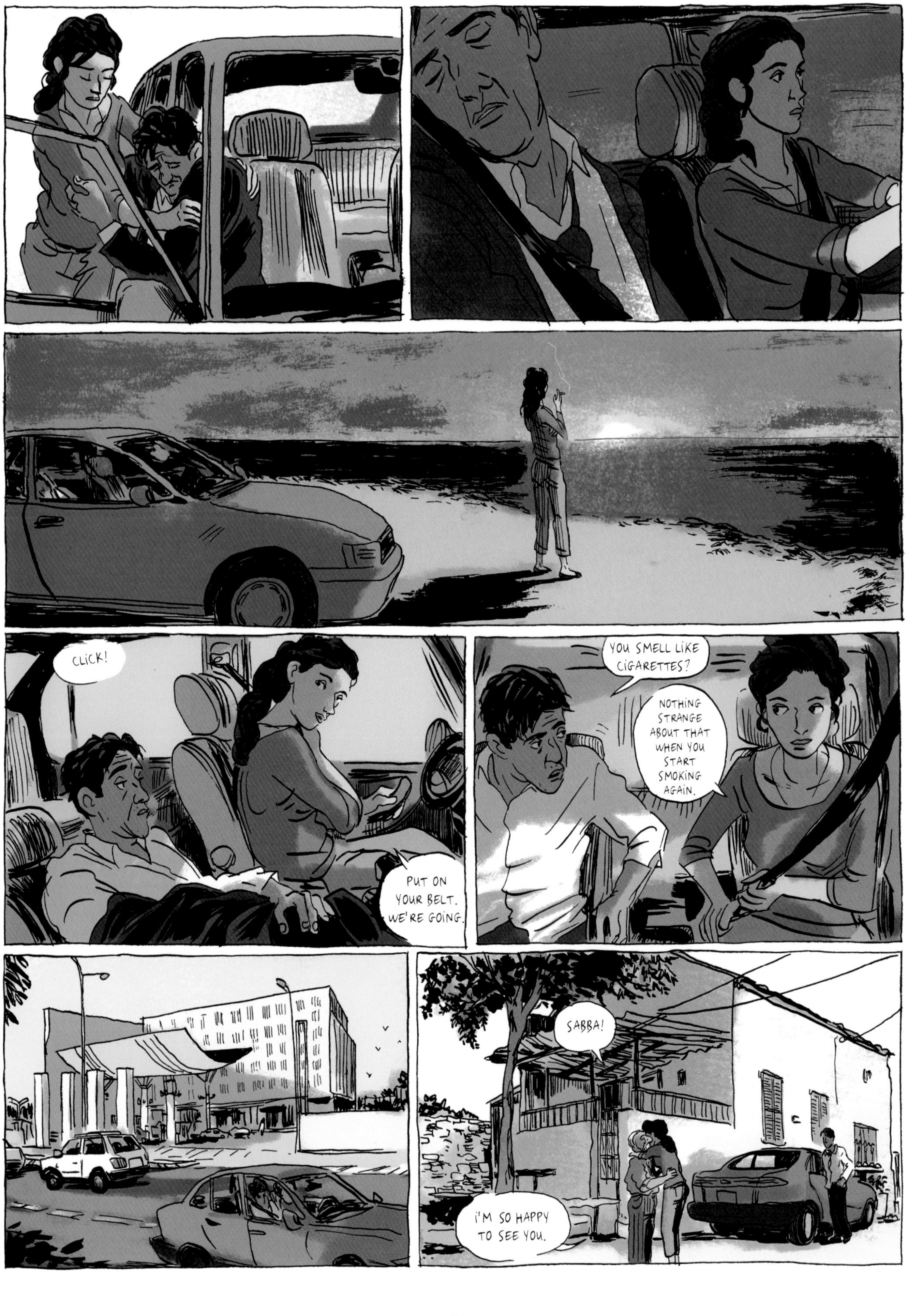
CLICK!
PUT ON YOUR BELT. WE'RE GOING.
YOU SMELL LIKE CIGARETTES?
NOTHING STRANGE ABOUT THAT WHEN YOU START SMOKING AGAIN.
SABBA!
I'M SO HAPPY TO SEE YOU.

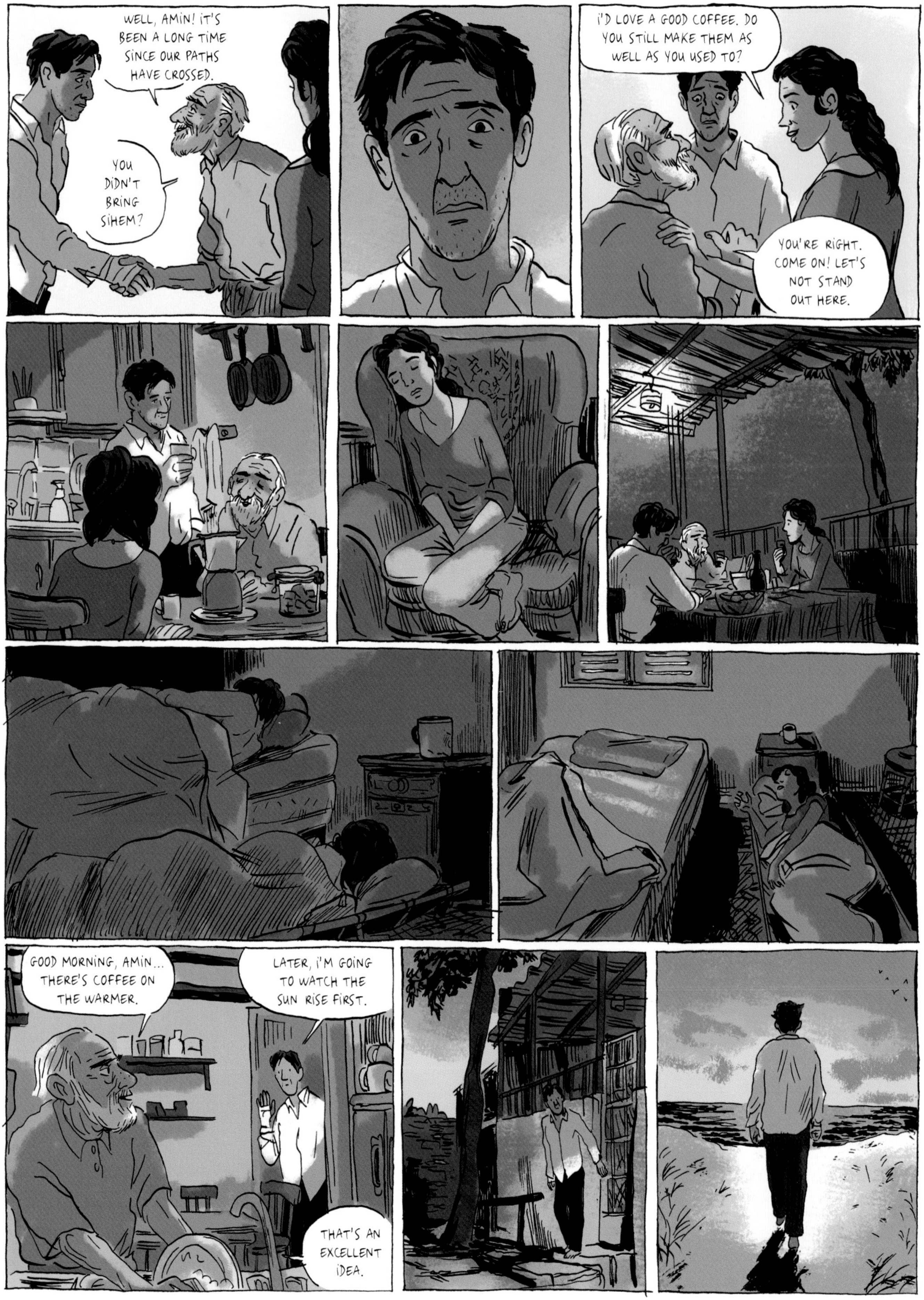
WELL, AMIN! IT'S BEEN A LONG TIME SINCE OUR PATHS HAVE CROSSED.
YOU DIDN'T BRING SIHEM?
I'D LOVE A GOOD COFFEE. DO YOU STILL MAKE THEM AS WELL AS YOU USED TO?
YOU'RE RIGHT. COME ON! LET'S NOT STAND OUT HERE.
GOOD MORNING, AMIN... THERE'S COFFEE ON THE WARMER.
LATER, I'M GOING TO WATCH THE SUN RISE FIRST.
THAT'S AN EXCELLENT IDEA.

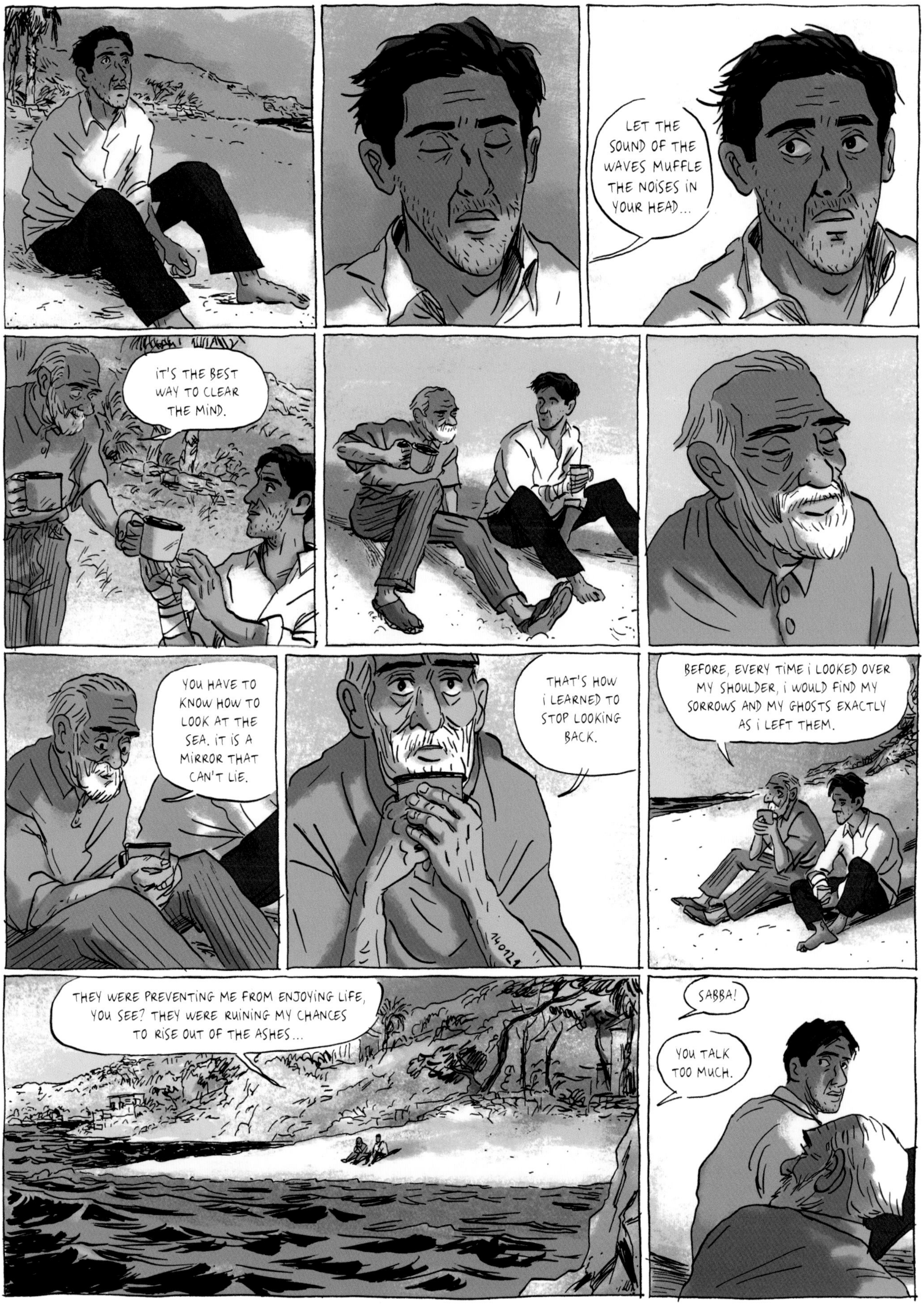
LET THE SOUND OF THE WAVES MUFFLE THE NOISES IN YOUR HEAD...
iT'S THE BEST WAY TO CLEAR THE MiND.
YOU HAVE TO KNOW HOW TO LOOK AT THE SEA. iT IS A MiRROR THAT CAN'T LiE.
THAT'S HOW i LEARNED TO STOP LOOKING BACK.
BEFORE, EVERY TiME i LOOKED OVER MY SHOULDER, i WOULD FiND MY SORROWS AND MY GHOSTS EXACTLY AS i LEFT THEM.
THEY WERE PREVENTiNG ME FROM ENJOYiNG LiFE, YOU SEE? THEY WERE RUiNiNG MY CHANCES TO RiSE OUT OF THE ASHES...
SABBA!
YOU TALK TOO MUCH.

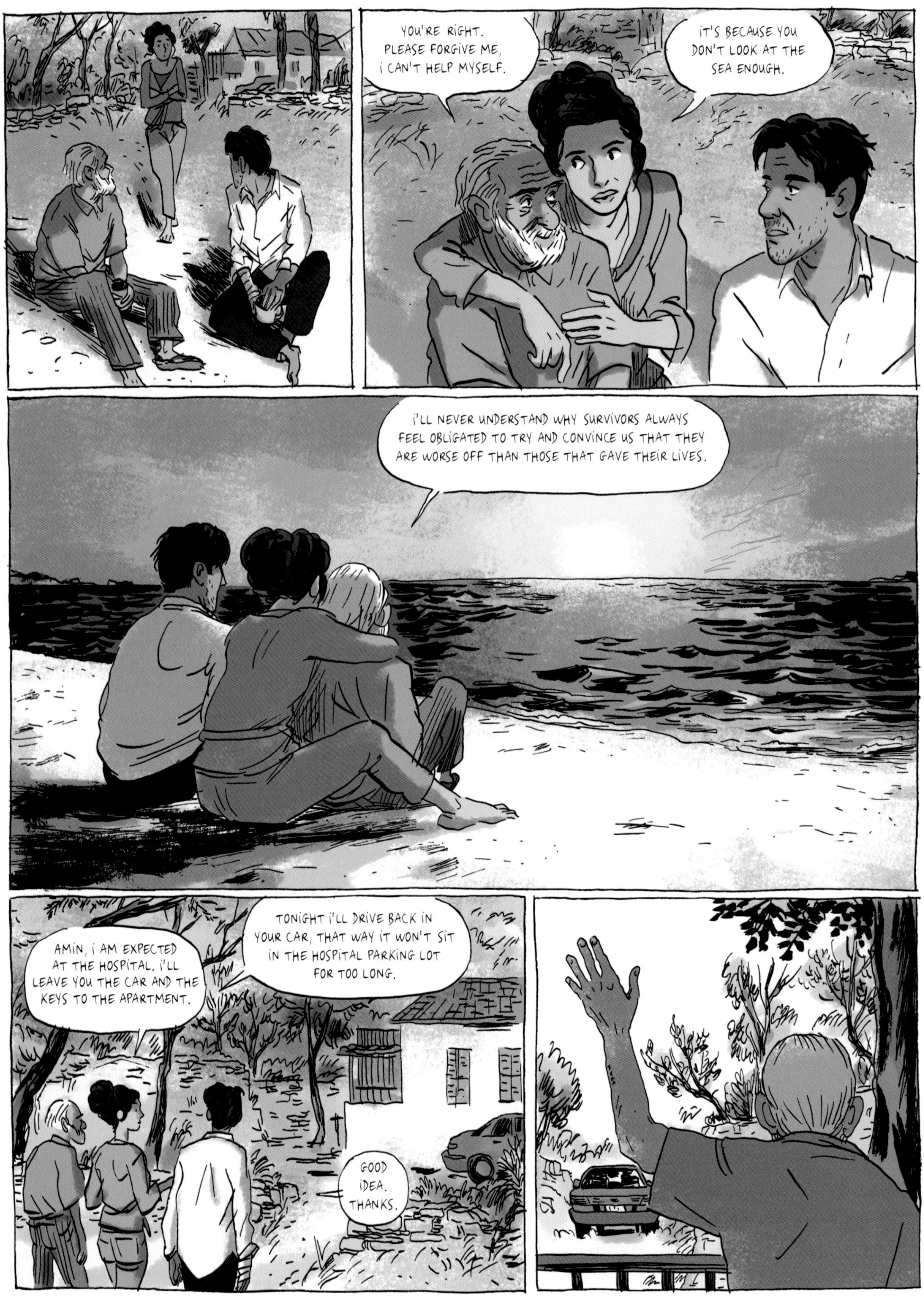
YOU'RE RIGHT. PLEASE FORGIVE ME, I CAN'T HELP MYSELF.
IT'S BECAUSE YOU DON'T LOOK AT THE SEA ENOUGH.
I'LL NEVER UNDERSTAND WHY SURVIVORS ALWAYS FEEL OBLIGATED TO TRY AND CONVINCE US THAT THEY ARE WORSE OFF THAN THOSE THAT GAVE THEIR LIVES.
AMIN, I AM EXPECTED AT THE HOSPITAL. I'LL LEAVE YOU THE CAR AND THE KEYS TO THE APARTMENT.
TONIGHT I'LL DRIVE BACK IN YOUR CAR, THAT WAY IT WON'T SIT IN THE HOSPITAL PARKING LOT FOR TOO LONG.
GOOD IDEA. THANKS.

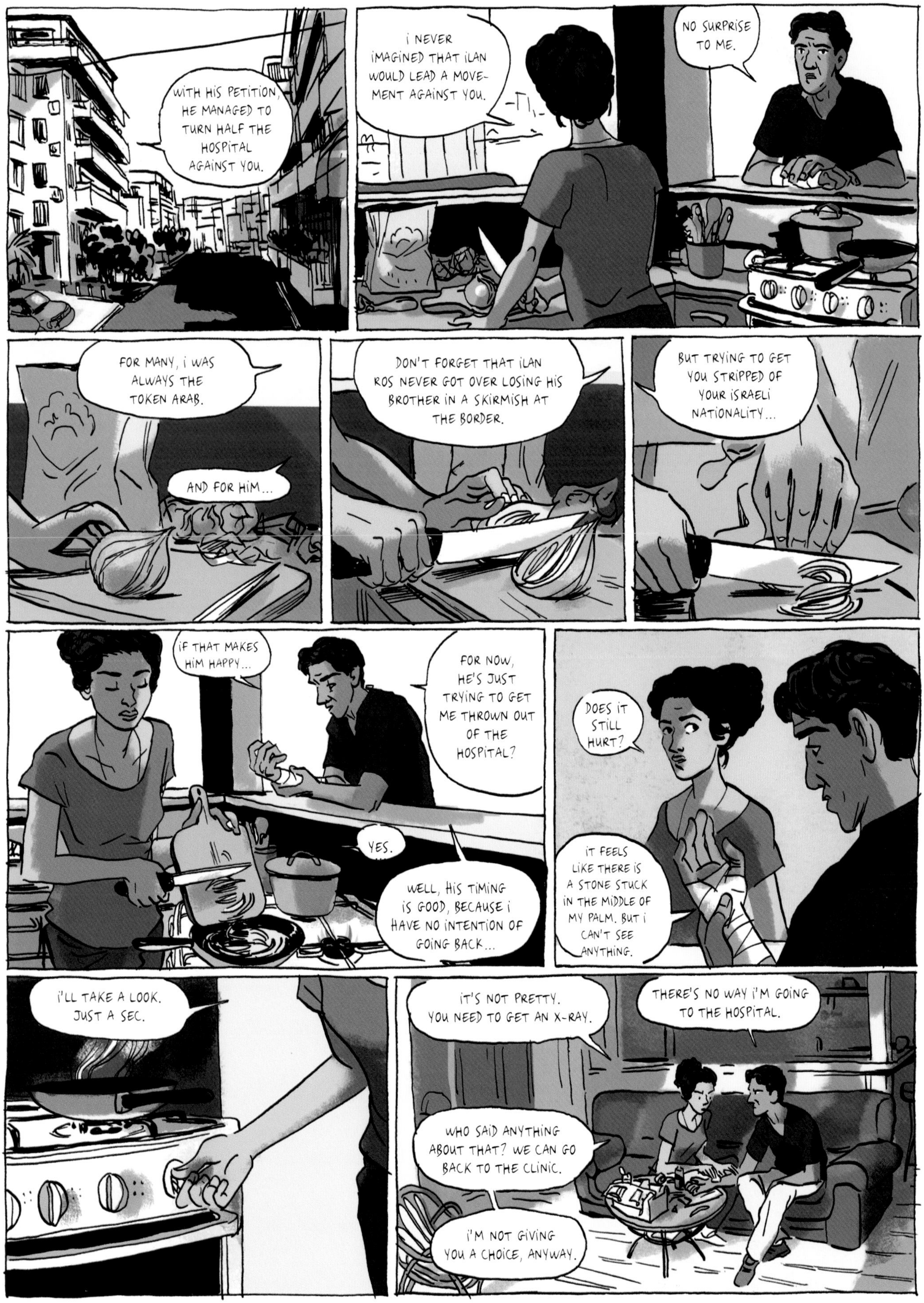
WITH HIS PETITION, HE MANAGED TO TURN HALF THE HOSPITAL AGAINST YOU.
I NEVER IMAGINED THAT ILAN WOULD LEAD A MOVEMENT AGAINST YOU.
NO SURPRISE TO ME.
FOR MANY, I WAS ALWAYS THE TOKEN ARAB.
AND FOR HIM...
DON'T FORGET THAT ILAN ROS NEVER GOT OVER LOSING HIS BROTHER IN A SKIRMISH AT THE BORDER.
BUT TRYING TO GET YOU STRIPPED OF YOUR ISRAELI NATIONALITY...
IF THAT MAKES HIM HAPPY...
FOR NOW, HE'S JUST TRYING TO GET ME THROWN OUT OF THE HOSPITAL?
YES.
WELL, HIS TIMING IS GOOD, BECAUSE I HAVE NO INTENTION OF GOING BACK...
DOES IT STILL HURT?
IT FEELS LIKE THERE IS A STONE STUCK IN THE MIDDLE OF MY PALM. BUT I CAN'T SEE ANYTHING.
I'LL TAKE A LOOK. JUST A SEC.
IT'S NOT PRETTY. YOU NEED TO GET AN X-RAY.
THERE'S NO WAY I'M GOING TO THE HOSPITAL.
WHO SAID ANYTHING ABOUT THAT? WE CAN GO BACK TO THE CLINIC.
I'M NOT GIVING YOU A CHOICE, ANYWAY.

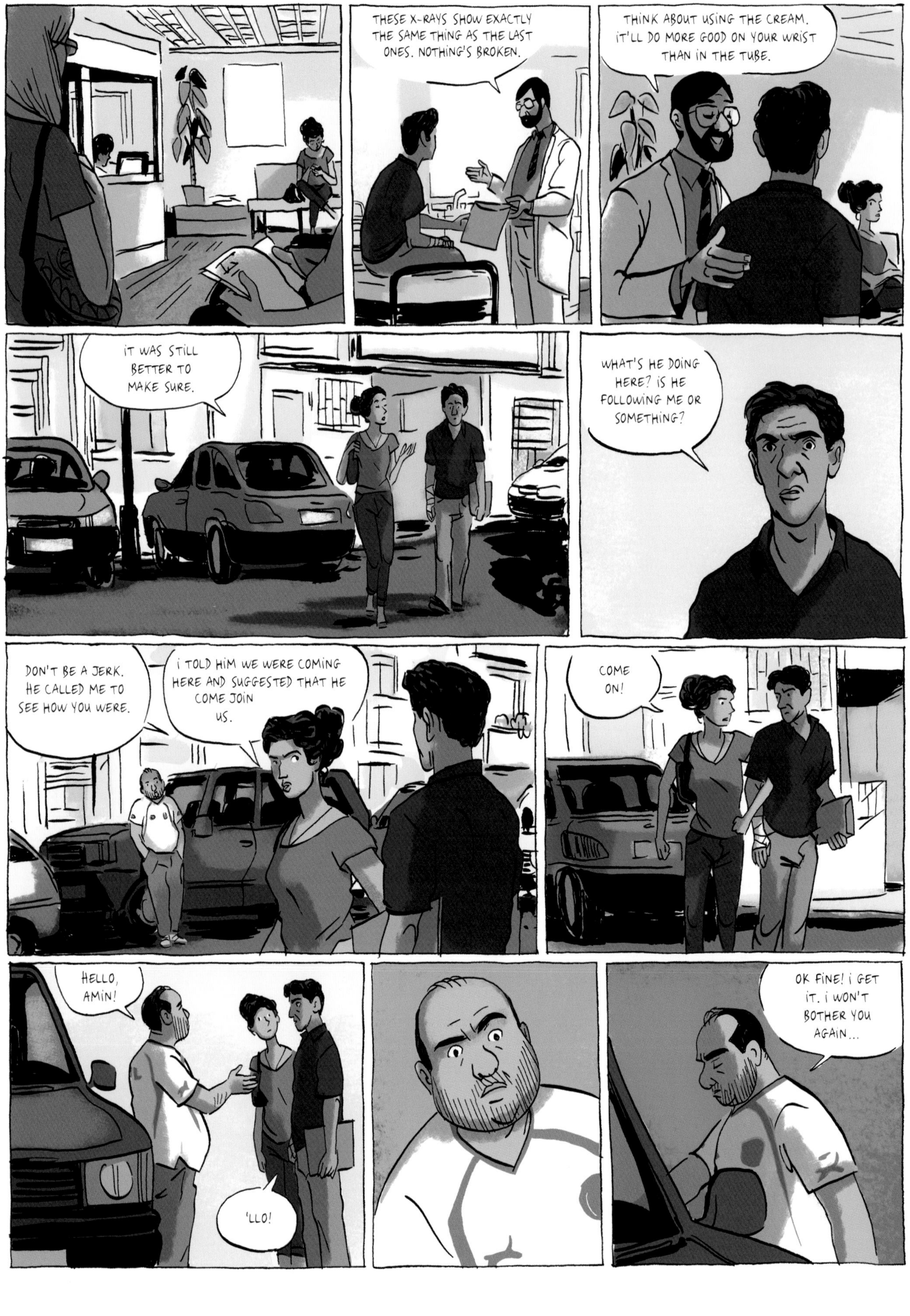
THESE X-RAYS SHOW EXACTLY THE SAME THING AS THE LAST ONES. NOTHING'S BROKEN.
THINK ABOUT USING THE CREAM. IT'LL DO MORE GOOD ON YOUR WRIST THAN IN THE TUBE.
IT WAS STILL BETTER TO MAKE SURE.
WHAT'S HE DOING HERE? IS HE FOLLOWING ME OR SOMETHING?
DON'T BE A JERK. HE CALLED ME TO SEE HOW YOU WERE.
I TOLD HIM WE WERE COMING HERE AND SUGGESTED THAT HE COME JOIN US.
COME ON!
HELLO, AMIN!
'LLO!
OK FINE! I GET IT. I WON'T BOTHER YOU AGAIN...

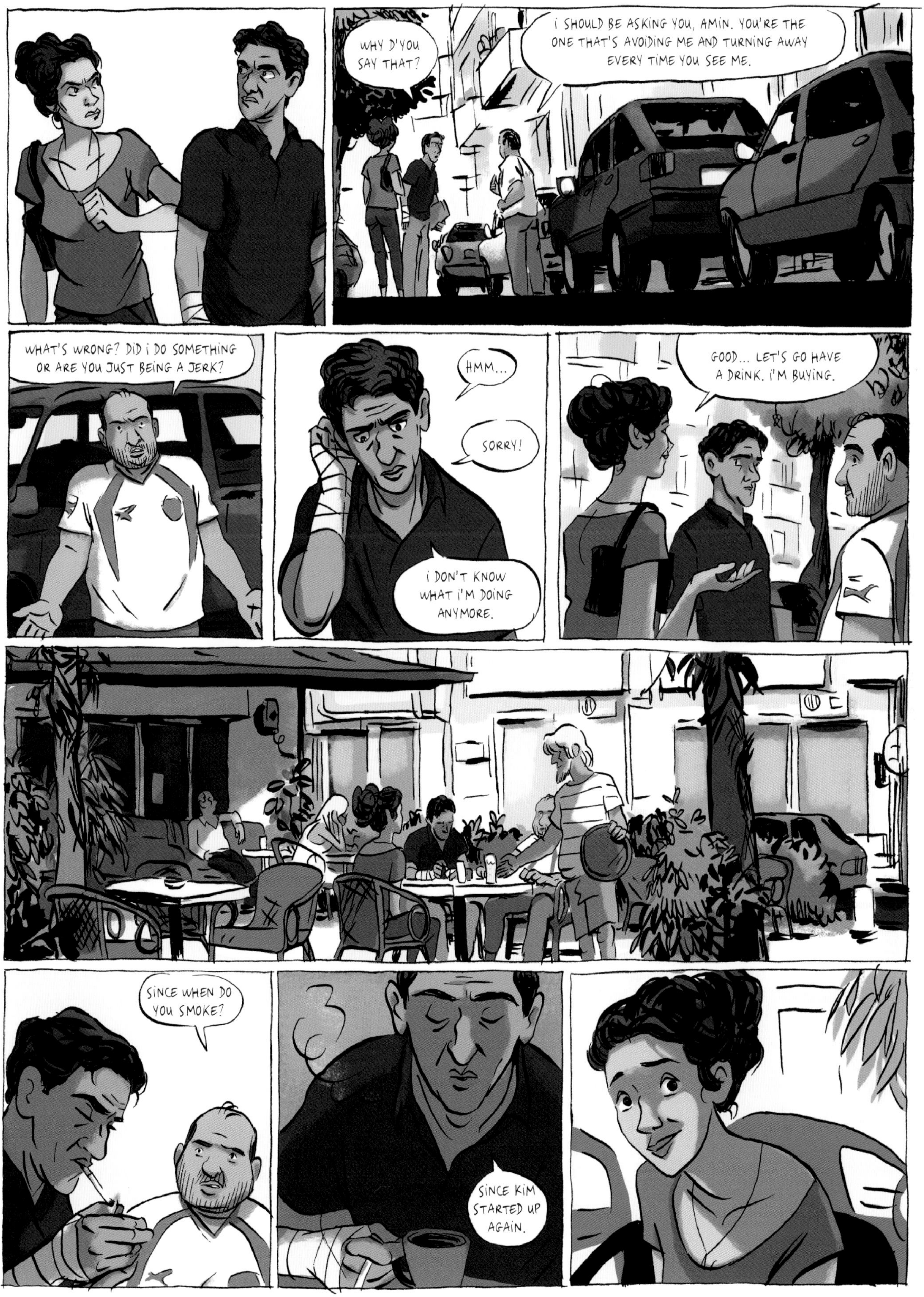
WHY D'YOU SAY THAT?
i SHOULD BE ASKiNG YOU, AMiN. YOU'RE THE ONE THAT'S AVOiDiNG ME AND TURNiNG AWAY EVERY TiME YOU SEE ME.
WHAT'S WRONG? DiD i DO SOMETHiNG OR ARE YOU JUST BEiNG A JERK?
HMM...
SORRY!
i DON'T KNOW WHAT i'M DOiNG ANYMORE.
GOOD... LET'S GO HAVE A DRiNK. i'M BUYiNG.
SiNCE WHEN DO YOU SMOKE?
SiNCE KiM STARTED UP AGAiN.

HOW'S MARGARET?

SHE'S COMPLETELY TAKEN UP BY EDEET'S WEDDING.

MMM! MARRIAGE. A GAME OF CHANCE.

AND YOU? HOW'S THE WRIST?

A BAD BRUISE, BUT NOTHING SERIOUS.

TELL ME...

HOW'S THE RESEARCH GOING?

I DON'T WANT TO ARGUE WITH YOU.

THAT'S NOT MY INTENTION EITHER, BUT I THINK I HAVE THE RIGHT TO KNOW.

TO KNOW WHAT EXACTLY? WHAT YOU DON'T WANT TO SEE?

NOT ANYMORE. I KNOW SHE DID IT.

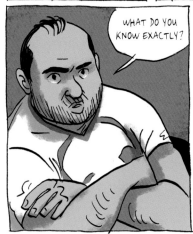

WHAT DO YOU KNOW EXACTLY?

THAT SHE BLEW HERSELF UP IN THE RESTAURANT.

AND SINCE WHEN DID YOU KNOW THAT?

IS THIS AN INTERROGATION, NAVID?

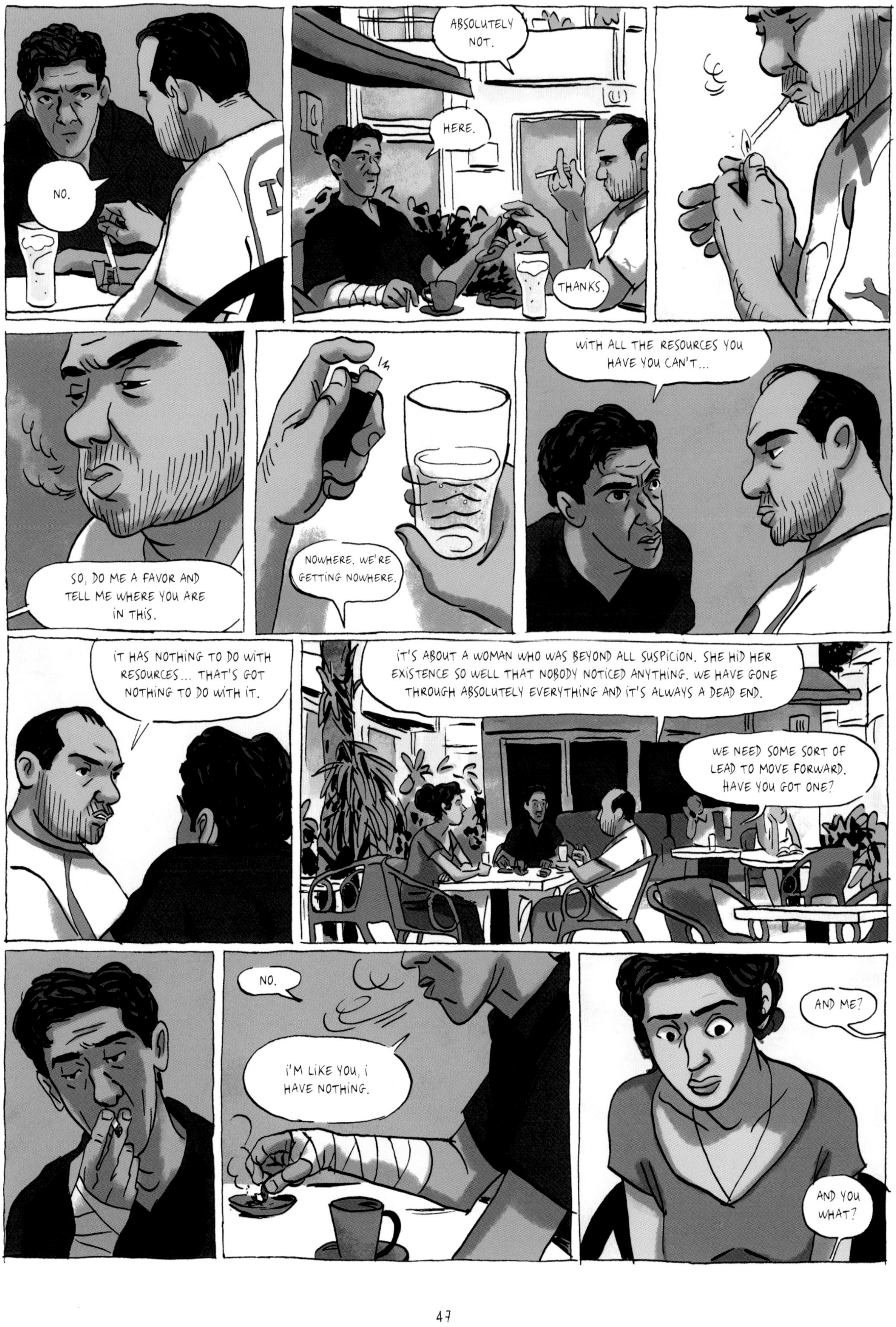
NO.
ABSOLUTELY NOT.
HERE.
THANKS.
SO, DO ME A FAVOR AND TELL ME WHERE YOU ARE IN THIS.
NOWHERE. WE'RE GETTING NOWHERE.
WITH ALL THE RESOURCES YOU HAVE YOU CAN'T...
IT HAS NOTHING TO DO WITH RESOURCES... THAT'S GOT NOTHING TO DO WITH IT.
IT'S ABOUT A WOMAN WHO WAS BEYOND ALL SUSPICION. SHE HID HER EXISTENCE SO WELL THAT NOBODY NOTICED ANYTHING. WE HAVE GONE THROUGH ABSOLUTELY EVERYTHING AND IT'S ALWAYS A DEAD END.
WE NEED SOME SORT OF LEAD TO MOVE FORWARD. HAVE YOU GOT ONE?
NO.
I'M LIKE YOU, I HAVE NOTHING.
AND ME?
AND YOU WHAT?

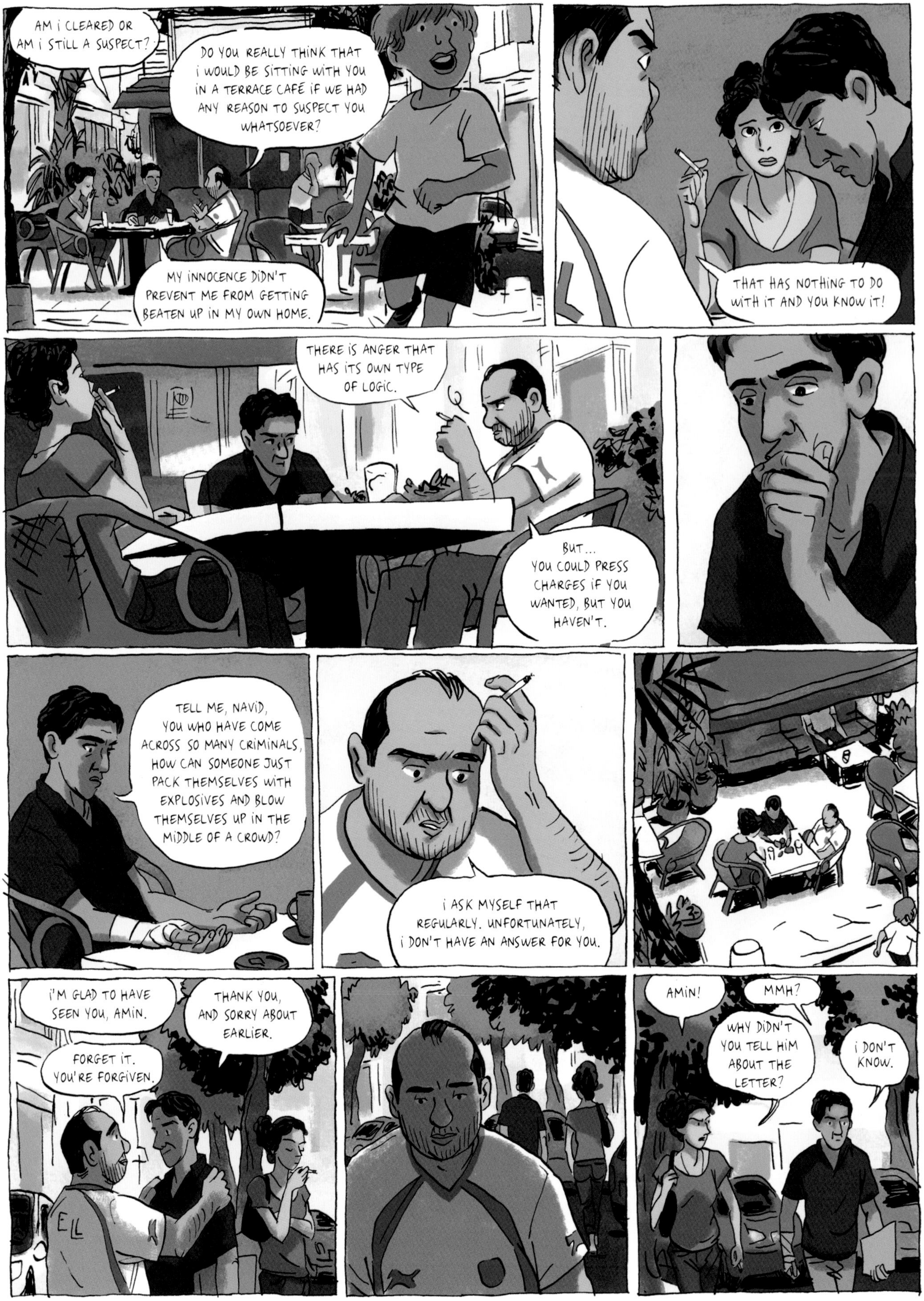
AM i CLEARED OR AM i STILL A SUSPECT?
DO YOU REALLY THiNK THAT i WOULD BE SiTTiNG WiTH YOU iN A TERRACE CAFÉ iF WE HAD ANY REASON TO SUSPECT YOU WHATSOEVER?
MY iNNOCENCE DiDN'T PREVENT ME FROM GETTiNG BEATEN UP iN MY OWN HOME.
THAT HAS NOTHiNG TO DO WiTH iT AND YOU KNOW iT!
THERE iS ANGER THAT HAS iTS OWN TYPE OF LOGiC.
BUT... YOU COULD PRESS CHARGES iF YOU WANTED, BUT YOU HAVEN'T.
TELL ME, NAViD, YOU WHO HAVE COME ACROSS SO MANY CRiMiNALS, HOW CAN SOMEONE JUST PACK THEMSELVES WiTH EXPLOSiVES AND BLOW THEMSELVES UP iN THE MiDDLE OF A CROWD?
i ASK MYSELF THAT REGULARLY. UNFORTUNATELY, i DON'T HAVE AN ANSWER FOR YOU.
i'M GLAD TO HAVE SEEN YOU, AMiN.
THANK YOU, AND SORRY ABOUT EARLiER.
FORGET iT. YOU'RE FORGiVEN.
AMiN!
MMH?
WHY DiDN'T YOU TELL HiM ABOUT THE LETTER?
i DON'T KNOW.

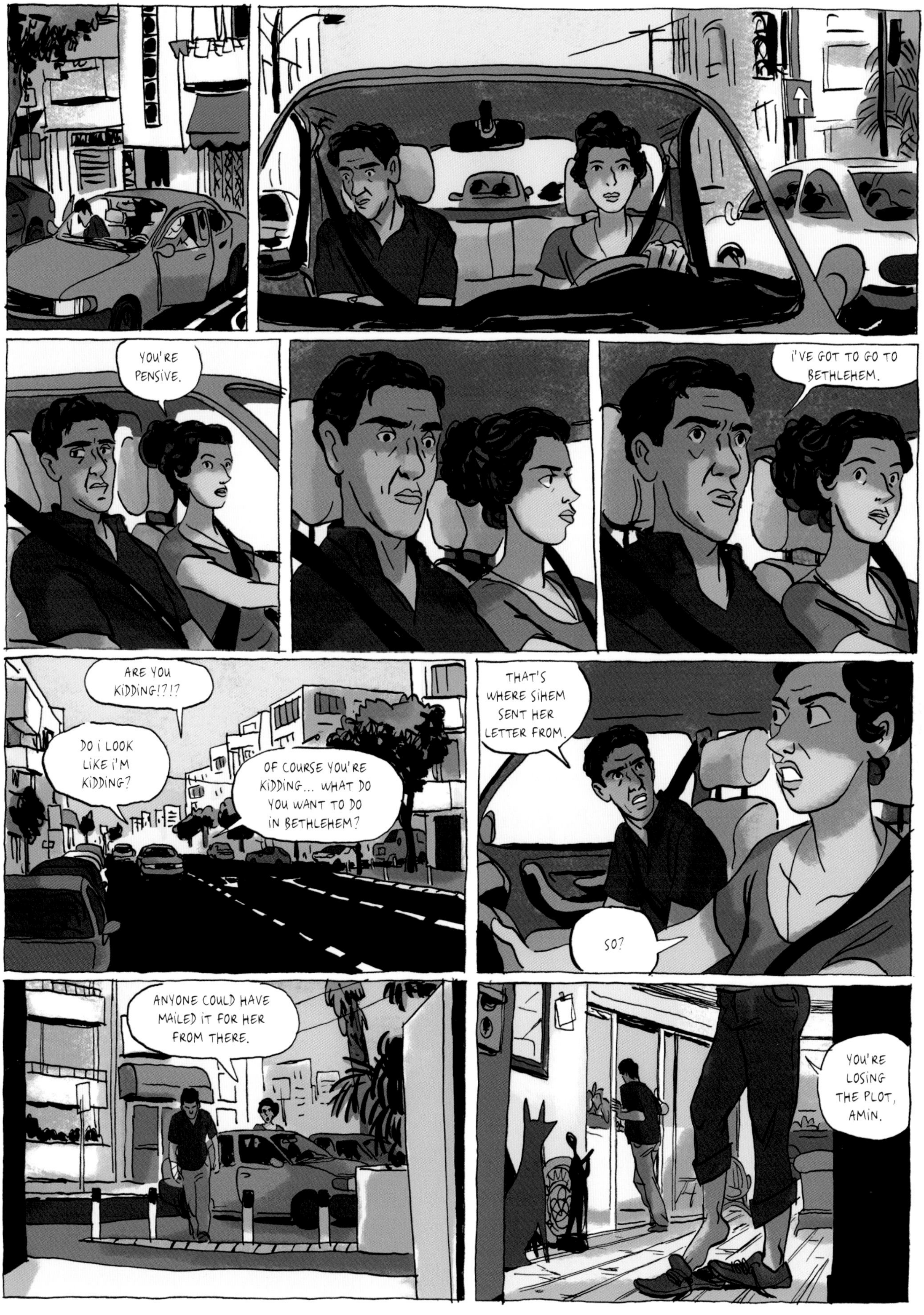
YOU'RE PENSIVE.
I'VE GOT TO GO TO BETHLEHEM.
ARE YOU KIDDING!?!?
DO I LOOK LIKE I'M KIDDING?
OF COURSE YOU'RE KIDDING... WHAT DO YOU WANT TO DO IN BETHLEHEM?
THAT'S WHERE SIHEM SENT HER LETTER FROM.
SO?
ANYONE COULD HAVE MAILED IT FOR HER FROM THERE.
YOU'RE LOSING THE PLOT, AMIN.

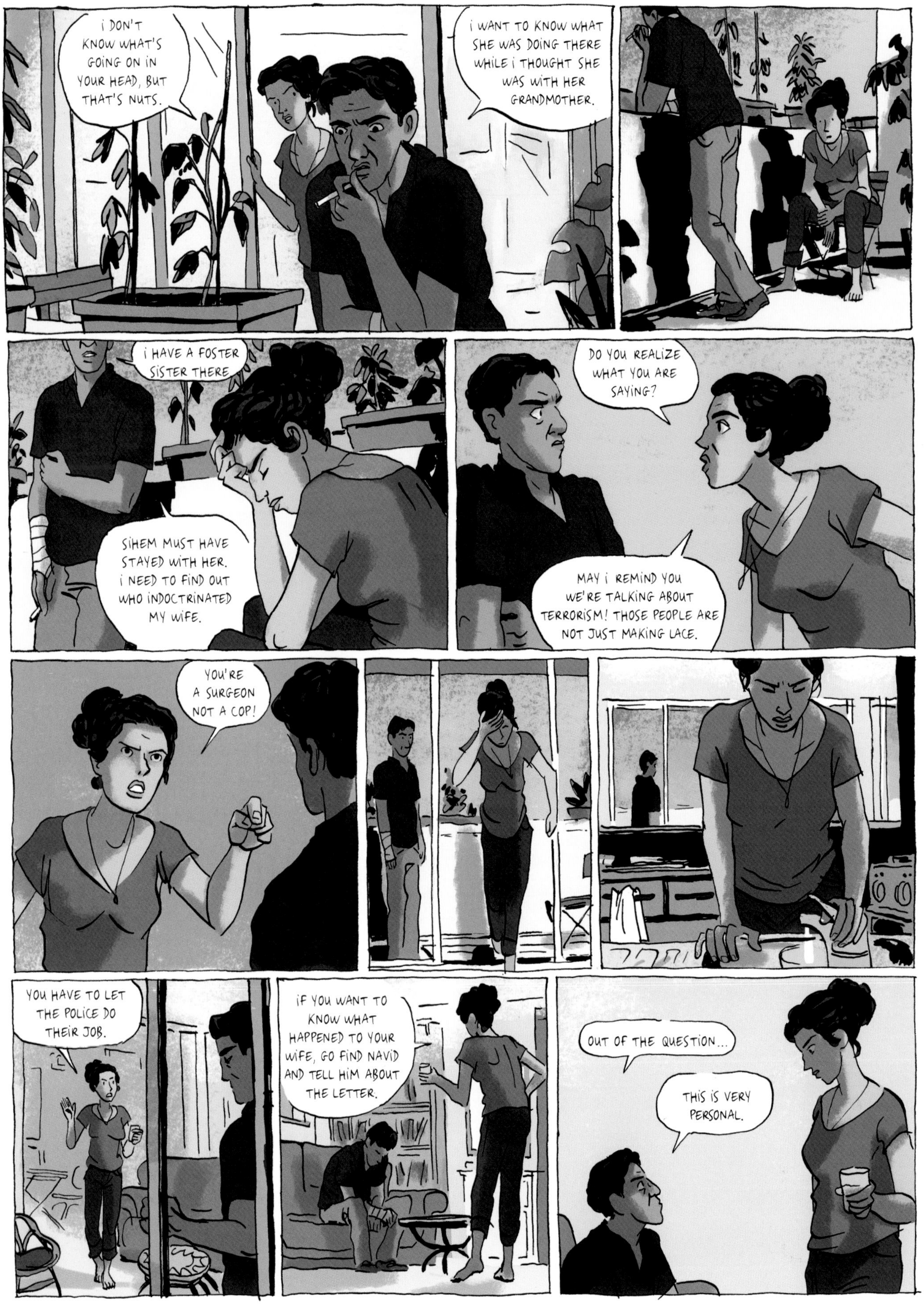
I DON'T KNOW WHAT'S GOING ON IN YOUR HEAD, BUT THAT'S NUTS.
I WANT TO KNOW WHAT SHE WAS DOING THERE WHILE I THOUGHT SHE WAS WITH HER GRANDMOTHER.
I HAVE A FOSTER SISTER THERE.
SIHEM MUST HAVE STAYED WITH HER. I NEED TO FIND OUT WHO INDOCTRINATED MY WIFE.
DO YOU REALIZE WHAT YOU ARE SAYING?
MAY I REMIND YOU WE'RE TALKING ABOUT TERRORISM! THOSE PEOPLE ARE NOT JUST MAKING LACE.
YOU'RE A SURGEON NOT A COP!
YOU HAVE TO LET THE POLICE DO THEIR JOB.
IF YOU WANT TO KNOW WHAT HAPPENED TO YOUR WIFE, GO FIND NAVID AND TELL HIM ABOUT THE LETTER.
OUT OF THE QUESTION...
THIS IS VERY PERSONAL.

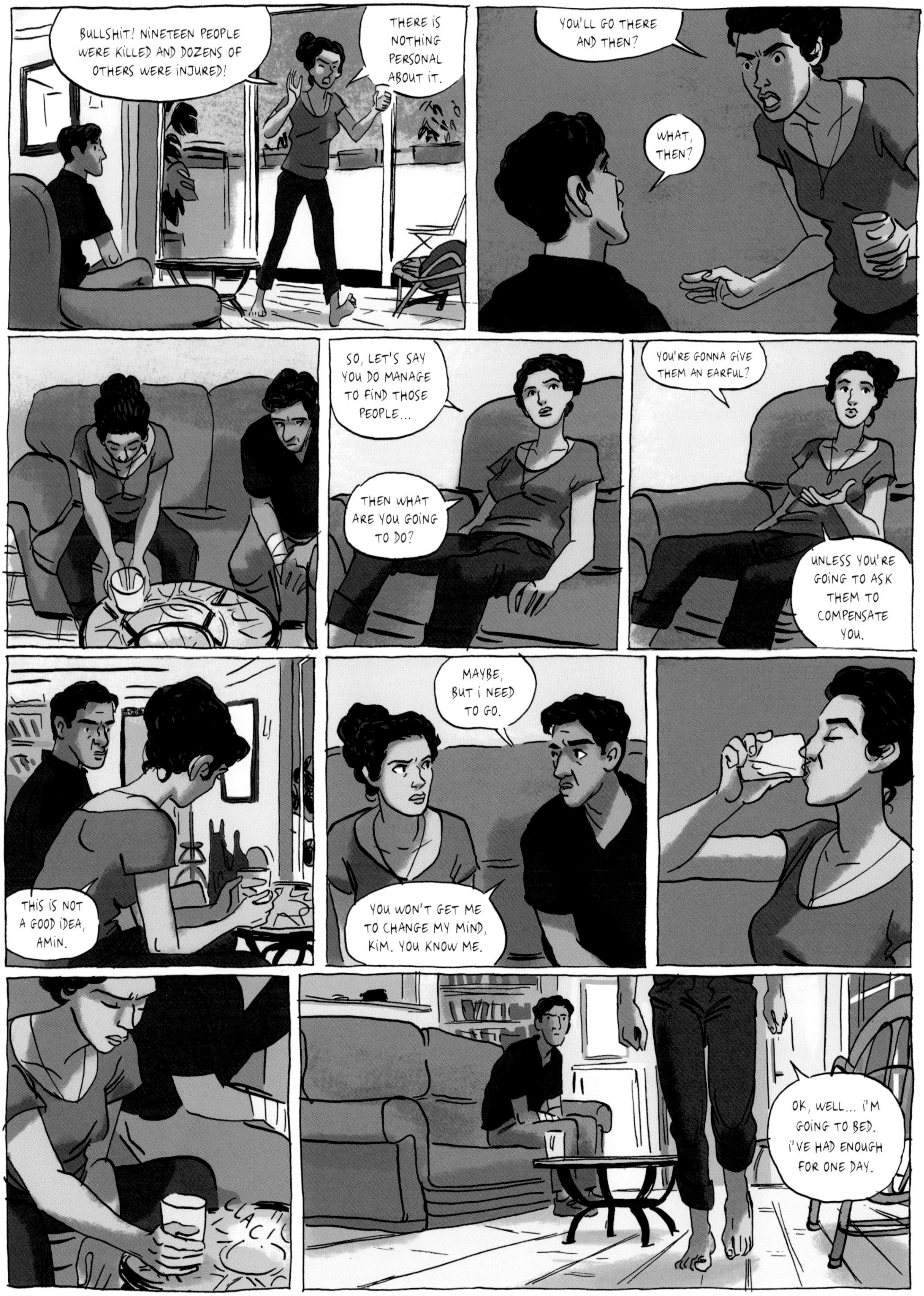
BULLSHIT! NINETEEN PEOPLE WERE KILLED AND DOZENS OF OTHERS WERE INJURED!
THERE IS NOTHING PERSONAL ABOUT IT.
YOU'LL GO THERE AND THEN?
WHAT, THEN?
SO, LET'S SAY YOU DO MANAGE TO FIND THOSE PEOPLE...
THEN WHAT ARE YOU GOING TO DO?
YOU'RE GONNA GIVE THEM AN EARFUL?
UNLESS YOU'RE GOING TO ASK THEM TO COMPENSATE YOU.
THIS IS NOT A GOOD IDEA, AMIN.
MAYBE, BUT I NEED TO GO.
YOU WON'T GET ME TO CHANGE MY MIND, KIM. YOU KNOW ME.
CLAC!
OK, WELL... I'M GOING TO BED. I'VE HAD ENOUGH FOR ONE DAY.

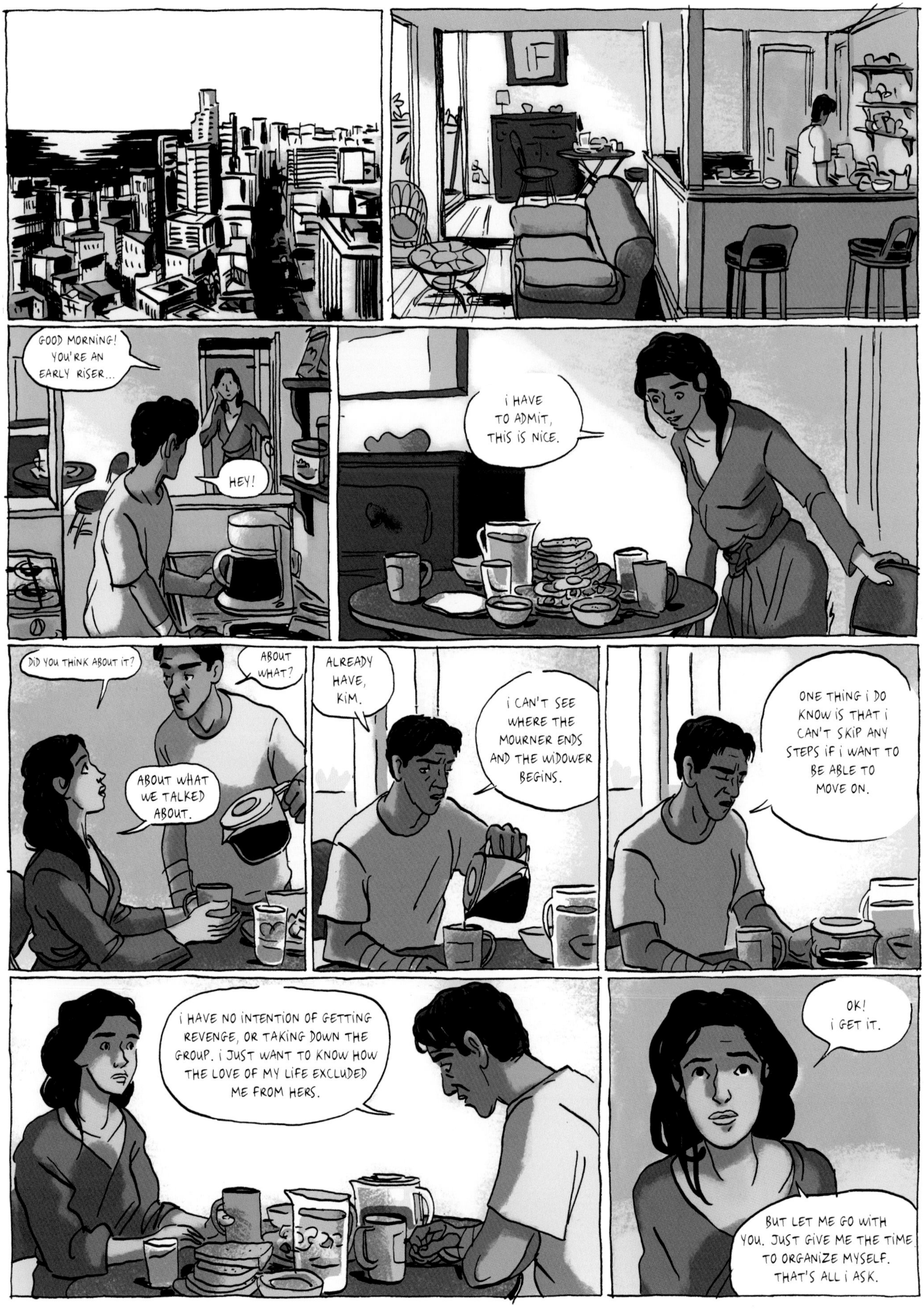
GOOD MORNING! YOU'RE AN EARLY RISER...
HEY!
I HAVE TO ADMIT, THIS IS NICE.
DID YOU THINK ABOUT IT?
ABOUT WHAT?
ABOUT WHAT WE TALKED ABOUT.
ALREADY HAVE, KIM.
I CAN'T SEE WHERE THE MOURNER ENDS AND THE WIDOWER BEGINS.
ONE THING I DO KNOW IS THAT I CAN'T SKIP ANY STEPS IF I WANT TO BE ABLE TO MOVE ON.
I HAVE NO INTENTION OF GETTING REVENGE, OR TAKING DOWN THE GROUP. I JUST WANT TO KNOW HOW THE LOVE OF MY LIFE EXCLUDED ME FROM HERS.
OK! I GET IT.
BUT LET ME GO WITH YOU. JUST GIVE ME THE TIME TO ORGANIZE MYSELF. THAT'S ALL I ASK.

OK! I'LL WAIT.

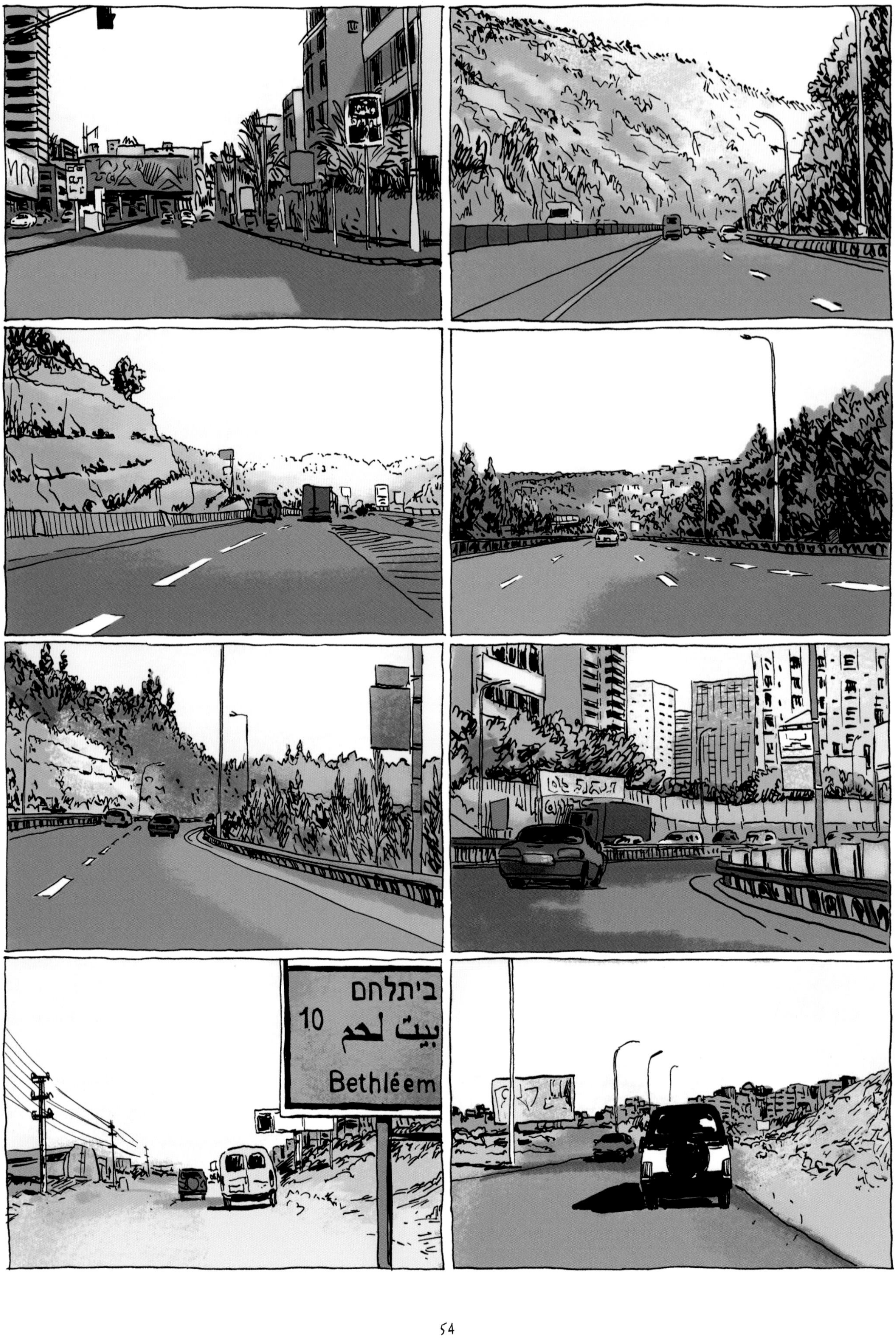
ביתלחם
10
بيت لحم
Bethléem

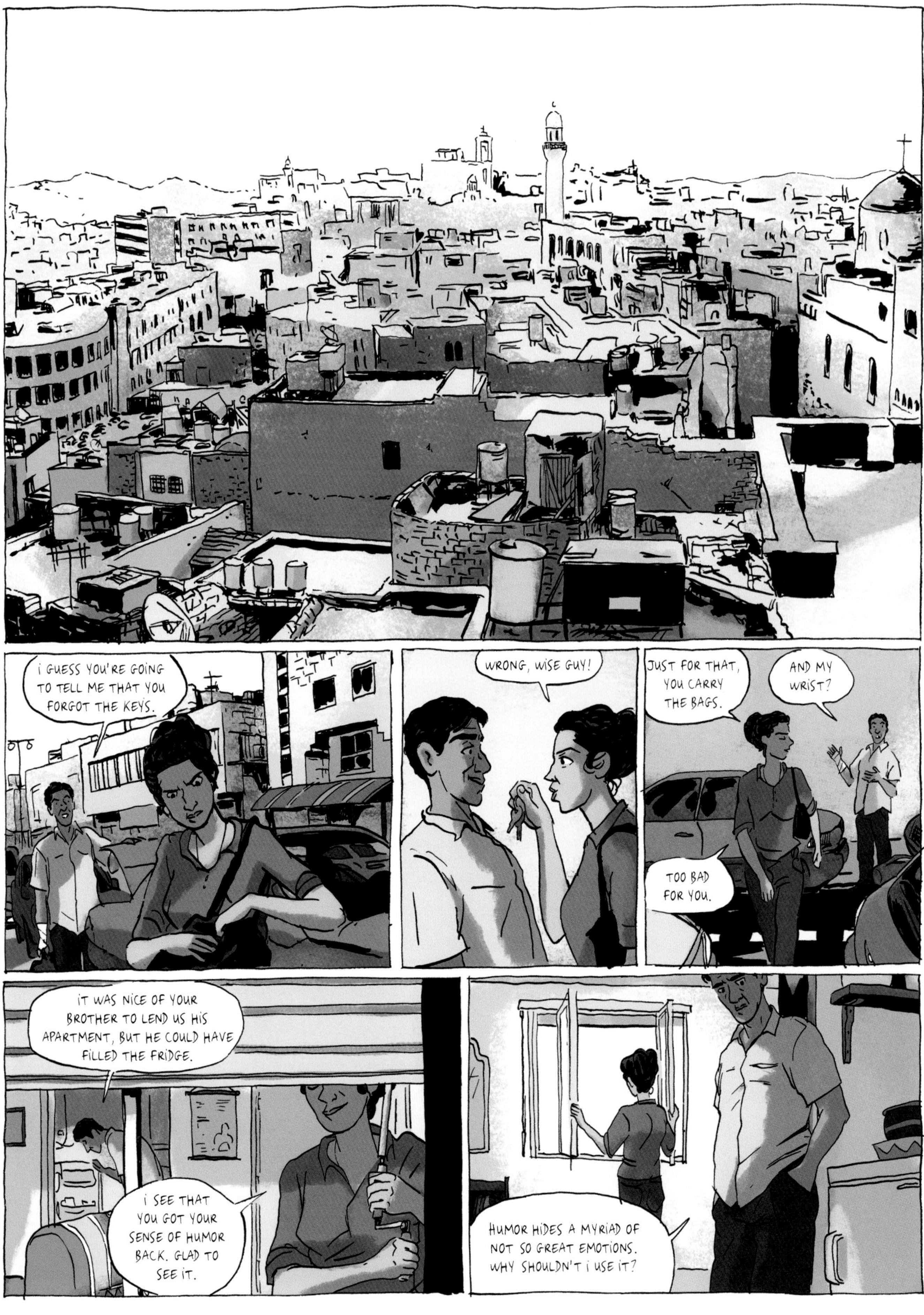
I GUESS YOU'RE GOING TO TELL ME THAT YOU FORGOT THE KEYS.
WRONG, WISE GUY!
JUST FOR THAT, YOU CARRY THE BAGS.
AND MY WRIST?
TOO BAD FOR YOU.
IT WAS NICE OF YOUR BROTHER TO LEND US HIS APARTMENT, BUT HE COULD HAVE FILLED THE FRIDGE.
I SEE THAT YOU GOT YOUR SENSE OF HUMOR BACK. GLAD TO SEE IT.
HUMOR HIDES A MYRIAD OF NOT SO GREAT EMOTIONS. WHY SHOULDN'T I USE IT?

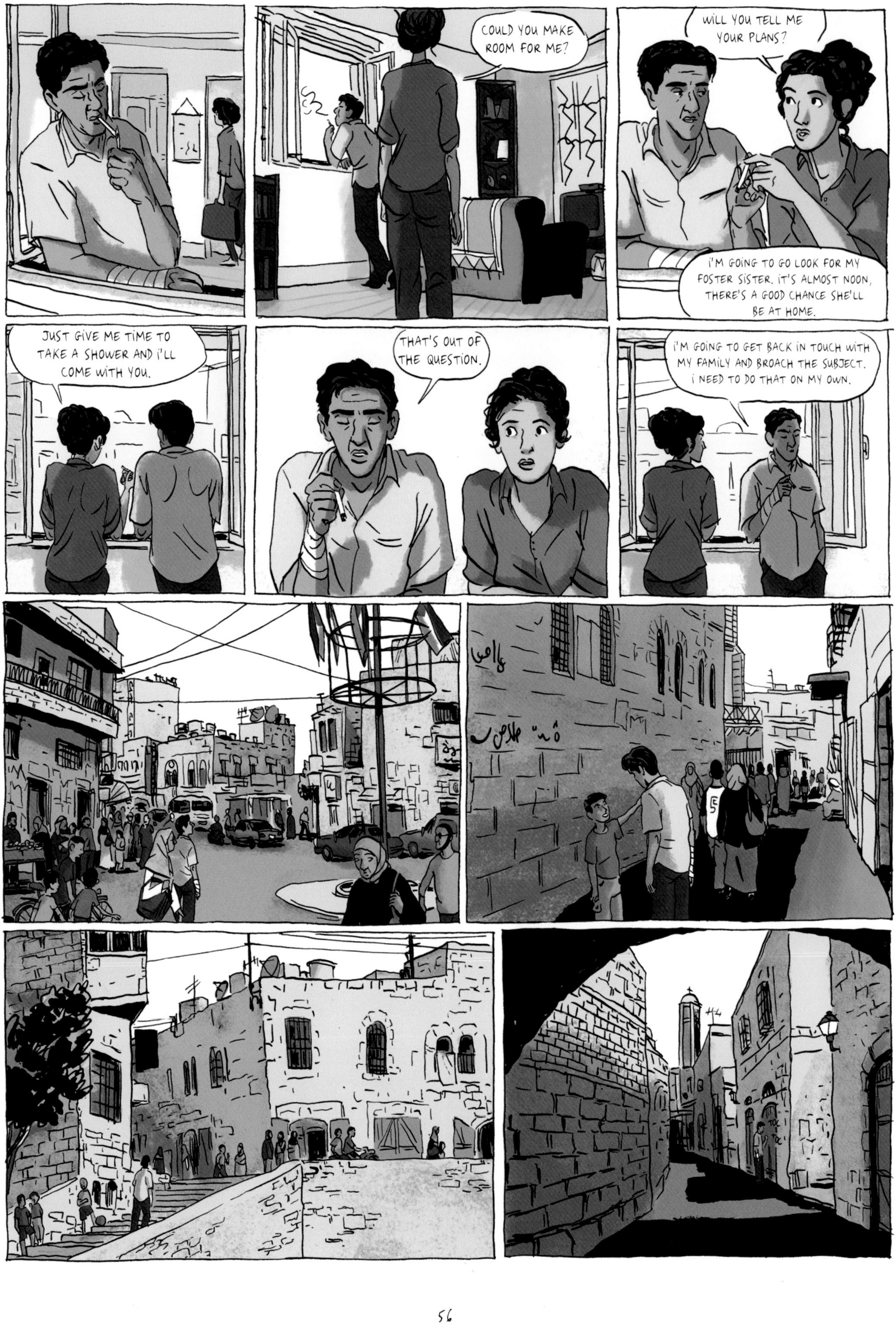
COULD YOU MAKE ROOM FOR ME?
WILL YOU TELL ME YOUR PLANS?
I'M GOING TO GO LOOK FOR MY FOSTER SISTER. IT'S ALMOST NOON, THERE'S A GOOD CHANCE SHE'LL BE AT HOME.
JUST GIVE ME TIME TO TAKE A SHOWER AND I'LL COME WITH YOU.
THAT'S OUT OF THE QUESTION.
I'M GOING TO GET BACK IN TOUCH WITH MY FAMILY AND BROACH THE SUBJECT. I NEED TO DO THAT ON MY OWN.

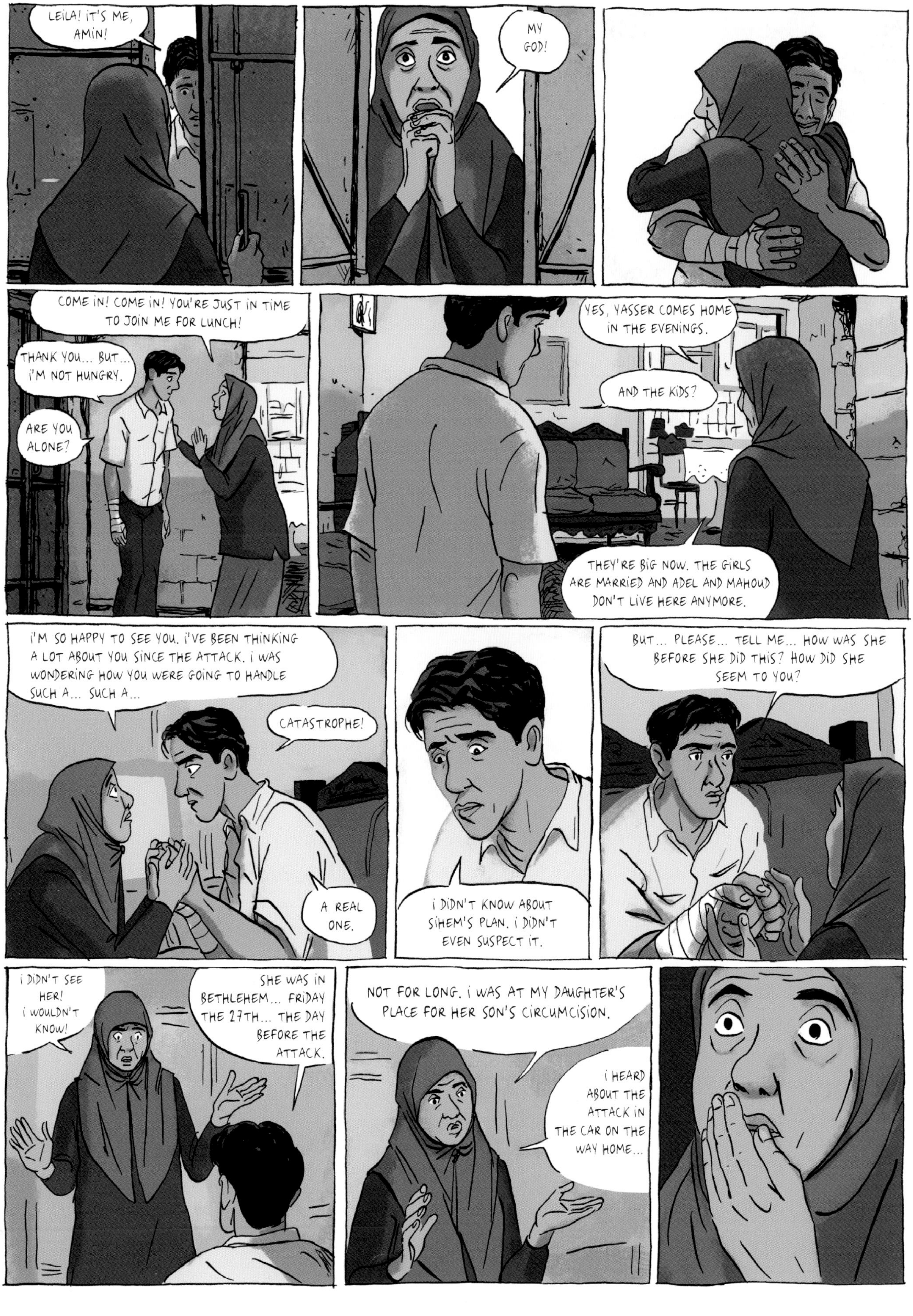
LEILA! IT'S ME, AMIN!
MY GOD!
COME IN! COME IN! YOU'RE JUST IN TIME TO JOIN ME FOR LUNCH!
THANK YOU... BUT... I'M NOT HUNGRY.
ARE YOU ALONE?
YES, YASSER COMES HOME IN THE EVENINGS.
AND THE KIDS?
THEY'RE BIG NOW. THE GIRLS ARE MARRIED AND ADEL AND MAHOUD DON'T LIVE HERE ANYMORE.
I'M SO HAPPY TO SEE YOU. I'VE BEEN THINKING A LOT ABOUT YOU SINCE THE ATTACK. I WAS WONDERING HOW YOU WERE GOING TO HANDLE SUCH A... SUCH A...
CATASTROPHE!
A REAL ONE.
I DIDN'T KNOW ABOUT SIHEM'S PLAN. I DIDN'T EVEN SUSPECT IT.
BUT... PLEASE... TELL ME... HOW WAS SHE BEFORE SHE DID THIS? HOW DID SHE SEEM TO YOU?
I DIDN'T SEE HER! I WOULDN'T KNOW!
SHE WAS IN BETHLEHEM... FRIDAY THE 27TH... THE DAY BEFORE THE ATTACK.
NOT FOR LONG. I WAS AT MY DAUGHTER'S PLACE FOR HER SON'S CIRCUMCISION.
I HEARD ABOUT THE ATTACK IN THE CAR ON THE WAY HOME...

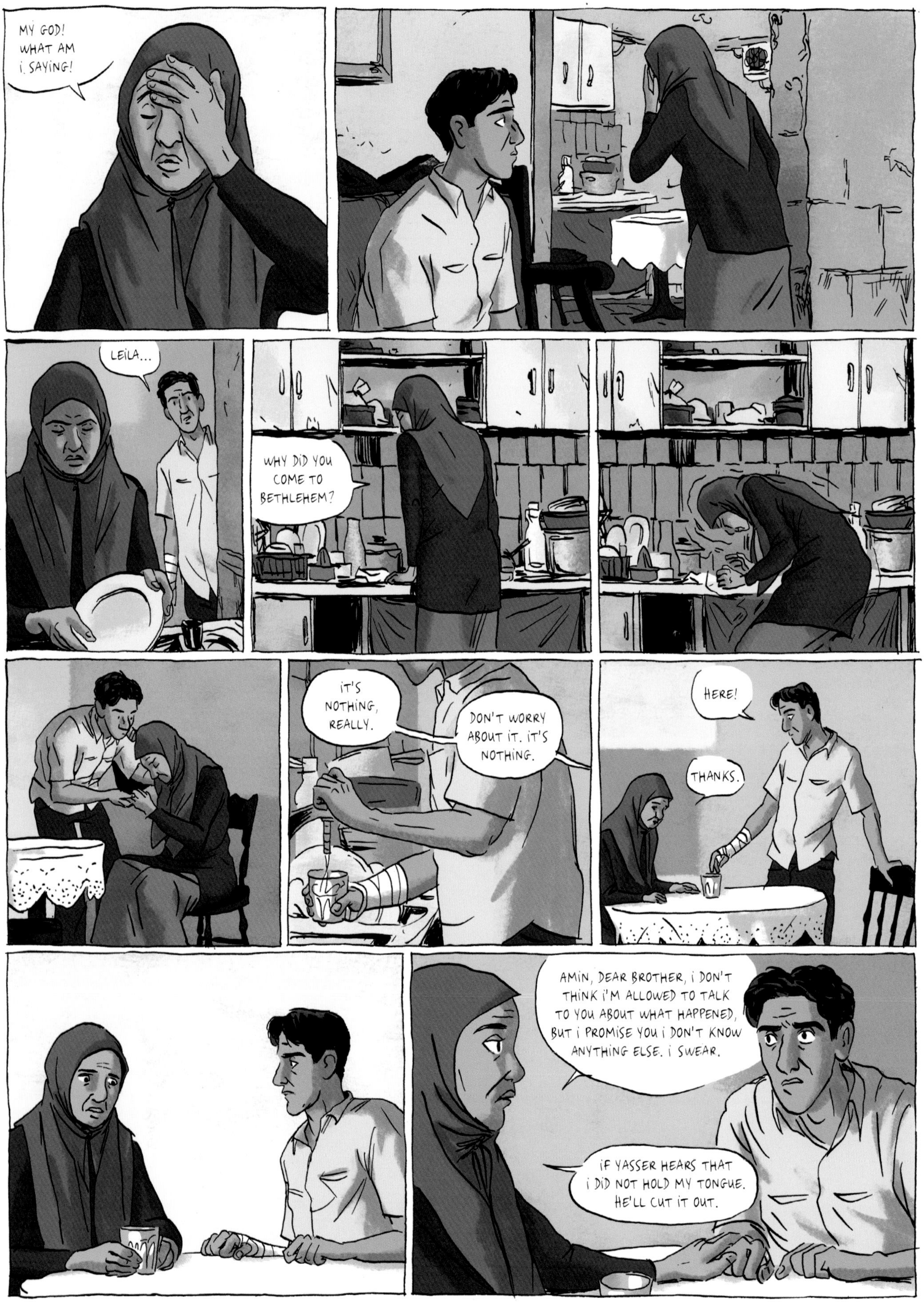
MY GOD! WHAT AM I SAYING!
LEILA...
WHY DID YOU COME TO BETHLEHEM?
IT'S NOTHING, REALLY.
DON'T WORRY ABOUT IT. IT'S NOTHING.
HERE!
THANKS.
AMIN, DEAR BROTHER, I DON'T THINK I'M ALLOWED TO TALK TO YOU ABOUT WHAT HAPPENED, BUT I PROMISE YOU I DON'T KNOW ANYTHING ELSE. I SWEAR.
IF YASSER HEARS THAT I DID NOT HOLD MY TONGUE, HE'LL CUT IT OUT.

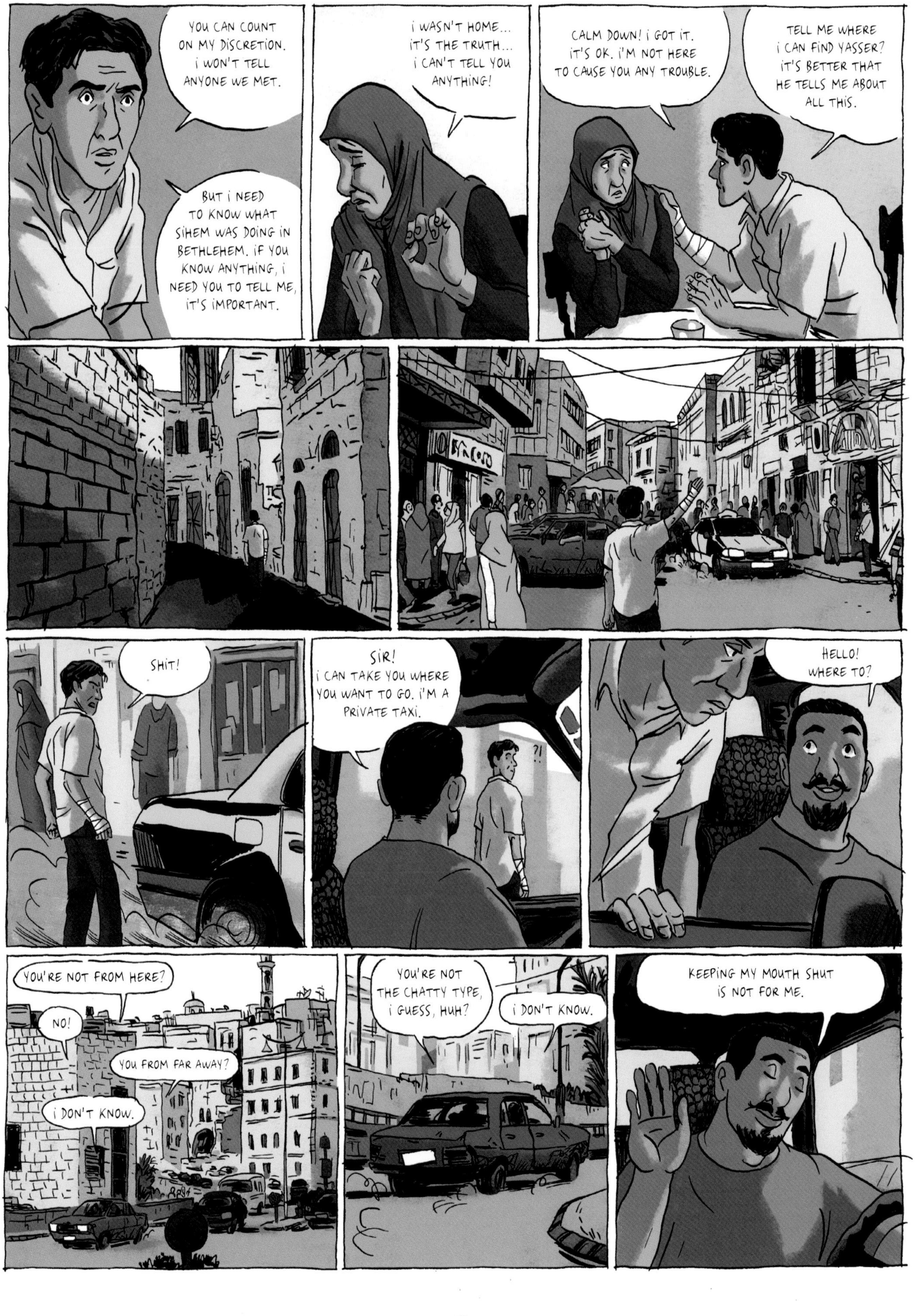

YOU CAN COUNT ON MY DISCRETION. i WON'T TELL ANYONE WE MET.
BUT i NEED TO KNOW WHAT SiHEM WAS DOING IN BETHLEHEM. iF YOU KNOW ANYTHING, i NEED YOU TO TELL ME, iT'S iMPORTANT.
i WASN'T HOME... iT'S THE TRUTH... i CAN'T TELL YOU ANYTHiNG!
CALM DOWN! i GOT iT. iT'S OK. i'M NOT HERE TO CAUSE YOU ANY TROUBLE.
TELL ME WHERE i CAN FiND YASSER? iT'S BETTER THAT HE TELLS ME ABOUT ALL THiS.
SHiT!
SiR! i CAN TAKE YOU WHERE YOU WANT TO GO. i'M A PRiVATE TAXi.
?!
HELLO! WHERE TO?
YOU'RE NOT FROM HERE?
NO!
YOU FROM FAR AWAY?
i DON'T KNOW.
YOU'RE NOT THE CHATTY TYPE, i GUESS, HUH?
i DON'T KNOW.
KEEPiNG MY MOUTH SHUT iS NOT FOR ME.

SINCE YOU'RE NOT GOING TO TALK, LISTEN TO THIS, MY FRIEND. ANYONE WHO HASN'T HEARD THE PREACHER SHEIKH MARWAN HASN'T LIVED. OPEN YOUR EARS TO THIS.

IS THERE, ON THIS VERSATILE AND INCONSISTENT LOWLY PLANET, OTHER SPLENDORS THAT ARE SUSCEPTIBLE TO TURNING US AWAY FROM ALLAH?

WHAT WILL WE SAY WHEN WE ARE ASKED, ALL OF US, BIG AND SMALL, WHAT HAVE YOU DONE WITH YOUR LIFE? WHAT HAVE YOU DONE TO MY PROPHETS AND MY GENEROSITY?

"EVERY DAY WE ARE DRAGGED THROUGH THE MUD OR THROUGH THE COURTS.

EVERY DAY THE WORLD SEES OUR MISERY...

CLAC!

HEY! WHAT ARE YOU DOING?!

I DON'T LIKE PREACHERS.

WHAT?!

HiiiiiRHi

YOU DON'T BELIEVE IN GOD!?

I DON'T BELIEVE IN HIS SAINTS.

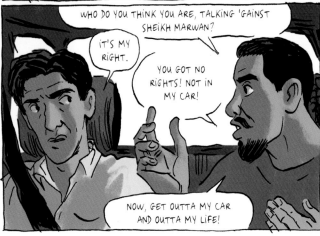
WHO DO YOU THINK YOU ARE, TALKING 'GAINST SHEIKH MARWAN?

IT'S MY RIGHT.

YOU GOT NO RIGHTS! NOT IN MY CAR!

NOW, GET OUTTA MY CAR AND OUTTA MY LIFE!

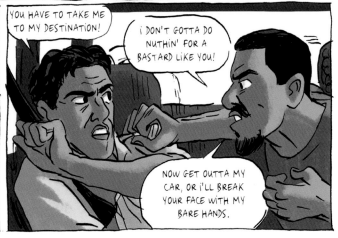
YOU HAVE TO TAKE ME TO MY DESTINATION!

I DON'T GOTTA DO NUTHIN' FOR A BASTARD LIKE YOU!

NOW GET OUTTA MY CAR, OR I'LL BREAK YOUR FACE WITH MY BARE HANDS.

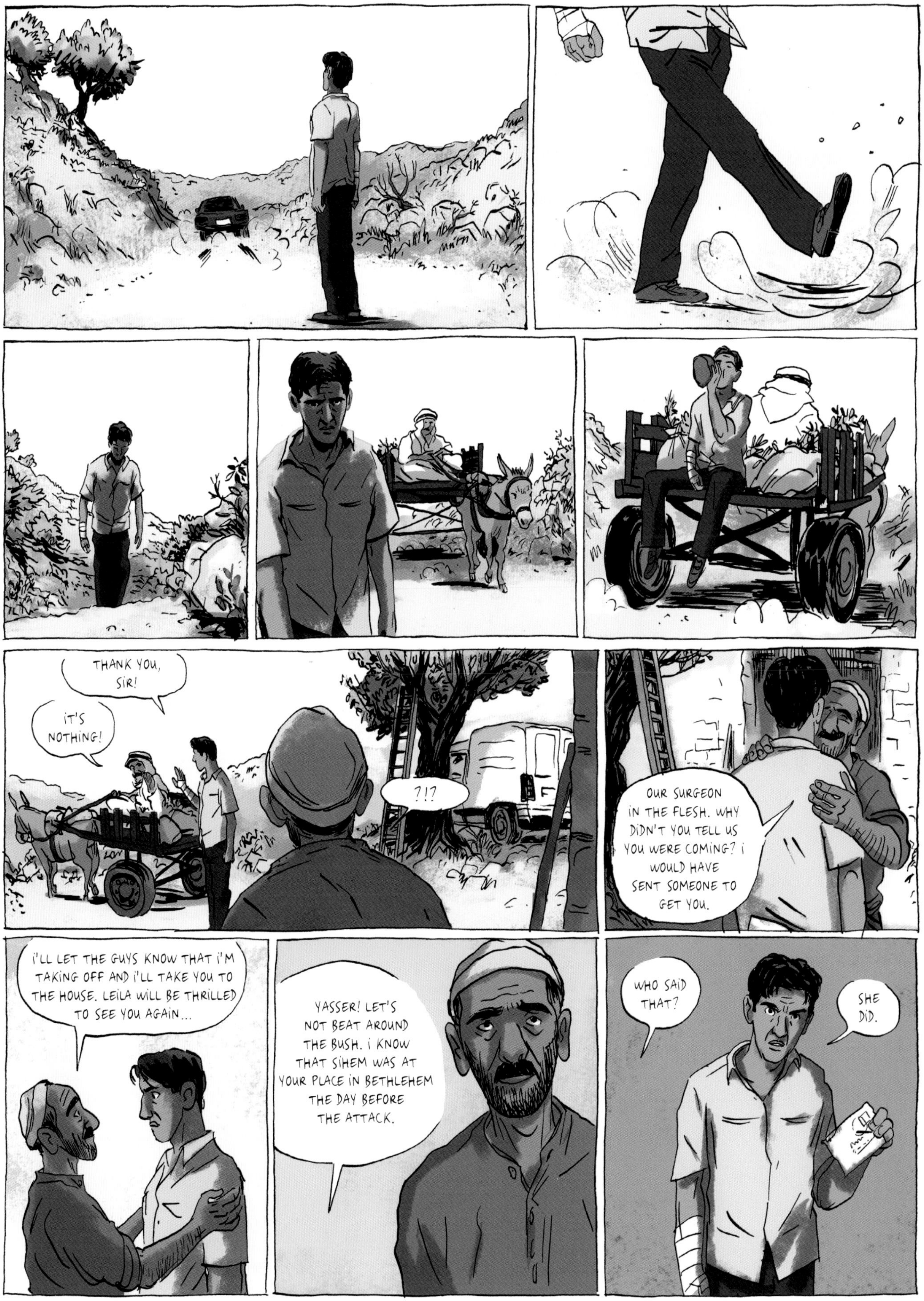
THANK YOU, SIR!
IT'S NOTHING!
?!?
OUR SURGEON IN THE FLESH. WHY DIDN'T YOU TELL US YOU WERE COMING? I WOULD HAVE SENT SOMEONE TO GET YOU.
I'LL LET THE GUYS KNOW THAT I'M TAKING OFF AND I'LL TAKE YOU TO THE HOUSE. LEILA WILL BE THRILLED TO SEE YOU AGAIN...
YASSER! LET'S NOT BEAT AROUND THE BUSH. I KNOW THAT SIHEM WAS AT YOUR PLACE IN BETHLEHEM THE DAY BEFORE THE ATTACK.
WHO SAID THAT?
SHE DID.

SHE DIDN'T STAY LONG... AND SHE WASN'T HERE TO SEE US. THAT FRIDAY SHEIKH MARWAN WAS GOING TO BE AT THE BIG MOSQUE. YOUR WIFE WANTED HIM TO BLESS HER.

IT WASN'T UNTIL WE SAW HER PICTURE IN THE PAPER THAT WE UNDERSTOOD.

YOU KNOW... WE ARE VERY PROUD OF HER.

PROUD OF WHAT? THAT SHE BLEW HERSELF TO BITS?

I DON'T WANT TO HEAR YOU TALKING LIKE THAT.

HOW CAN WE BE PROUD OF KILLING OTHERS SO THAT WE CAN LIVE FREE AND HAPPY?

MY DREAMS WERE DESTROYED FROM ONE DAY TO THE NEXT! I LOST EVERYTHING, FOR NOTHING!

AMIN! CALM DOWN, PLEASE.

CALM DOWN?! ME? DID... DID YOU THINK OF MY SUFFERING WHEN YOU WERE JUMPING FOR JOY AFTER HAVING HEARD THAT SIHEM BLEW HERSELF UP?

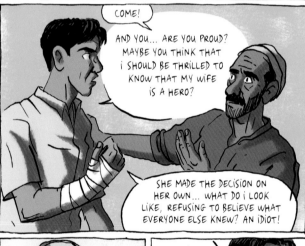

COME!

AND YOU... ARE YOU PROUD? MAYBE YOU THINK THAT I SHOULD BE THRILLED TO KNOW THAT MY WIFE IS A HERO?

SHE MADE THE DECISION ON HER OWN... WHAT DO I LOOK LIKE, REFUSING TO BELIEVE WHAT EVERYONE ELSE KNEW? AN IDIOT!

LET GO OF ME!

AMIN, I THINK YOU'VE GOT THE WRONG GUY. I HAD NOTHING TO DO WITH IT.

YOU SAID YOU WERE PROUD OF HER!

WHAT DID YOU EXPECT ME TO SAY? I DIDN'T KNOW THAT YOU DIDN'T KNOW.

I'M REALLY CONFUSED, AMIN. I'M SORRY...

THEN SHUT UP. THAT WAY YOU CAN BE SURE NOT TO SAY SOMETHING STUPID.

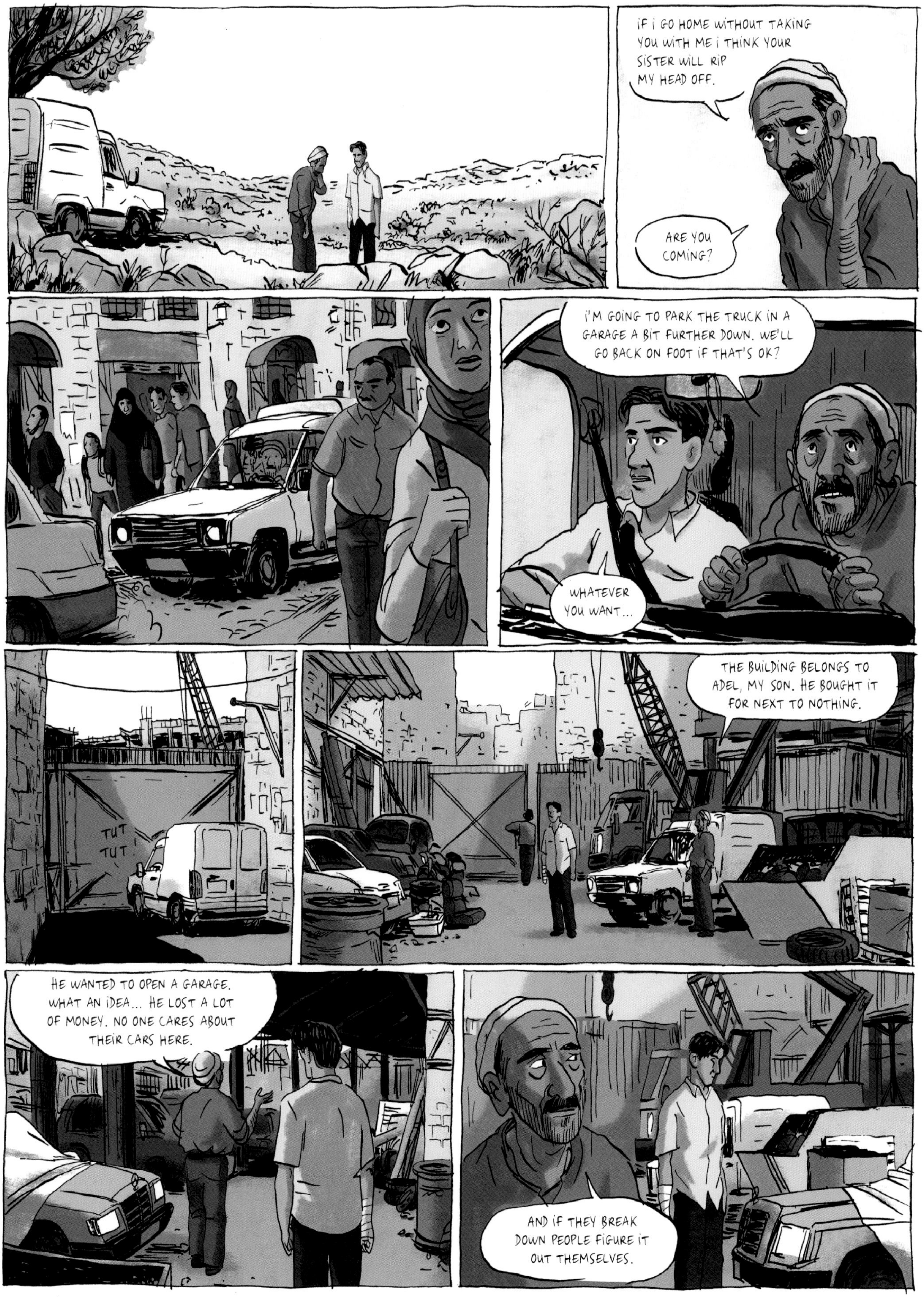
IF I GO HOME WITHOUT TAKING YOU WITH ME I THINK YOUR SISTER WILL RIP MY HEAD OFF.
ARE YOU COMING?
I'M GOING TO PARK THE TRUCK IN A GARAGE A BIT FURTHER DOWN. WE'LL GO BACK ON FOOT IF THAT'S OK?
WHATEVER YOU WANT...
TUT TUT
THE BUILDING BELONGS TO ADEL, MY SON. HE BOUGHT IT FOR NEXT TO NOTHING.
HE WANTED TO OPEN A GARAGE. WHAT AN IDEA... HE LOST A LOT OF MONEY. NO ONE CARES ABOUT THEIR CARS HERE.
AND IF THEY BREAK DOWN PEOPLE FIGURE IT OUT THEMSELVES.

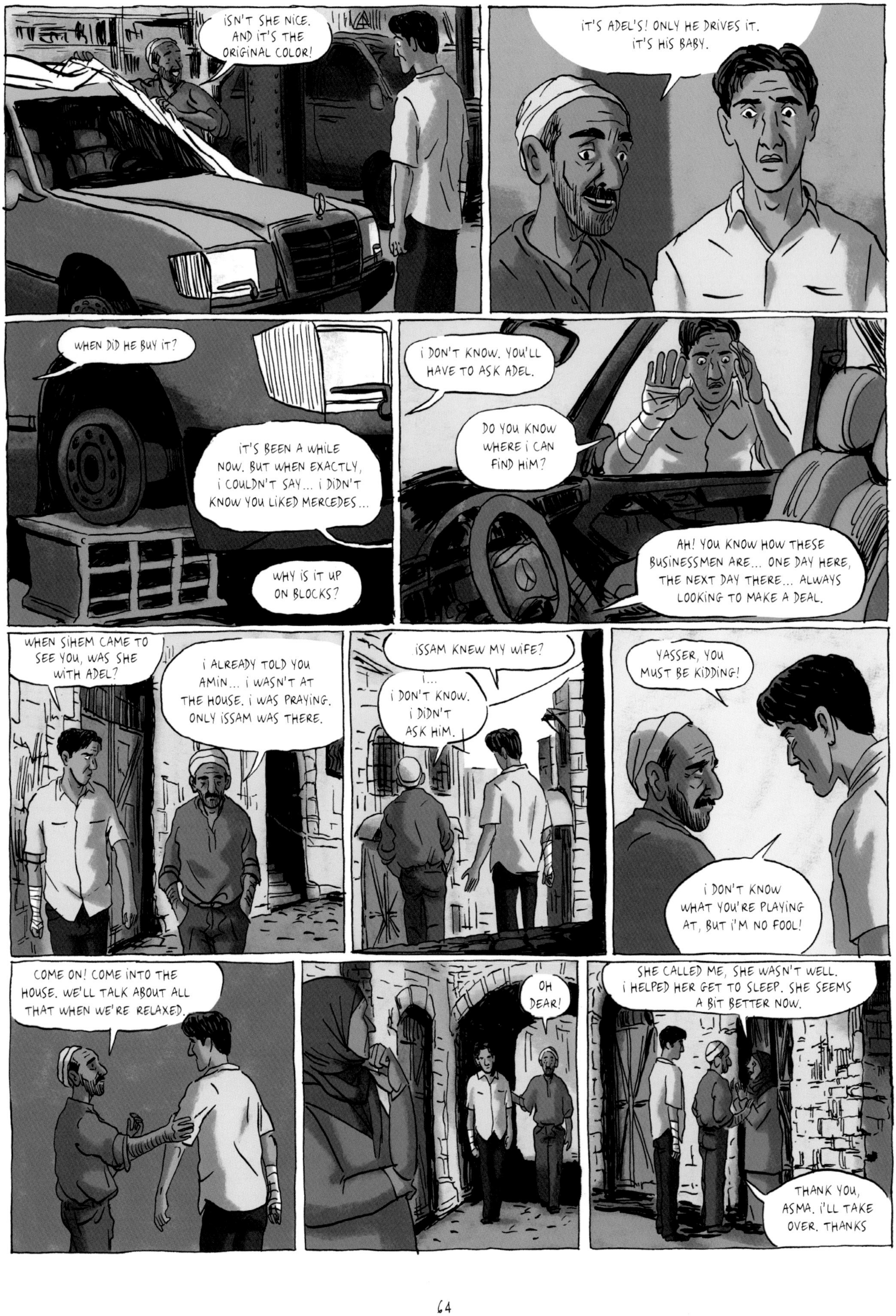
ISN'T SHE NICE. AND IT'S THE ORIGINAL COLOR!
IT'S ADEL'S! ONLY HE DRIVES IT. IT'S HIS BABY.
WHEN DID HE BUY IT?
IT'S BEEN A WHILE NOW. BUT WHEN EXACTLY, I COULDN'T SAY... I DIDN'T KNOW YOU LIKED MERCEDES...
WHY IS IT UP ON BLOCKS?
I DON'T KNOW. YOU'LL HAVE TO ASK ADEL.
DO YOU KNOW WHERE I CAN FIND HIM?
AH! YOU KNOW HOW THESE BUSINESSMEN ARE... ONE DAY HERE, THE NEXT DAY THERE... ALWAYS LOOKING TO MAKE A DEAL.
WHEN SIHEM CAME TO SEE YOU, WAS SHE WITH ADEL?
I ALREADY TOLD YOU AMIN... I WASN'T AT THE HOUSE. I WAS PRAYING. ONLY ISSAM WAS THERE.
ISSAM KNEW MY WIFE?
I... I DON'T KNOW. I DIDN'T ASK HIM.
YASSER, YOU MUST BE KIDDING!
I DON'T KNOW WHAT YOU'RE PLAYING AT, BUT I'M NO FOOL!
COME ON! COME INTO THE HOUSE. WE'LL TALK ABOUT ALL THAT WHEN WE'RE RELAXED.
OH DEAR!
SHE CALLED ME, SHE WASN'T WELL. I HELPED HER GET TO SLEEP. SHE SEEMS A BIT BETTER NOW.
THANK YOU, ASMA. I'LL TAKE OVER. THANKS

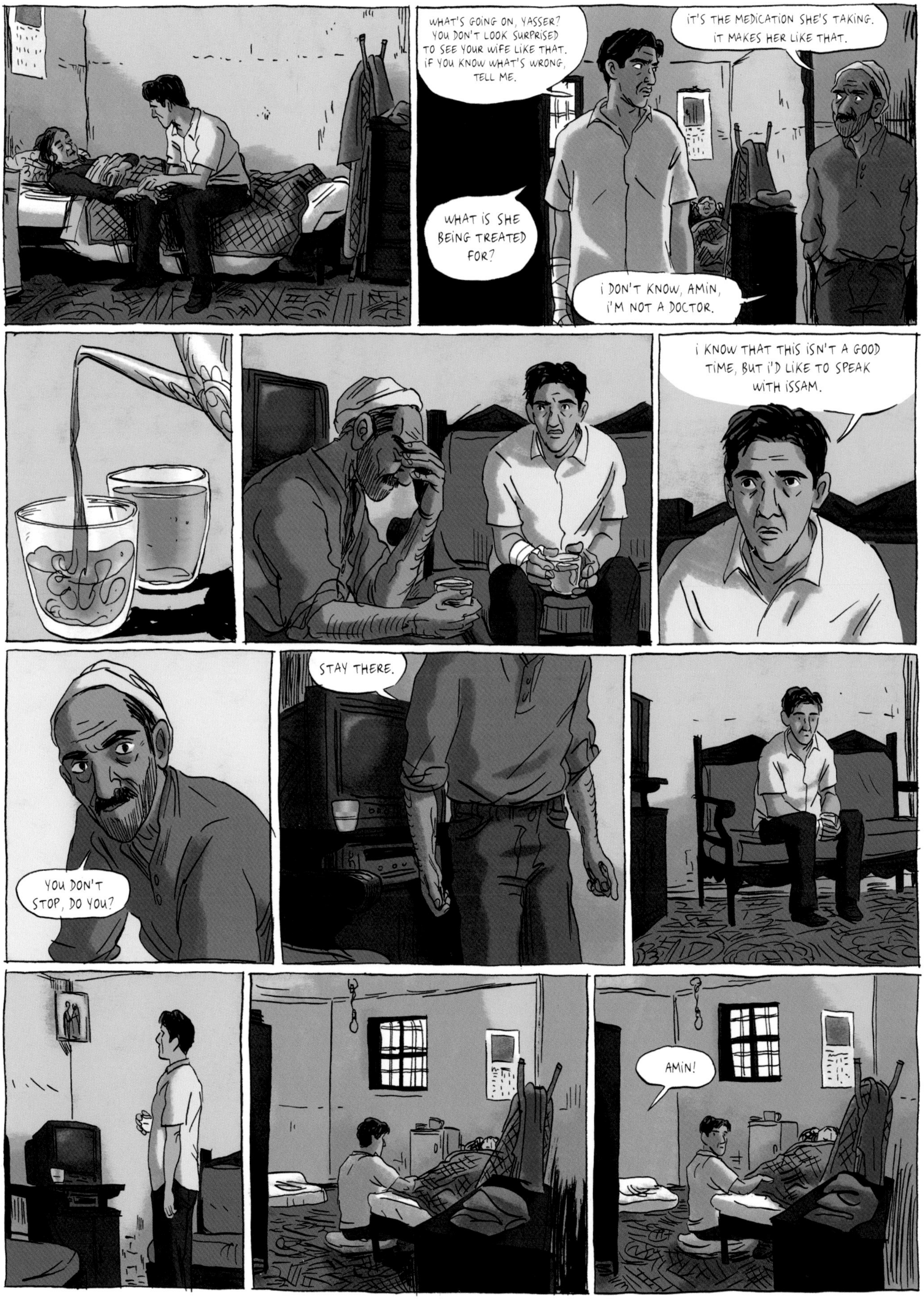
WHAT'S GOING ON, YASSER? YOU DON'T LOOK SURPRISED TO SEE YOUR WIFE LIKE THAT. IF YOU KNOW WHAT'S WRONG, TELL ME.
IT'S THE MEDICATION SHE'S TAKING. IT MAKES HER LIKE THAT.
WHAT IS SHE BEING TREATED FOR?
I DON'T KNOW, AMIN, I'M NOT A DOCTOR.
I KNOW THAT THIS ISN'T A GOOD TIME, BUT I'D LIKE TO SPEAK WITH ISSAM.
YOU DON'T STOP, DO YOU?
STAY THERE.
AMIN!

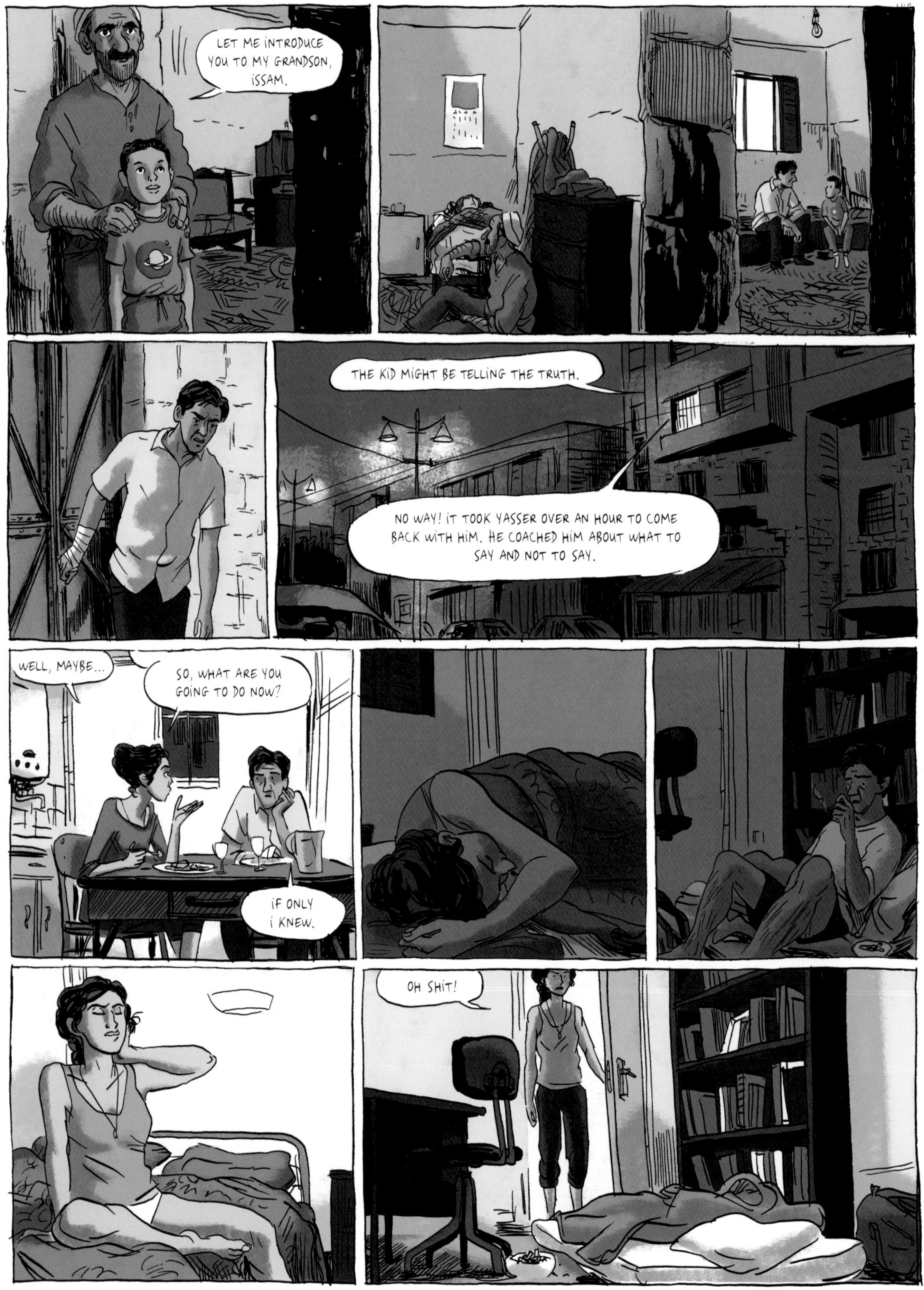
LET ME INTRODUCE YOU TO MY GRANDSON, ISSAM.
THE KID MIGHT BE TELLING THE TRUTH.
NO WAY! IT TOOK YASSER OVER AN HOUR TO COME BACK WITH HIM. HE COACHED HIM ABOUT WHAT TO SAY AND NOT TO SAY.
WELL, MAYBE...
SO, WHAT ARE YOU GOING TO DO NOW?
IF ONLY I KNEW.
OH SHIT!

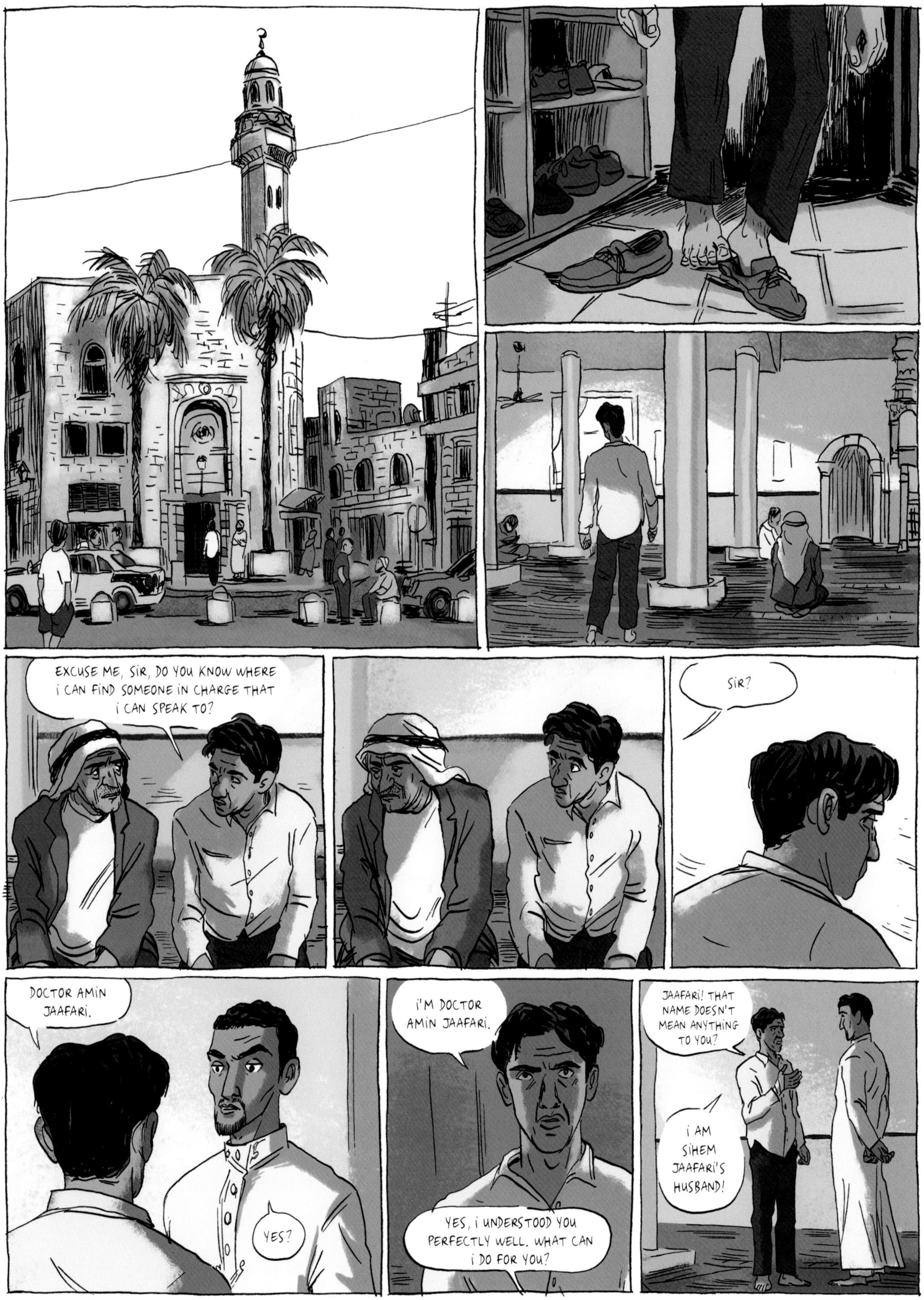
EXCUSE ME, SIR, DO YOU KNOW WHERE i CAN FIND SOMEONE IN CHARGE THAT i CAN SPEAK TO?
SIR?
DOCTOR AMIN JAAFARI.
YES?
i'M DOCTOR AMIN JAAFARI.
YES, i UNDERSTOOD YOU PERFECTLY WELL. WHAT CAN i DO FOR YOU?
JAAFARi! THAT NAME DOESN'T MEAN ANYTHING TO YOU?
i AM SiHEM JAAFARi'S HUSBAND!

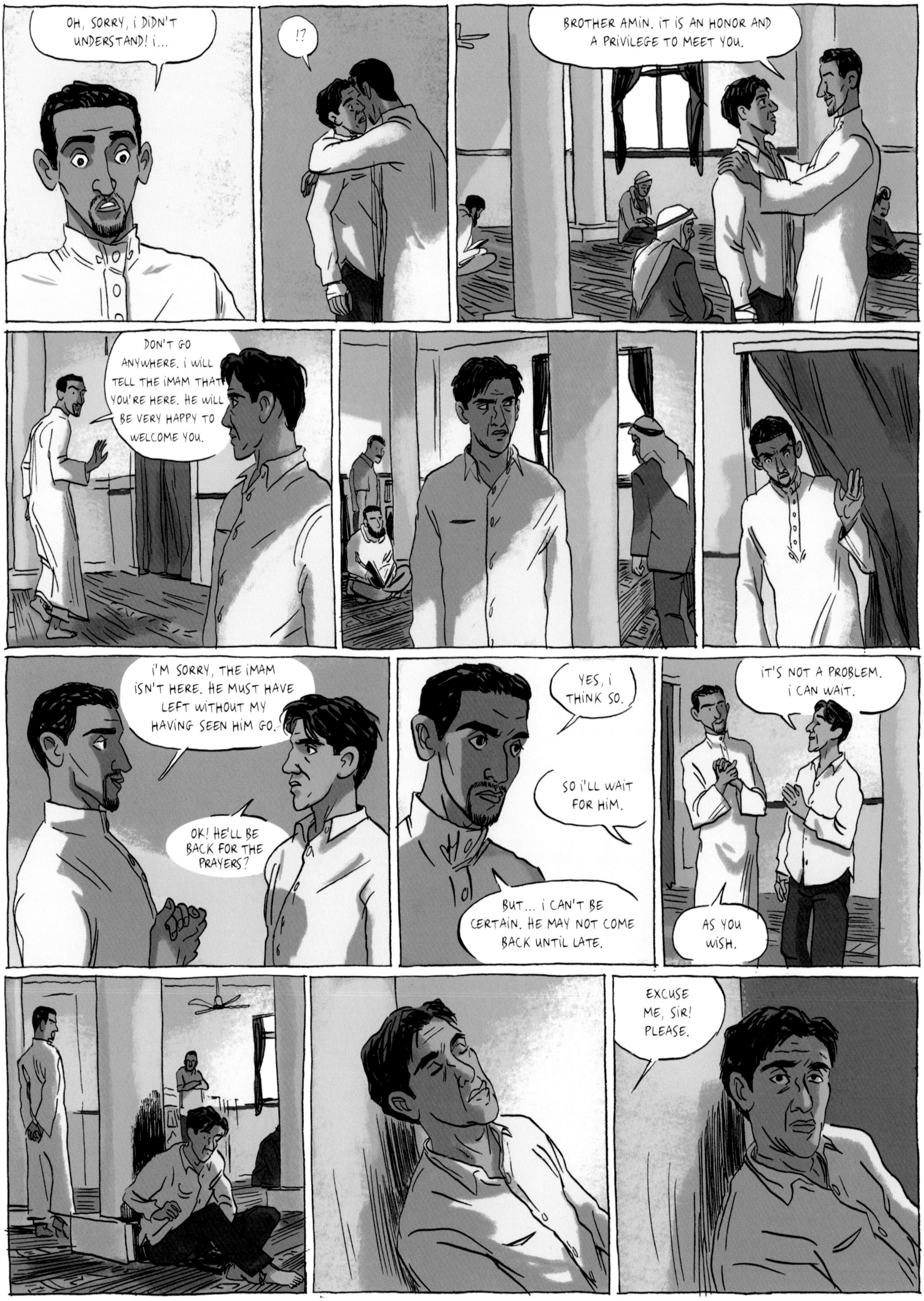
OH, SORRY, I DIDN'T UNDERSTAND! I...
!?
BROTHER AMIN. IT IS AN HONOR AND A PRIVILEGE TO MEET YOU.
DON'T GO ANYWHERE. I WILL TELL THE IMAM THAT YOU'RE HERE. HE WILL BE VERY HAPPY TO WELCOME YOU.
I'M SORRY, THE IMAM ISN'T HERE. HE MUST HAVE LEFT WITHOUT MY HAVING SEEN HIM GO.
OK! HE'LL BE BACK FOR THE PRAYERS?
YES, I THINK SO.
SO I'LL WAIT FOR HIM.
BUT... I CAN'T BE CERTAIN. HE MAY NOT COME BACK UNTIL LATE.
IT'S NOT A PROBLEM. I CAN WAIT.
AS YOU WISH.
EXCUSE ME, SIR! PLEASE.

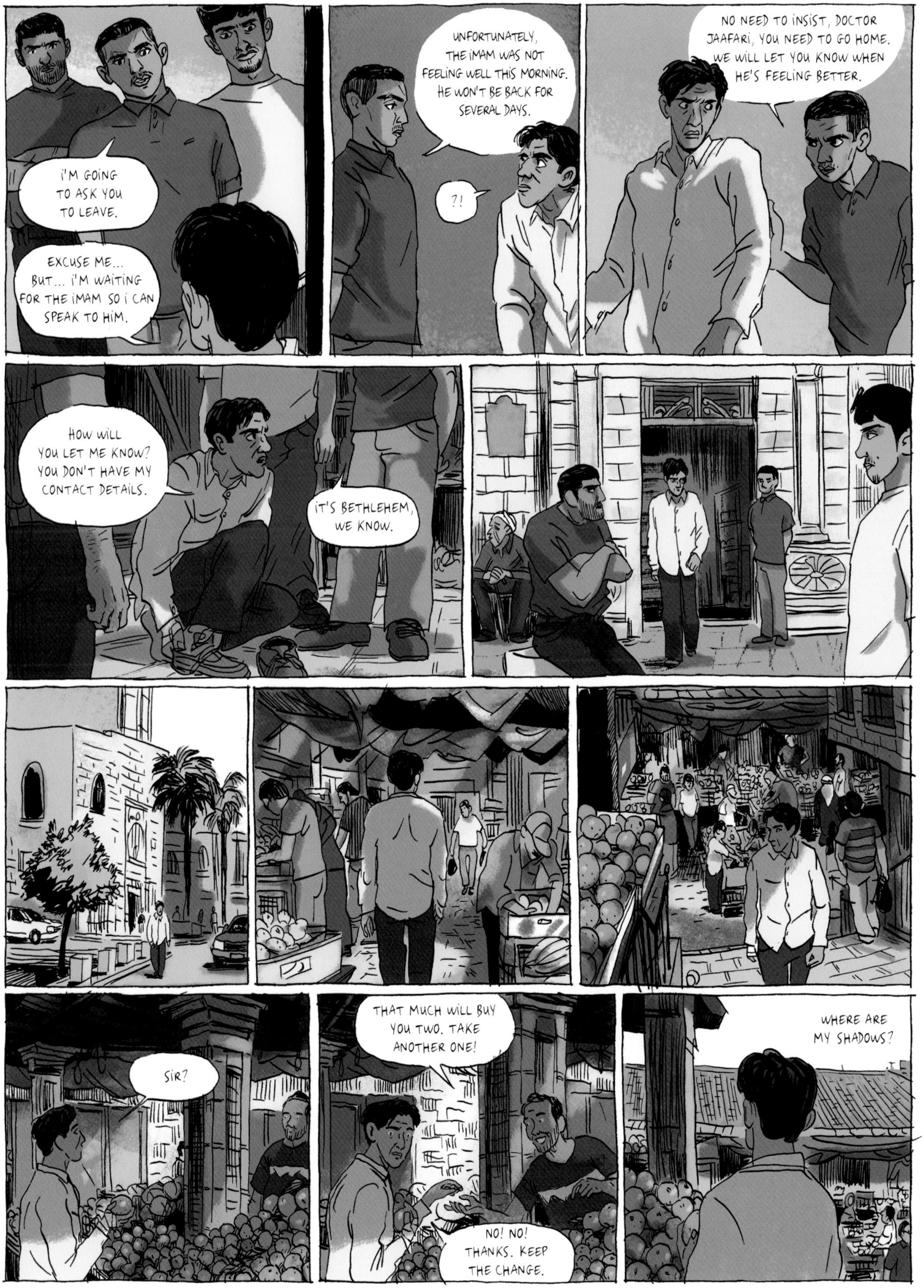
I'M GOING TO ASK YOU TO LEAVE.
EXCUSE ME... BUT... I'M WAITING FOR THE IMAM SO I CAN SPEAK TO HIM.
UNFORTUNATELY, THE IMAM WAS NOT FEELING WELL THIS MORNING. HE WON'T BE BACK FOR SEVERAL DAYS.
?!
NO NEED TO INSIST, DOCTOR JAAFARI, YOU NEED TO GO HOME. WE WILL LET YOU KNOW WHEN HE'S FEELING BETTER.
HOW WILL YOU LET ME KNOW? YOU DON'T HAVE MY CONTACT DETAILS.
IT'S BETHLEHEM, WE KNOW.
SIR?
THAT MUCH WILL BUY YOU TWO. TAKE ANOTHER ONE!
NO! NO! THANKS. KEEP THE CHANGE.
WHERE ARE MY SHADOWS?

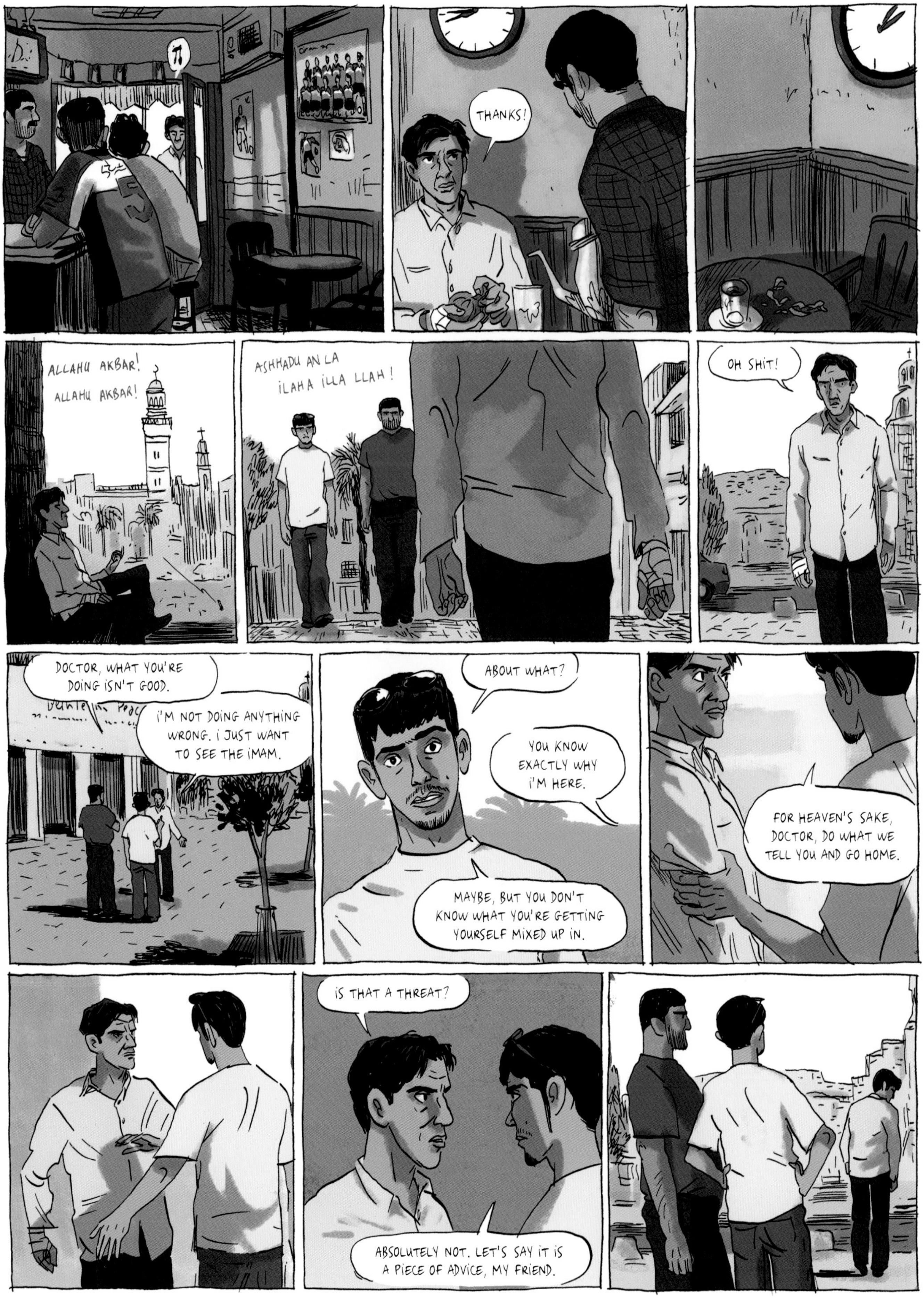
THANKS!
ALLAHU AKBAR!
ALLAHU AKBAR!
ASHHADU AN LA
iLAHA iLLA LLAH!
OH SHiT!
DOCTOR, WHAT YOU'RE DOiNG iSN'T GOOD.
i'M NOT DOiNG ANYTHiNG WRONG. i JUST WANT TO SEE THE iMAM.
ABOUT WHAT?
YOU KNOW EXACTLY WHY i'M HERE.
MAYBE, BUT YOU DON'T KNOW WHAT YOU'RE GETTiNG YOURSELF MiXED UP iN.
FOR HEAVEN'S SAKE, DOCTOR, DO WHAT WE TELL YOU AND GO HOME.
iS THAT A THREAT?
ABSOLUTELY NOT. LET'S SAY iT iS A PiECE OF ADViCE, MY FRIEND.

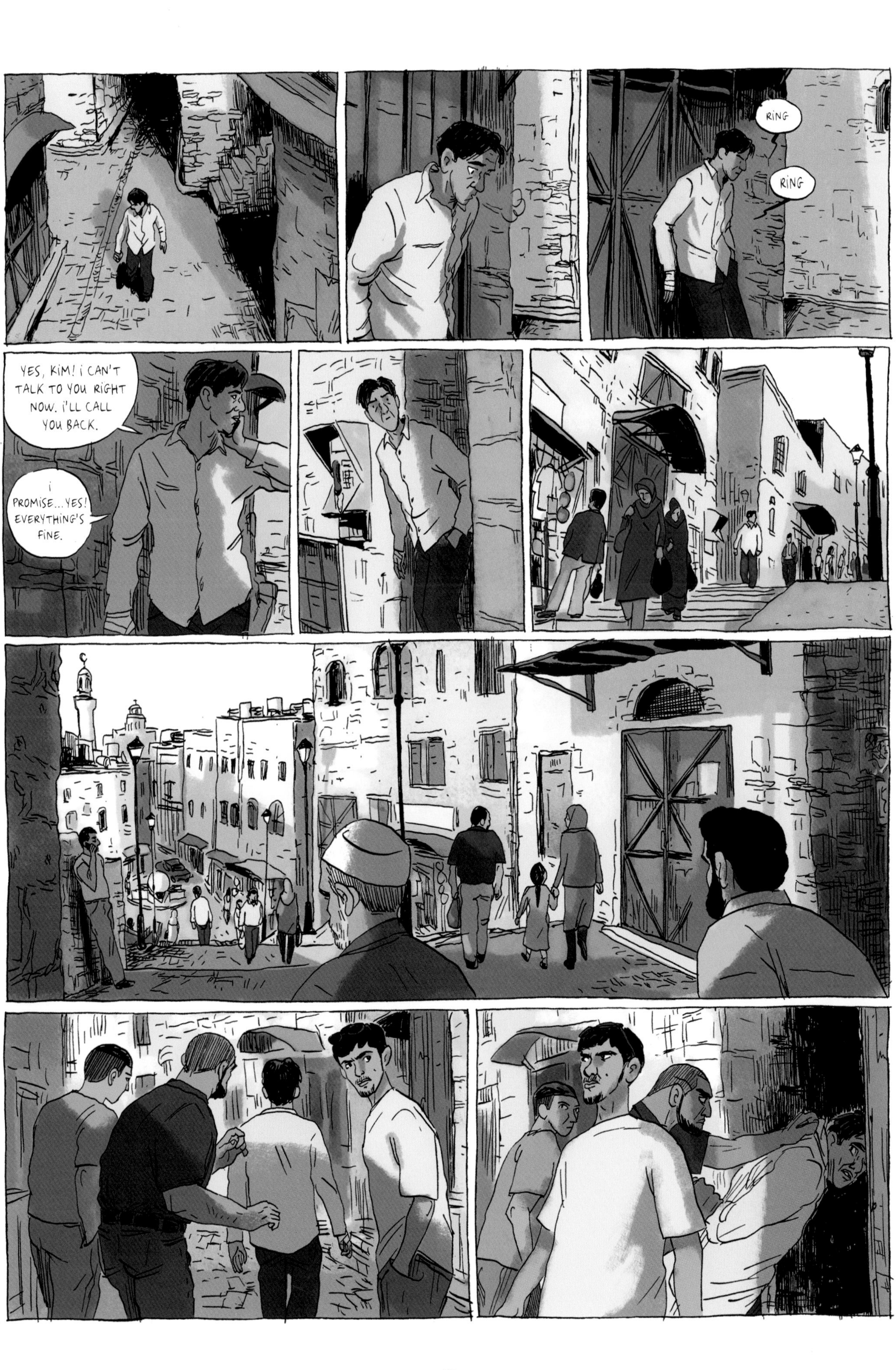
RING
RING
YES, KIM! I CAN'T TALK TO YOU RIGHT NOW. I'LL CALL YOU BACK.
I PROMISE... YES! EVERYTHING'S FINE.

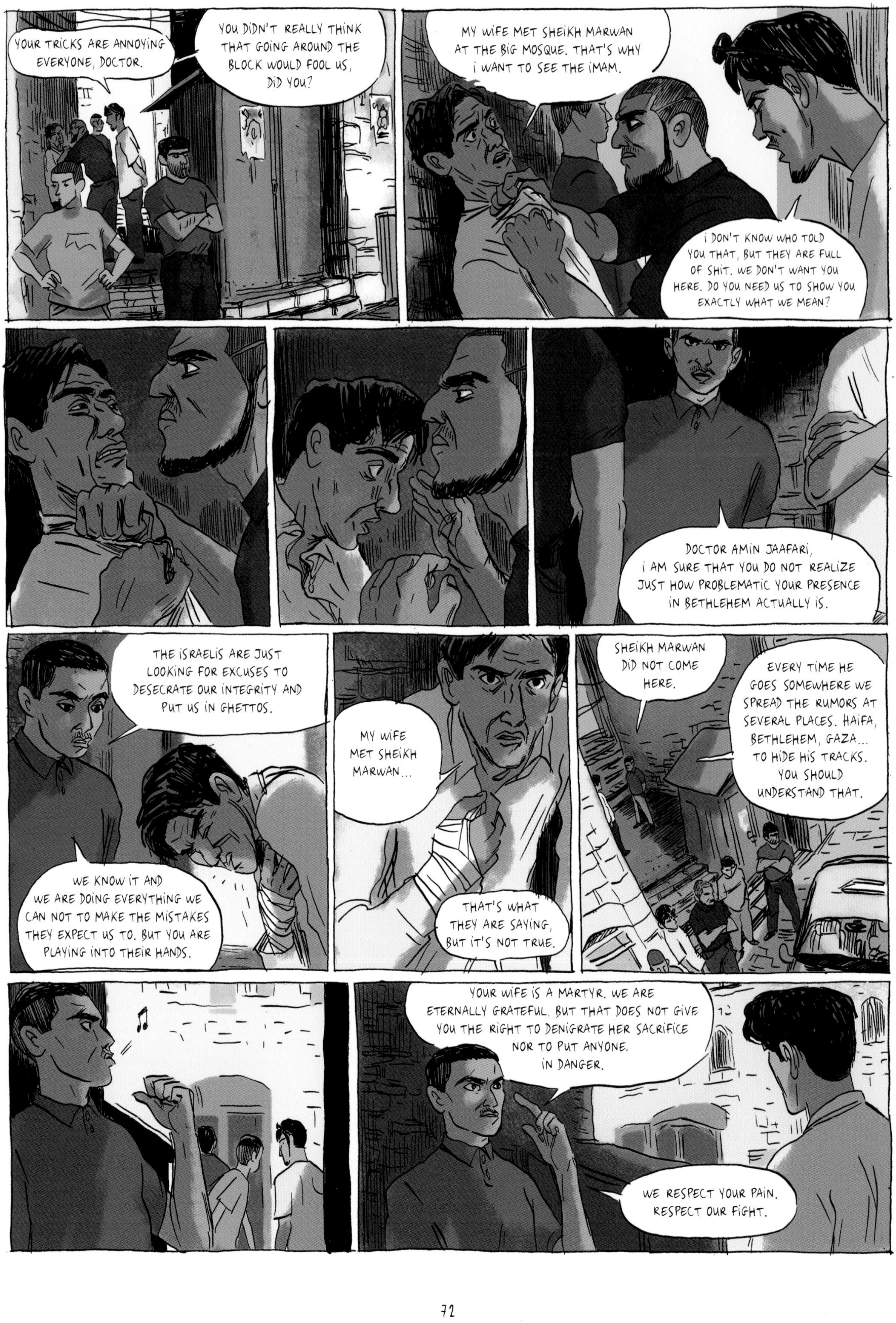
YOUR TRICKS ARE ANNOYING EVERYONE, DOCTOR.
YOU DIDN'T REALLY THINK THAT GOING AROUND THE BLOCK WOULD FOOL US, DID YOU?
MY WIFE MET SHEIKH MARWAN AT THE BIG MOSQUE. THAT'S WHY I WANT TO SEE THE IMAM.
I DON'T KNOW WHO TOLD YOU THAT, BUT THEY ARE FULL OF SHIT. WE DON'T WANT YOU HERE. DO YOU NEED US TO SHOW YOU EXACTLY WHAT WE MEAN?
DOCTOR AMIN JAAFARI, I AM SURE THAT YOU DO NOT REALIZE JUST HOW PROBLEMATIC YOUR PRESENCE IN BETHLEHEM ACTUALLY IS.
THE ISRAELIS ARE JUST LOOKING FOR EXCUSES TO DESECRATE OUR INTEGRITY AND PUT US IN GHETTOS.
WE KNOW IT AND WE ARE DOING EVERYTHING WE CAN NOT TO MAKE THE MISTAKES THEY EXPECT US TO. BUT YOU ARE PLAYING INTO THEIR HANDS.
MY WIFE MET SHEIKH MARWAN...
THAT'S WHAT THEY ARE SAYING, BUT IT'S NOT TRUE.
SHEIKH MARWAN DID NOT COME HERE.
EVERY TIME HE GOES SOMEWHERE WE SPREAD THE RUMORS AT SEVERAL PLACES. HAIFA, BETHLEHEM, GAZA... TO HIDE HIS TRACKS. YOU SHOULD UNDERSTAND THAT.
YOUR WIFE IS A MARTYR. WE ARE ETERNALLY GRATEFUL. BUT THAT DOES NOT GIVE YOU THE RIGHT TO DENIGRATE HER SACRIFICE NOR TO PUT ANYONE IN DANGER.
WE RESPECT YOUR PAIN. RESPECT OUR FIGHT.

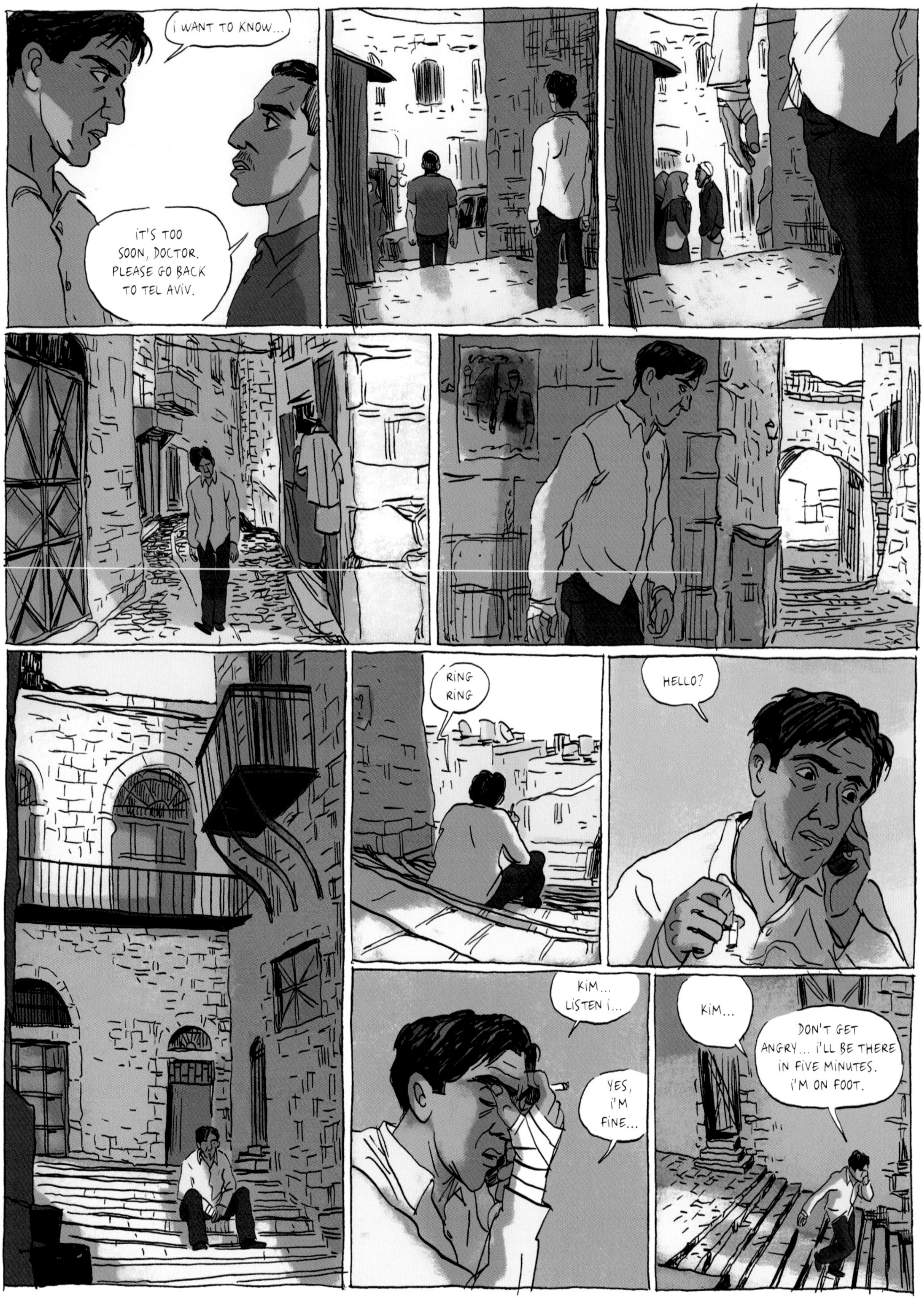
I WANT TO KNOW...
IT'S TOO SOON, DOCTOR. PLEASE GO BACK TO TEL AVIV.
RING RING
HELLO?
KIM... LISTEN I...
YES, I'M FINE...
KIM...
DON'T GET ANGRY... I'LL BE THERE IN FIVE MINUTES. I'M ON FOOT.

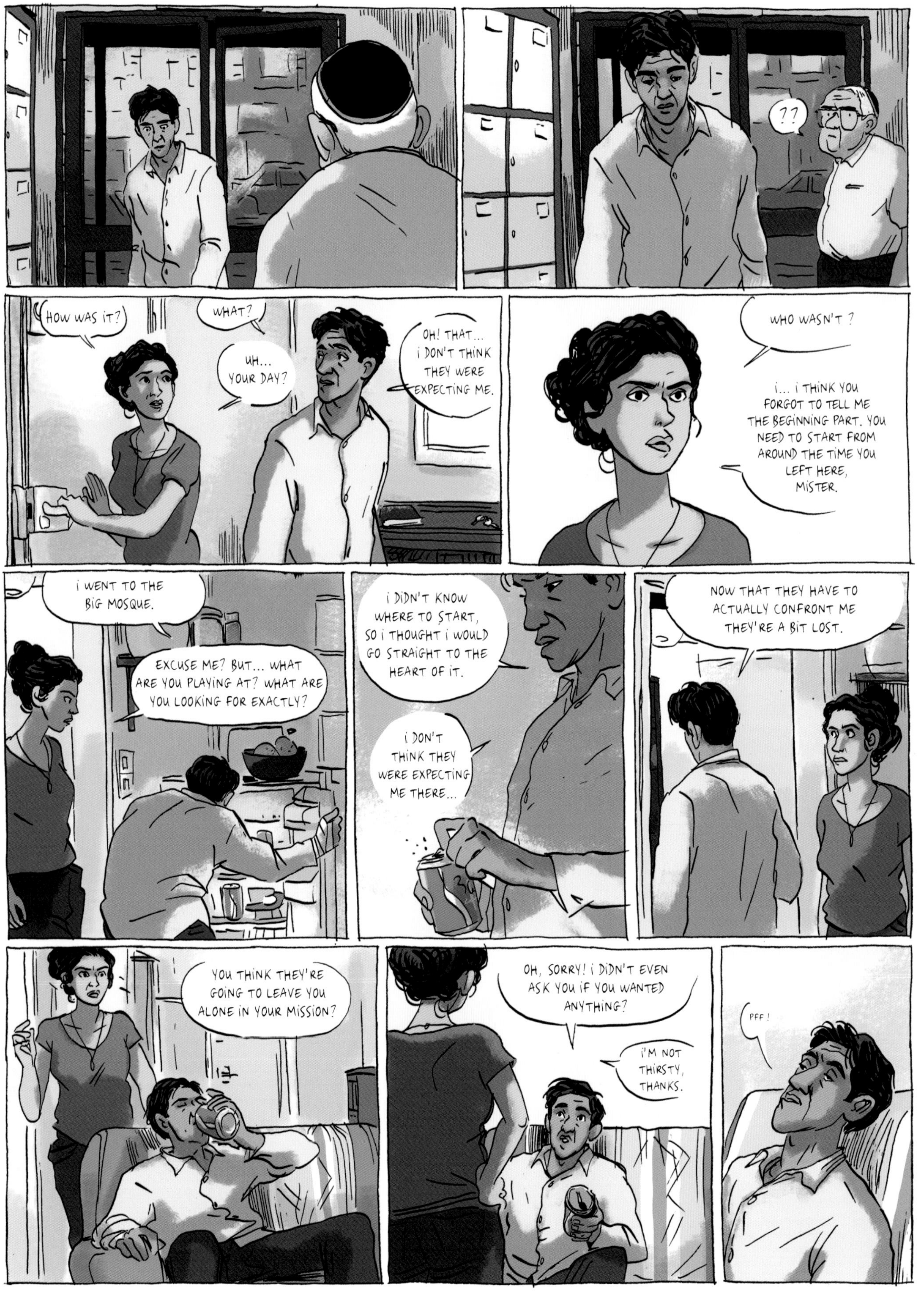
??
HOW WAS iT?
WHAT?
UH... YOUR DAY?
OH! THAT... i DON'T THINK THEY WERE EXPECTING ME.
WHO WASN'T ?
i... i THiNK YOU FORGOT TO TELL ME THE BEGiNNiNG PART. YOU NEED TO START FROM AROUND THE TiME YOU LEFT HERE, MiSTER.
i WENT TO THE BiG MOSQUE.
EXCUSE ME? BUT... WHAT ARE YOU PLAYiNG AT? WHAT ARE YOU LOOKiNG FOR EXACTLY?
i DiDN'T KNOW WHERE TO START, SO i THOUGHT i WOULD GO STRAiGHT TO THE HEART OF iT.
i DON'T THiNK THEY WERE EXPECTiNG ME THERE...
NOW THAT THEY HAVE TO ACTUALLY CONFRONT ME THEY'RE A BiT LOST.
YOU THiNK THEY'RE GOiNG TO LEAVE YOU ALONE iN YOUR MiSSiON?
OH, SORRY! i DiDN'T EVEN ASK YOU iF YOU WANTED ANYTHiNG?
i'M NOT THiRSTY, THANKS.
PFF!

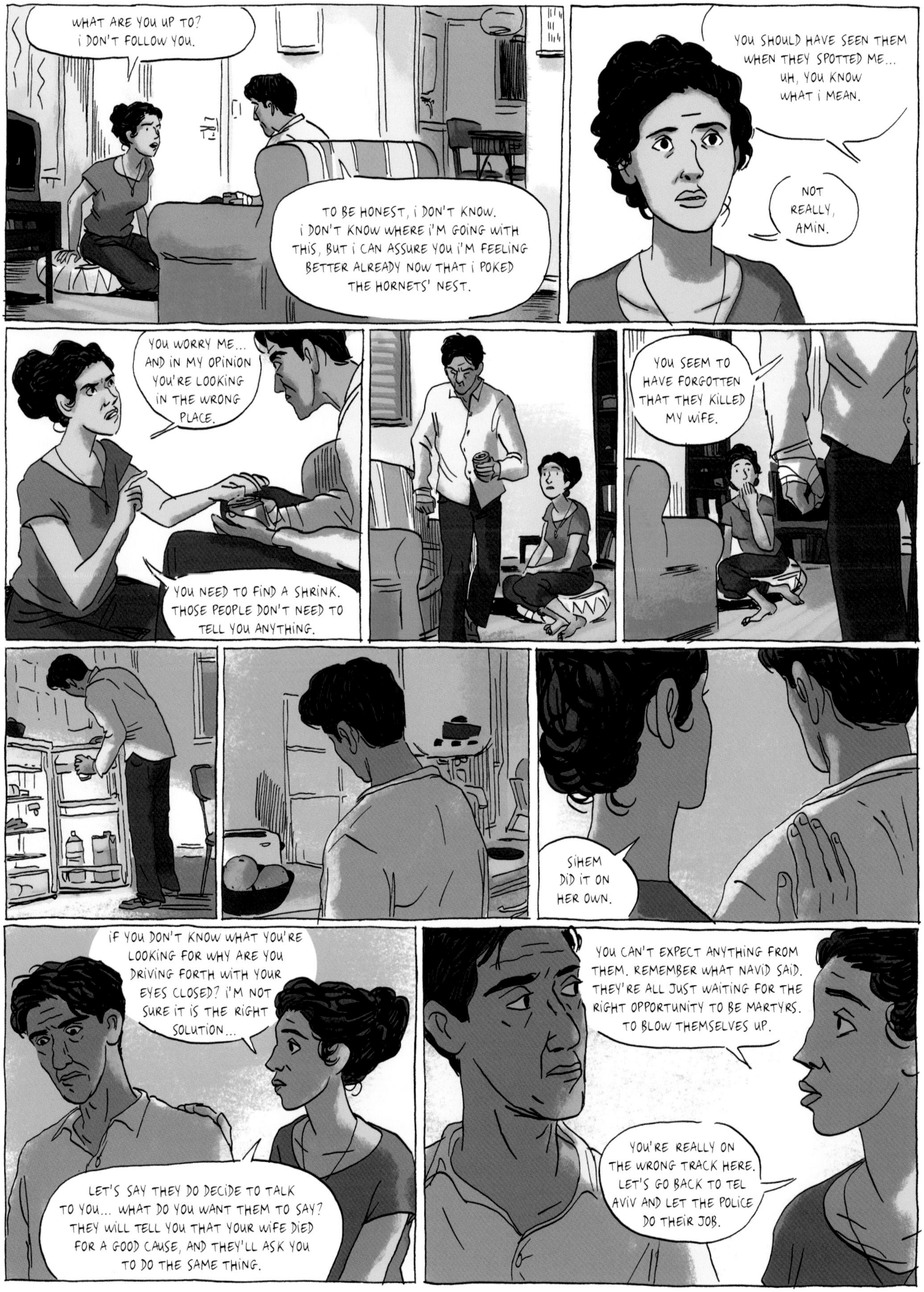
WHAT ARE YOU UP TO? I DON'T FOLLOW YOU.
TO BE HONEST, I DON'T KNOW. I DON'T KNOW WHERE I'M GOING WITH THIS, BUT I CAN ASSURE YOU I'M FEELING BETTER ALREADY NOW THAT I POKED THE HORNETS' NEST.
YOU SHOULD HAVE SEEN THEM WHEN THEY SPOTTED ME... UH, YOU KNOW WHAT I MEAN.
NOT REALLY, AMIN.
YOU WORRY ME... AND IN MY OPINION YOU'RE LOOKING IN THE WRONG PLACE.
YOU NEED TO FIND A SHRINK. THOSE PEOPLE DON'T NEED TO TELL YOU ANYTHING.
YOU SEEM TO HAVE FORGOTTEN THAT THEY KILLED MY WIFE.
SIHEM DID IT ON HER OWN.
IF YOU DON'T KNOW WHAT YOU'RE LOOKING FOR WHY ARE YOU DRIVING FORTH WITH YOUR EYES CLOSED? I'M NOT SURE IT IS THE RIGHT SOLUTION...
LET'S SAY THEY DO DECIDE TO TALK TO YOU... WHAT DO YOU WANT THEM TO SAY? THEY WILL TELL YOU THAT YOUR WIFE DIED FOR A GOOD CAUSE, AND THEY'LL ASK YOU TO DO THE SAME THING.
YOU CAN'T EXPECT ANYTHING FROM THEM. REMEMBER WHAT NAVID SAID. THEY'RE ALL JUST WAITING FOR THE RIGHT OPPORTUNITY TO BE MARTYRS. TO BLOW THEMSELVES UP.
YOU'RE REALLY ON THE WRONG TRACK HERE. LET'S GO BACK TO TEL AVIV AND LET THE POLICE DO THEIR JOB.

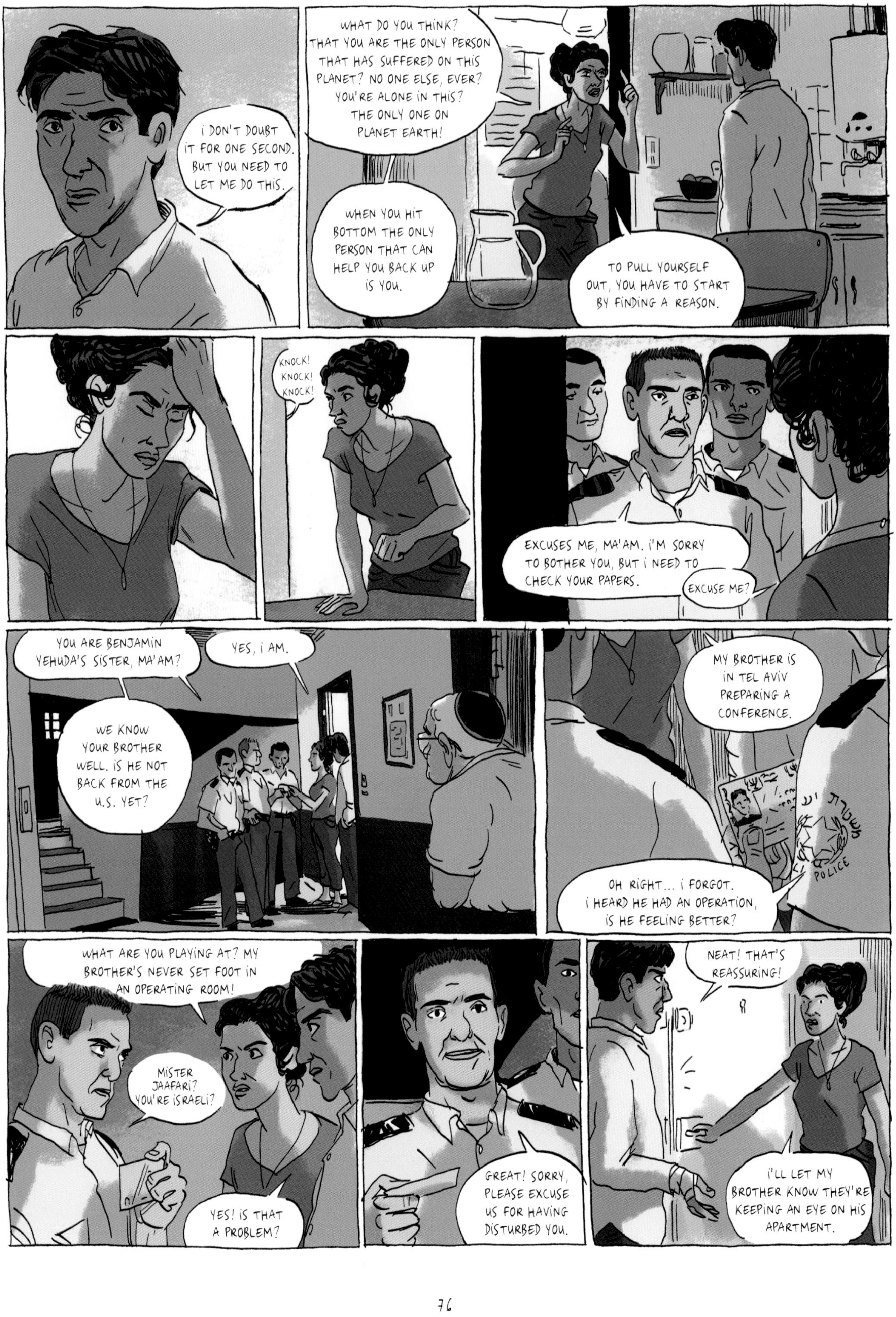
I DON'T DOUBT IT FOR ONE SECOND. BUT YOU NEED TO LET ME DO THIS.
WHAT DO YOU THINK? THAT YOU ARE THE ONLY PERSON THAT HAS SUFFERED ON THIS PLANET? NO ONE ELSE, EVER? YOU'RE ALONE IN THIS? THE ONLY ONE ON PLANET EARTH!
WHEN YOU HIT BOTTOM THE ONLY PERSON THAT CAN HELP YOU BACK UP IS YOU.
TO PULL YOURSELF OUT, YOU HAVE TO START BY FINDING A REASON.
KNOCK! KNOCK! KNOCK!
EXCUSES ME, MA'AM. I'M SORRY TO BOTHER YOU, BUT I NEED TO CHECK YOUR PAPERS.
EXCUSE ME?
YOU ARE BENJAMIN YEHUDA'S SISTER, MA'AM?
YES, I AM.
WE KNOW YOUR BROTHER WELL. IS HE NOT BACK FROM THE U.S. YET?
MY BROTHER IS IN TEL AVIV PREPARING A CONFERENCE.
POLICE
OH RIGHT... I FORGOT. I HEARD HE HAD AN OPERATION, IS HE FEELING BETTER?
WHAT ARE YOU PLAYING AT? MY BROTHER'S NEVER SET FOOT IN AN OPERATING ROOM!
MISTER JAAFARI? YOU'RE ISRAELI?
YES! IS THAT A PROBLEM?
GREAT! SORRY, PLEASE EXCUSE US FOR HAVING DISTURBED YOU.
NEAT! THAT'S REASSURING!
I'LL LET MY BROTHER KNOW THEY'RE KEEPING AN EYE ON HIS APARTMENT.

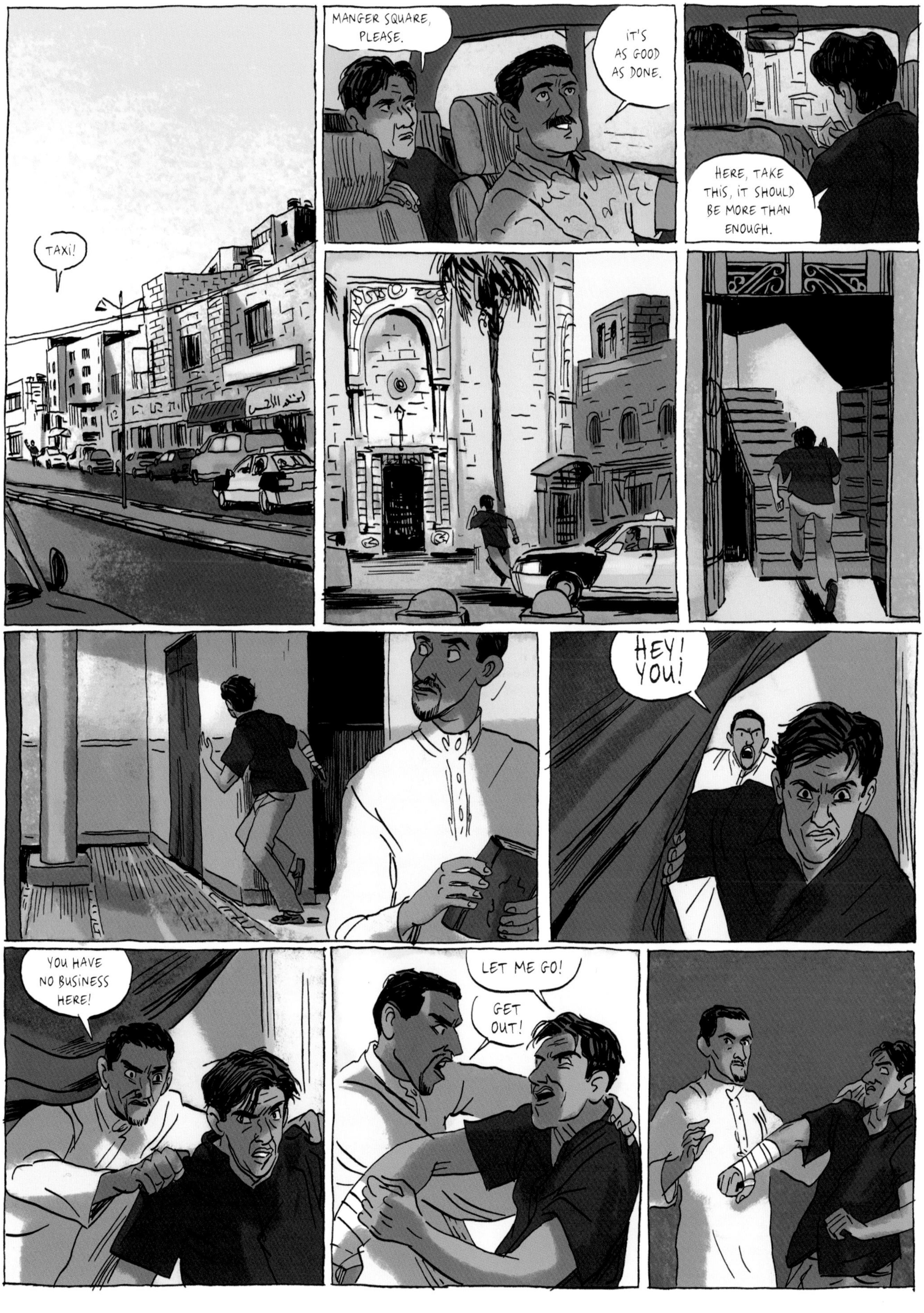
TAXI!
MANGER SQUARE, PLEASE.
IT'S AS GOOD AS DONE.
HERE, TAKE THIS, IT SHOULD BE MORE THAN ENOUGH.
HEY! YOU!
YOU HAVE NO BUSINESS HERE!
LET ME GO!
GET OUT!

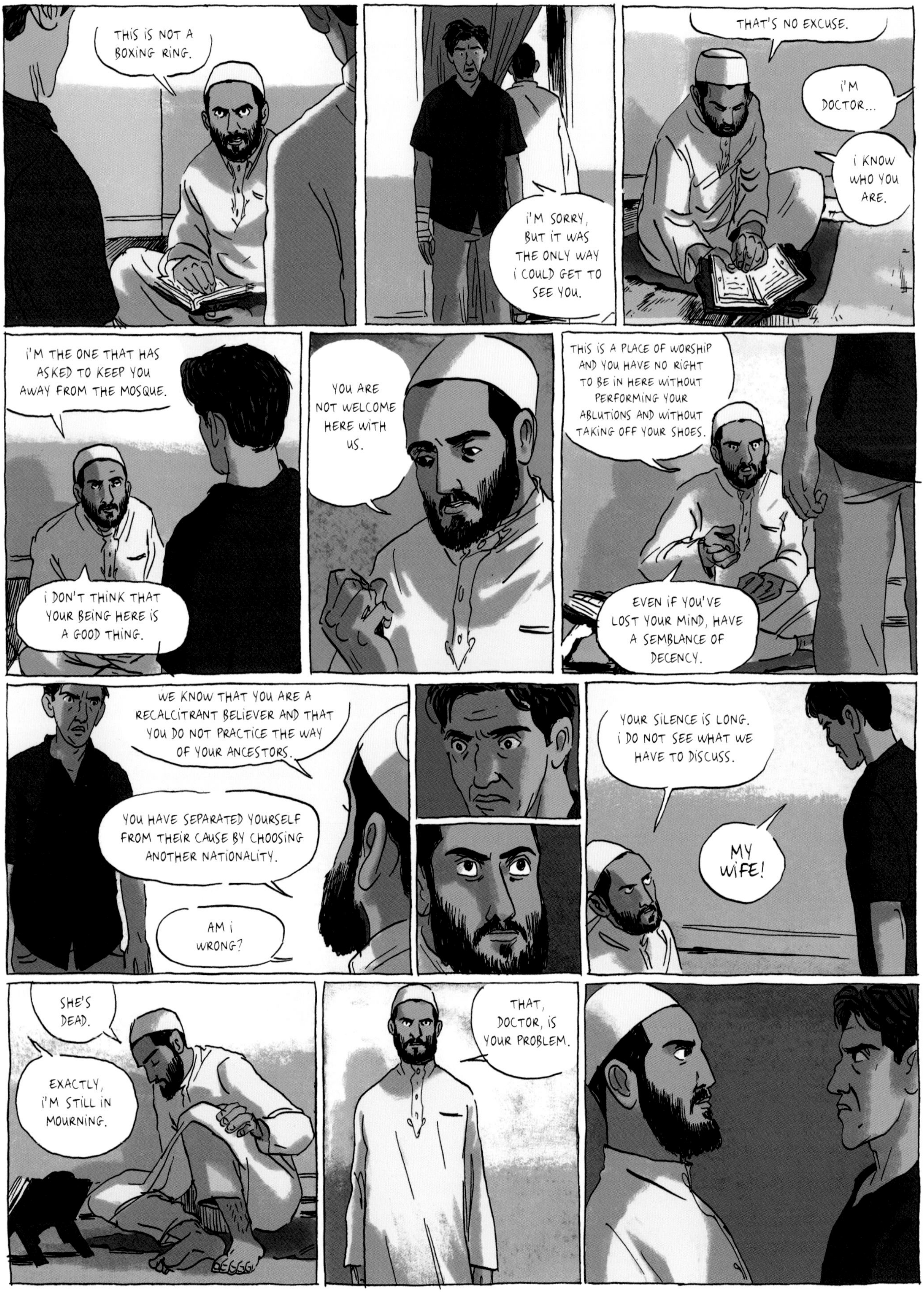
THIS IS NOT A BOXING RING.
I'M SORRY, BUT IT WAS THE ONLY WAY I COULD GET TO SEE YOU.
THAT'S NO EXCUSE.
I'M DOCTOR...
I KNOW WHO YOU ARE.
I'M THE ONE THAT HAS ASKED TO KEEP YOU AWAY FROM THE MOSQUE.
I DON'T THINK THAT YOUR BEING HERE IS A GOOD THING.
YOU ARE NOT WELCOME HERE WITH US.
THIS IS A PLACE OF WORSHIP AND YOU HAVE NO RIGHT TO BE IN HERE WITHOUT PERFORMING YOUR ABLUTIONS AND WITHOUT TAKING OFF YOUR SHOES.
EVEN IF YOU'VE LOST YOUR MIND, HAVE A SEMBLANCE OF DECENCY.
WE KNOW THAT YOU ARE A RECALCITRANT BELIEVER AND THAT YOU DO NOT PRACTICE THE WAY OF YOUR ANCESTORS.
YOU HAVE SEPARATED YOURSELF FROM THEIR CAUSE BY CHOOSING ANOTHER NATIONALITY.
AM I WRONG?
YOUR SILENCE IS LONG. I DO NOT SEE WHAT WE HAVE TO DISCUSS.
MY WIFE!
SHE'S DEAD.
EXACTLY, I'M STILL IN MOURNING.
THAT, DOCTOR, IS YOUR PROBLEM.

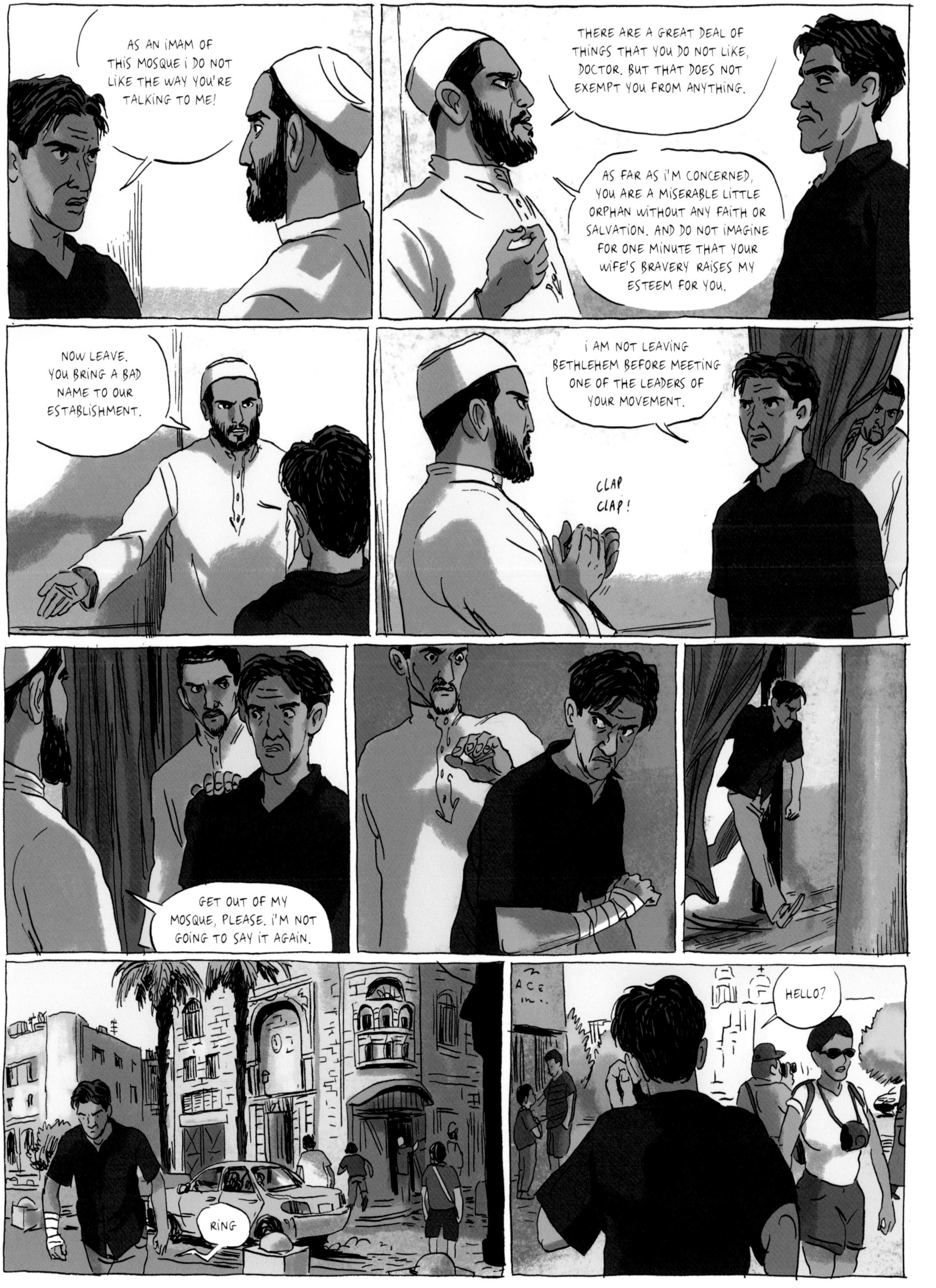
AS AN IMAM OF THIS MOSQUE I DO NOT LIKE THE WAY YOU'RE TALKING TO ME!
THERE ARE A GREAT DEAL OF THINGS THAT YOU DO NOT LIKE, DOCTOR. BUT THAT DOES NOT EXEMPT YOU FROM ANYTHING.
AS FAR AS I'M CONCERNED, YOU ARE A MISERABLE LITTLE ORPHAN WITHOUT ANY FAITH OR SALVATION. AND DO NOT IMAGINE FOR ONE MINUTE THAT YOUR WIFE'S BRAVERY RAISES MY ESTEEM FOR YOU.
NOW LEAVE. YOU BRING A BAD NAME TO OUR ESTABLISHMENT.
I AM NOT LEAVING BETHLEHEM BEFORE MEETING ONE OF THE LEADERS OF YOUR MOVEMENT.
CLAP CLAP!
GET OUT OF MY MOSQUE, PLEASE. I'M NOT GOING TO SAY IT AGAIN.
RING
HELLO?

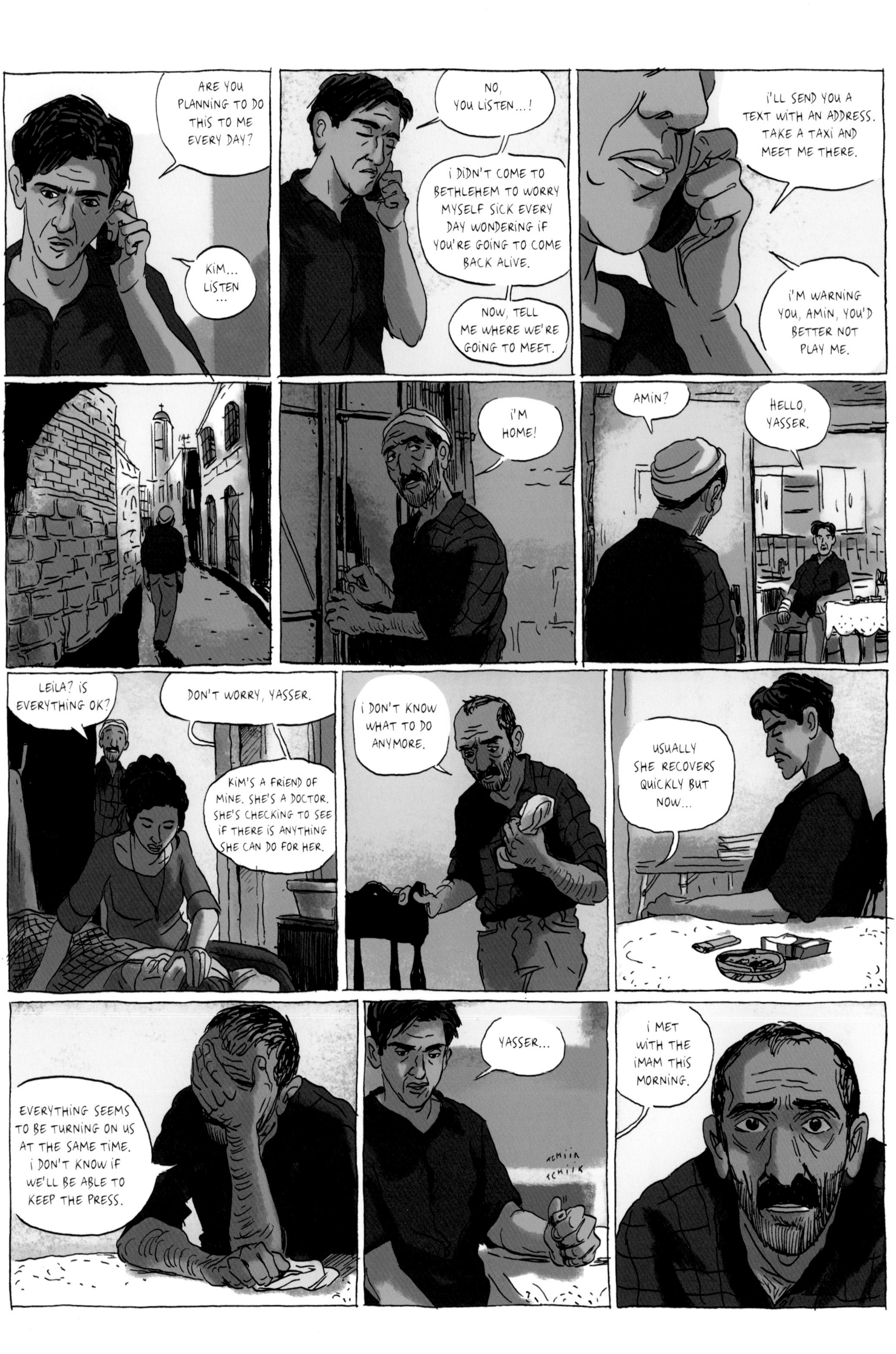
ARE YOU PLANNING TO DO THIS TO ME EVERY DAY?
KIM... LISTEN ...
NO, YOU LISTEN...!
I DIDN'T COME TO BETHLEHEM TO WORRY MYSELF SICK EVERY DAY WONDERING IF YOU'RE GOING TO COME BACK ALIVE.
NOW, TELL ME WHERE WE'RE GOING TO MEET.
I'LL SEND YOU A TEXT WITH AN ADDRESS. TAKE A TAXI AND MEET ME THERE.
I'M WARNING YOU, AMIN, YOU'D BETTER NOT PLAY ME.
I'M HOME!
AMIN?
HELLO, YASSER.
LEILA? IS EVERYTHING OK?
DON'T WORRY, YASSER.
KIM'S A FRIEND OF MINE. SHE'S A DOCTOR. SHE'S CHECKING TO SEE IF THERE IS ANYTHING SHE CAN DO FOR HER.
I DON'T KNOW WHAT TO DO ANYMORE.
USUALLY SHE RECOVERS QUICKLY BUT NOW...
EVERYTHING SEEMS TO BE TURNING ON US AT THE SAME TIME. I DON'T KNOW IF WE'LL BE ABLE TO KEEP THE PRESS.
YASSER...
TCHIIK TCHIIK
I MET WITH THE IMAM THIS MORNING.

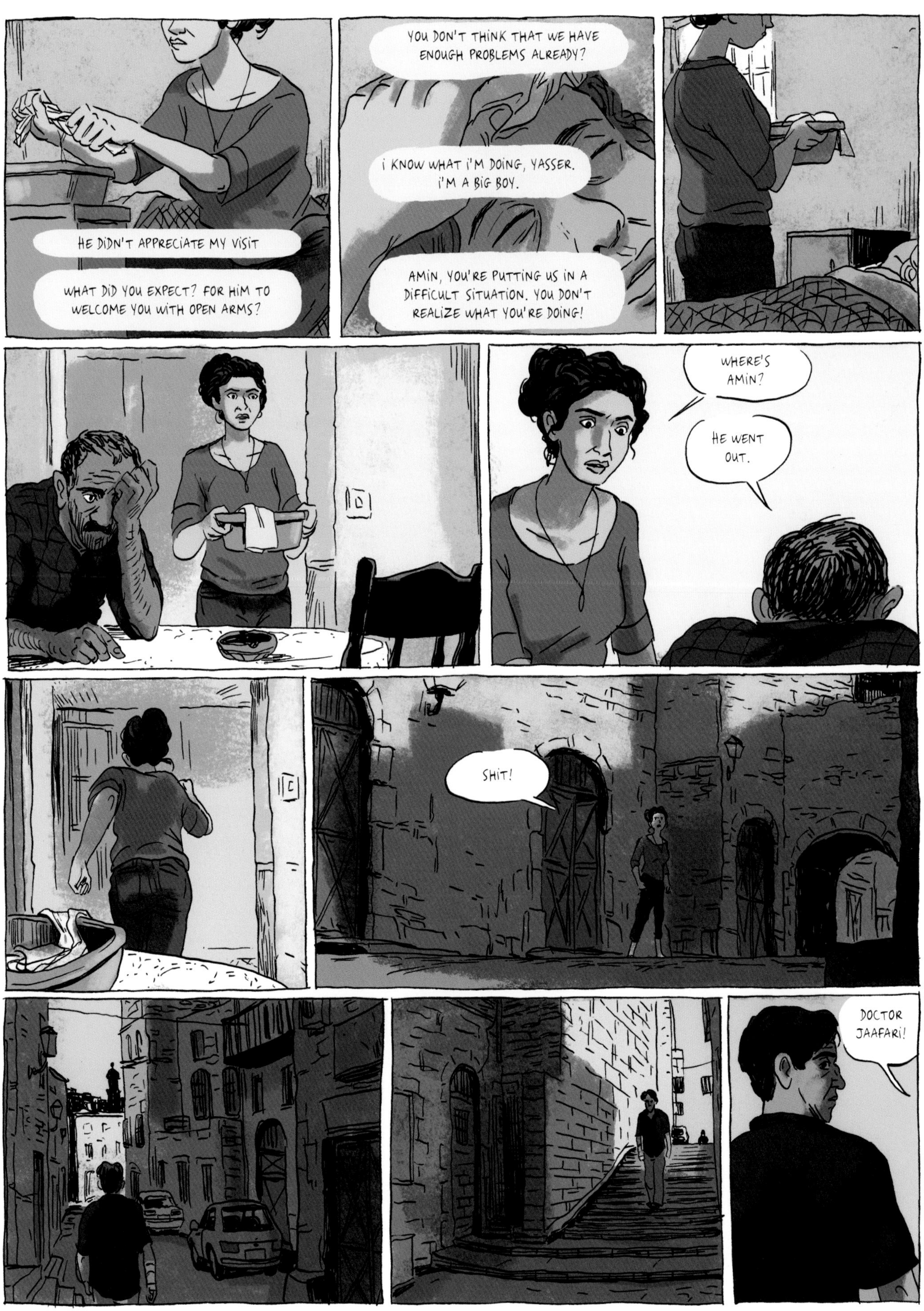
HE DIDN'T APPRECIATE MY VISIT
WHAT DID YOU EXPECT? FOR HIM TO WELCOME YOU WITH OPEN ARMS?
YOU DON'T THINK THAT WE HAVE ENOUGH PROBLEMS ALREADY?
I KNOW WHAT I'M DOING, YASSER. I'M A BIG BOY.
AMIN, YOU'RE PUTTING US IN A DIFFICULT SITUATION. YOU DON'T REALIZE WHAT YOU'RE DOING!
WHERE'S AMIN?
HE WENT OUT.
SHIT!
DOCTOR JAAFARI!

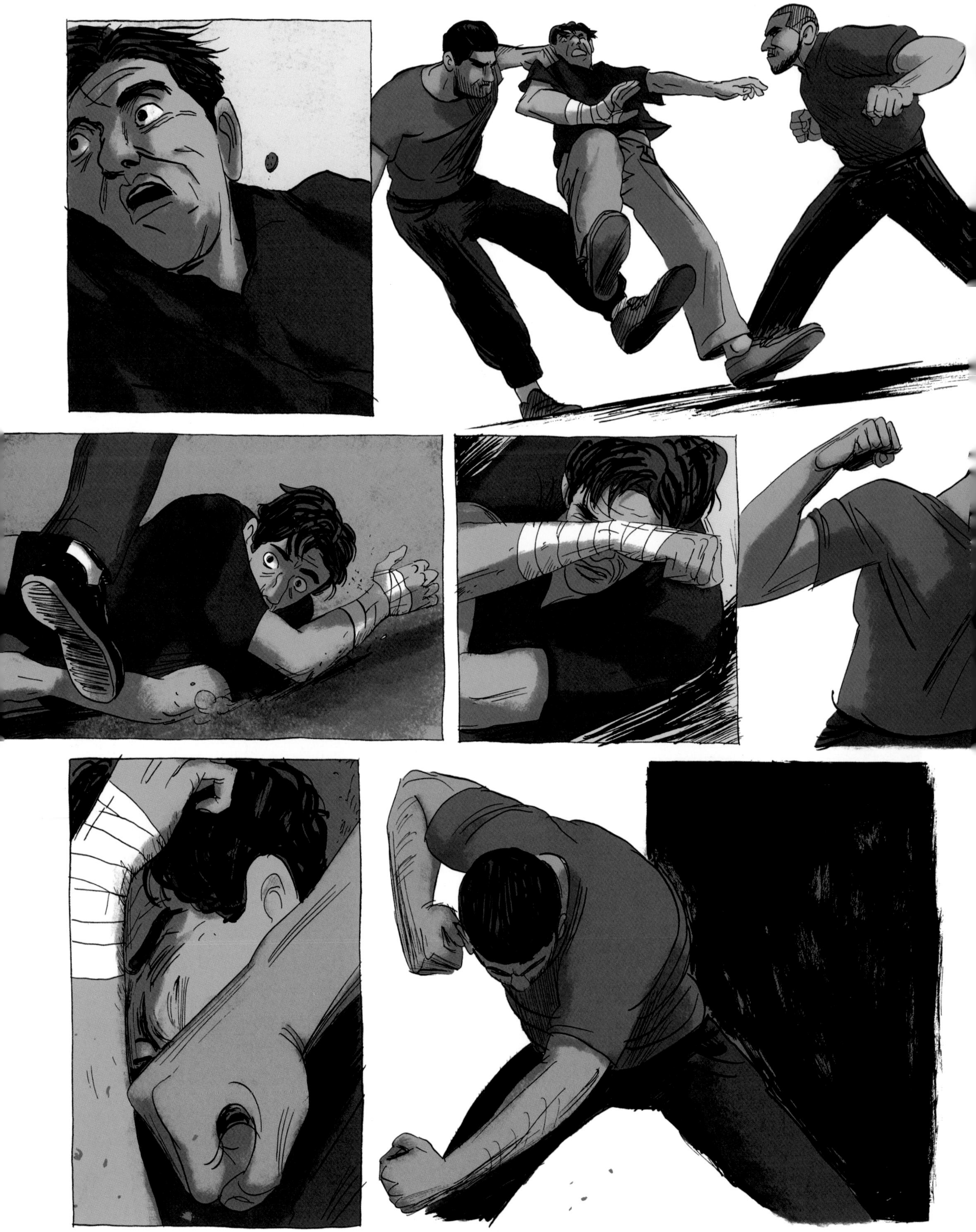

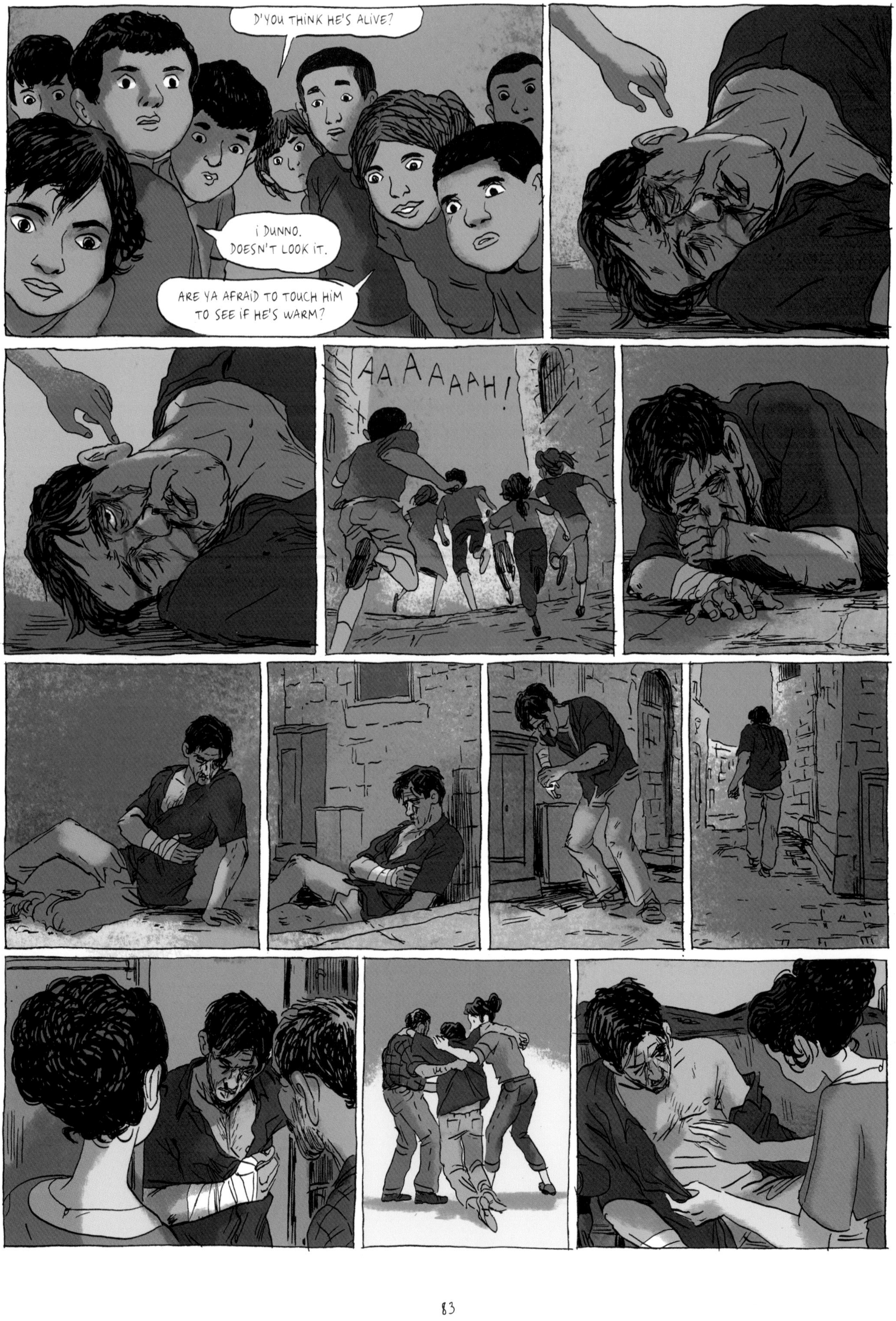
D'YOU THINK HE'S ALIVE?
I DUNNO. DOESN'T LOOK IT.
ARE YA AFRAID TO TOUCH HIM TO SEE IF HE'S WARM?
AAAAAAH!

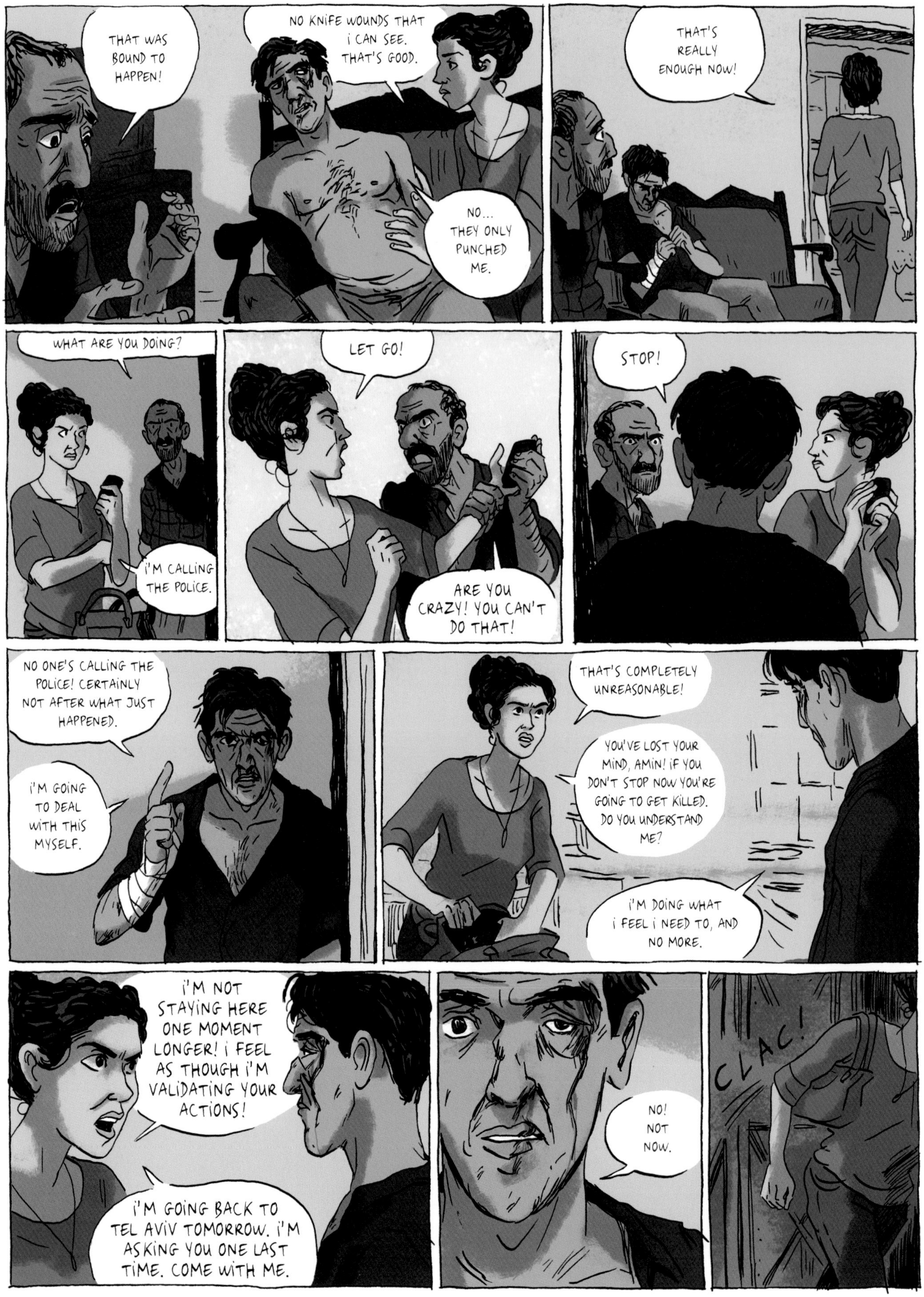
THAT WAS BOUND TO HAPPEN!
NO KNIFE WOUNDS THAT I CAN SEE. THAT'S GOOD.
NO... THEY ONLY PUNCHED ME.
THAT'S REALLY ENOUGH NOW!
WHAT ARE YOU DOING?
I'M CALLING THE POLICE.
LET GO!
ARE YOU CRAZY! YOU CAN'T DO THAT!
STOP!
NO ONE'S CALLING THE POLICE! CERTAINLY NOT AFTER WHAT JUST HAPPENED.
I'M GOING TO DEAL WITH THIS MYSELF.
THAT'S COMPLETELY UNREASONABLE!
YOU'VE LOST YOUR MIND, AMIN! IF YOU DON'T STOP NOW YOU'RE GOING TO GET KILLED. DO YOU UNDERSTAND ME?
I'M DOING WHAT I FEEL I NEED TO, AND NO MORE.
I'M NOT STAYING HERE ONE MOMENT LONGER! I FEEL AS THOUGH I'M VALIDATING YOUR ACTIONS!
I'M GOING BACK TO TEL AVIV TOMORROW. I'M ASKING YOU ONE LAST TIME. COME WITH ME.
NO! NOT NOW.
CLAC!

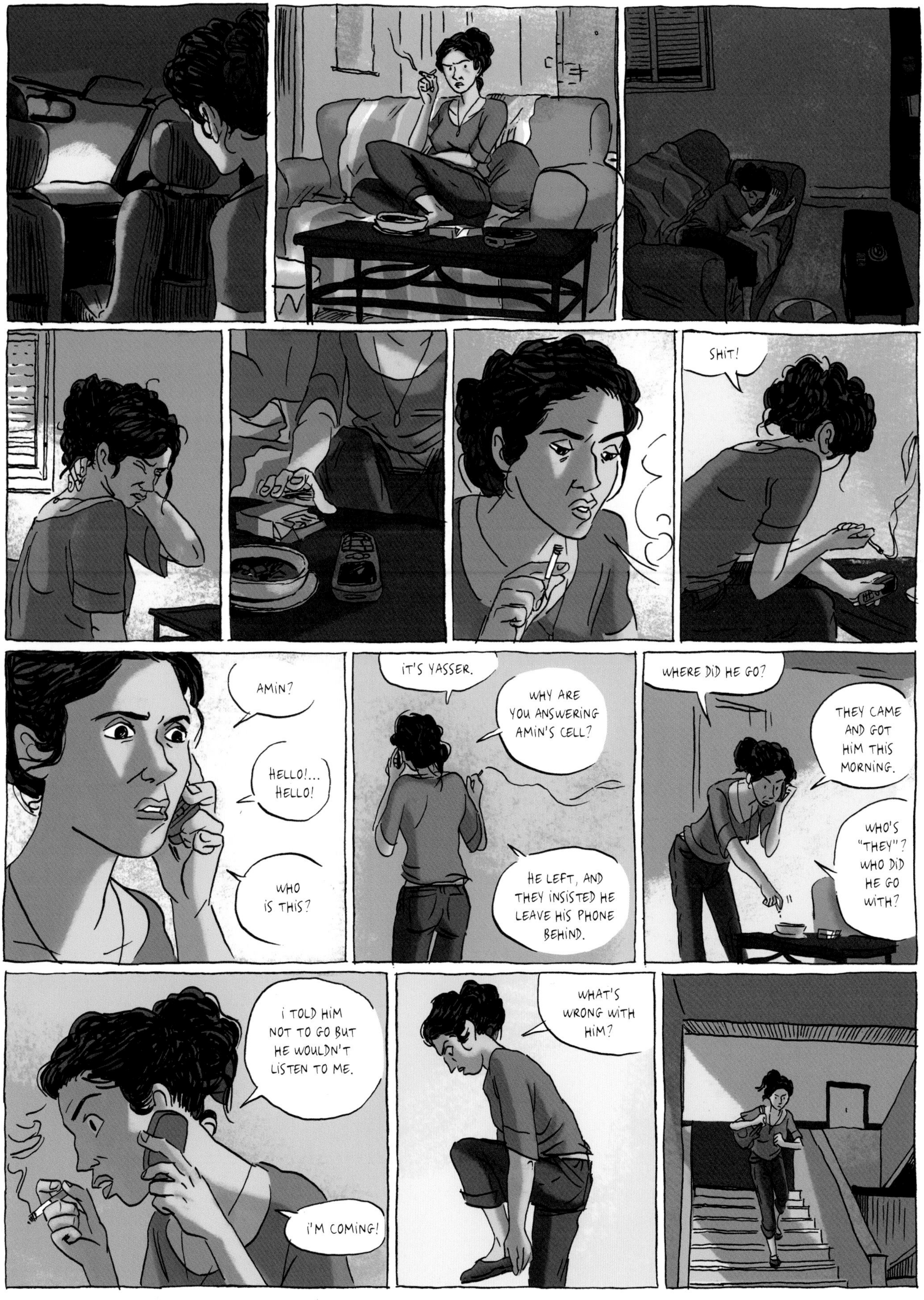

SHIT!
AMIN?
HELLO!... HELLO!
WHO IS THIS?
IT'S YASSER.
WHY ARE YOU ANSWERING AMIN'S CELL?
HE LEFT, AND THEY INSISTED HE LEAVE HIS PHONE BEHIND.
WHERE DID HE GO?
THEY CAME AND GOT HIM THIS MORNING.
WHO'S "THEY"? WHO DID HE GO WITH?
I TOLD HIM NOT TO GO BUT HE WOULDN'T LISTEN TO ME.
I'M COMING!
WHAT'S WRONG WITH HIM?

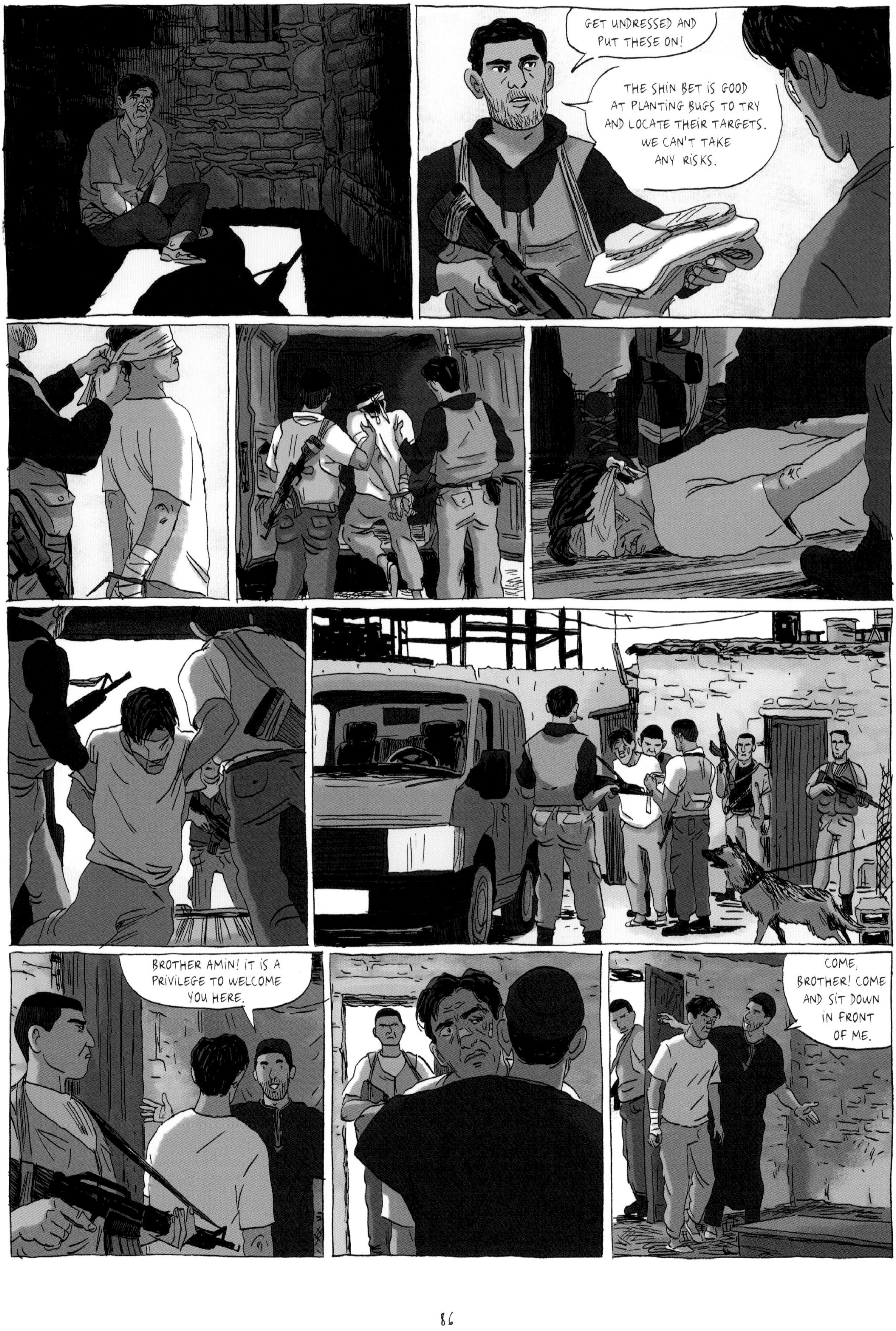
GET UNDRESSED AND PUT THESE ON!
THE SHIN BET IS GOOD AT PLANTING BUGS TO TRY AND LOCATE THEIR TARGETS. WE CAN'T TAKE ANY RISKS.
BROTHER AMIN! IT IS A PRIVILEGE TO WELCOME YOU HERE.
COME, BROTHER! COME AND SIT DOWN IN FRONT OF ME.

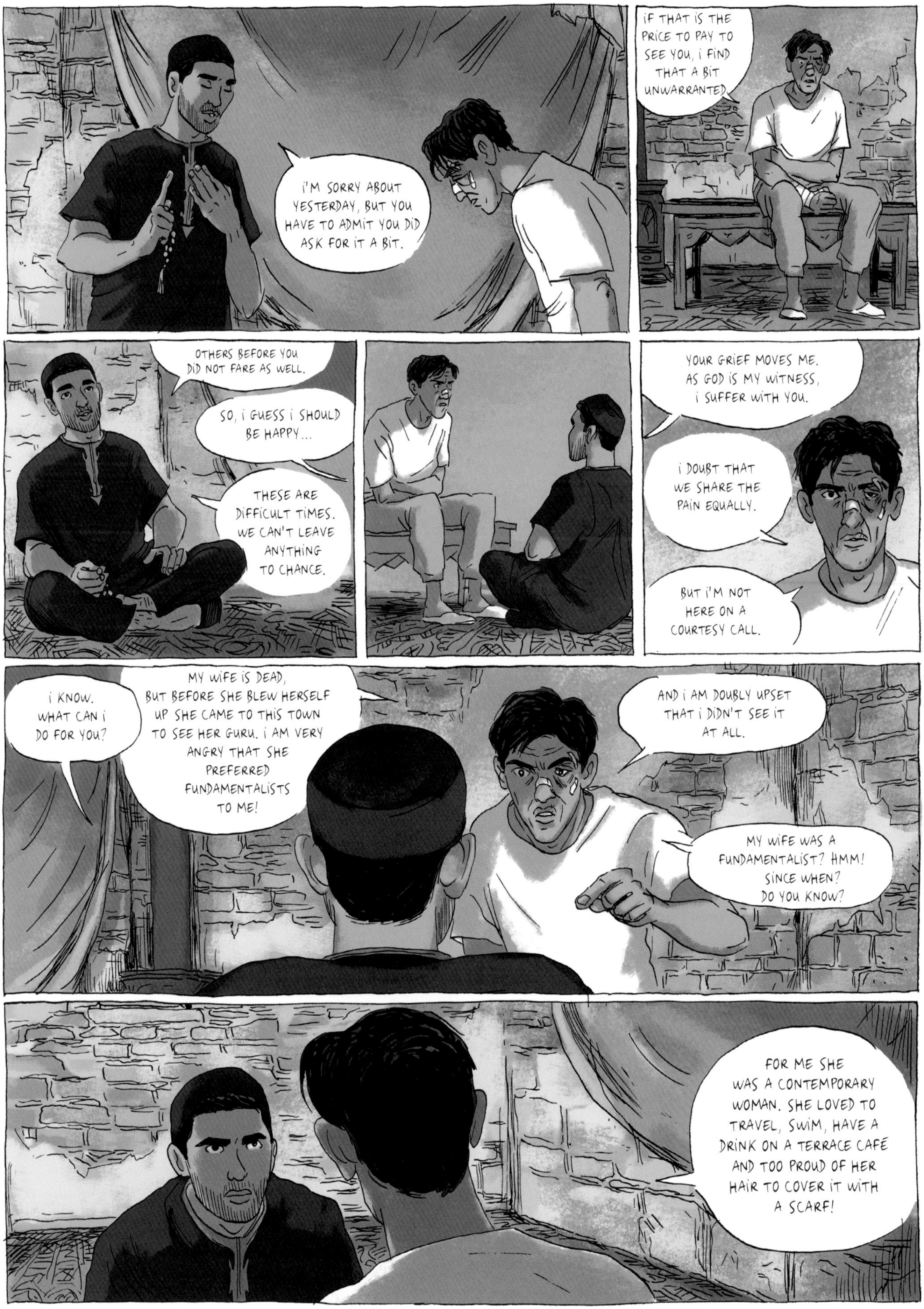
I'M SORRY ABOUT YESTERDAY, BUT YOU HAVE TO ADMIT YOU DID ASK FOR IT A BIT.
IF THAT IS THE PRICE TO PAY TO SEE YOU, I FIND THAT A BIT UNWARRANTED.
OTHERS BEFORE YOU DID NOT FARE AS WELL.
SO, I GUESS I SHOULD BE HAPPY...
THESE ARE DIFFICULT TIMES. WE CAN'T LEAVE ANYTHING TO CHANCE.
YOUR GRIEF MOVES ME. AS GOD IS MY WITNESS, I SUFFER WITH YOU.
I DOUBT THAT WE SHARE THE PAIN EQUALLY.
BUT I'M NOT HERE ON A COURTESY CALL.
MY WIFE IS DEAD, BUT BEFORE SHE BLEW HERSELF UP SHE CAME TO THIS TOWN TO SEE HER GURU. I AM VERY ANGRY THAT SHE PREFERRED FUNDAMENTALISTS TO ME!
I KNOW. WHAT CAN I DO FOR YOU?
AND I AM DOUBLY UPSET THAT I DIDN'T SEE IT AT ALL.
MY WIFE WAS A FUNDAMENTALIST? HMM! SINCE WHEN? DO YOU KNOW?
FOR ME SHE WAS A CONTEMPORARY WOMAN. SHE LOVED TO TRAVEL, SWIM, HAVE A DRINK ON A TERRACE CAFÉ AND TOO PROUD OF HER HAIR TO COVER IT WITH A SCARF!

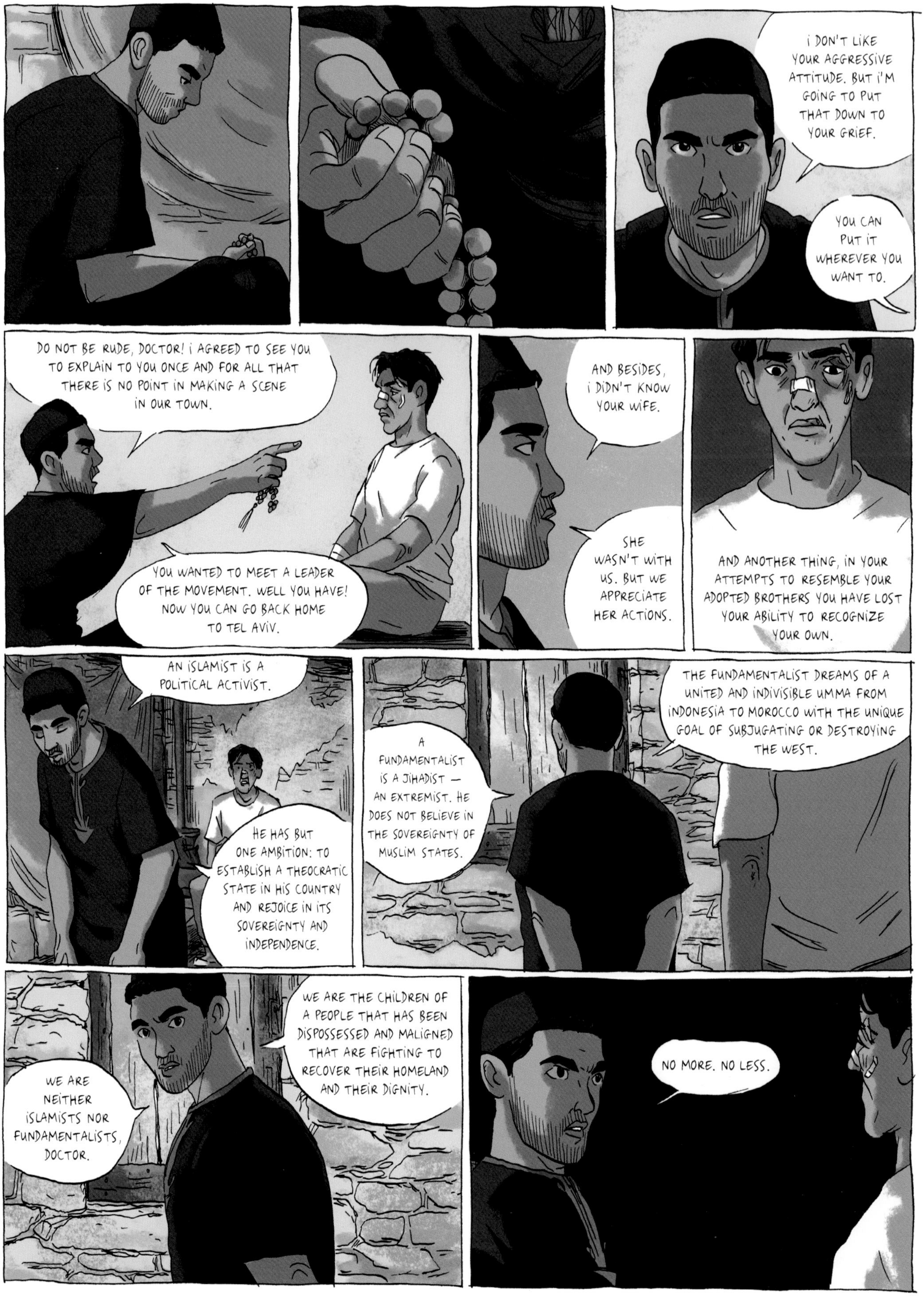
I DON'T LIKE YOUR AGGRESSIVE ATTITUDE. BUT I'M GOING TO PUT THAT DOWN TO YOUR GRIEF.
YOU CAN PUT IT WHEREVER YOU WANT TO.
DO NOT BE RUDE, DOCTOR! I AGREED TO SEE YOU TO EXPLAIN TO YOU ONCE AND FOR ALL THAT THERE IS NO POINT IN MAKING A SCENE IN OUR TOWN.
YOU WANTED TO MEET A LEADER OF THE MOVEMENT. WELL YOU HAVE! NOW YOU CAN GO BACK HOME TO TEL AVIV.
AND BESIDES, I DIDN'T KNOW YOUR WIFE.
SHE WASN'T WITH US. BUT WE APPRECIATE HER ACTIONS.
AND ANOTHER THING, IN YOUR ATTEMPTS TO RESEMBLE YOUR ADOPTED BROTHERS YOU HAVE LOST YOUR ABILITY TO RECOGNIZE YOUR OWN.
AN ISLAMIST IS A POLITICAL ACTIVIST.
HE HAS BUT ONE AMBITION: TO ESTABLISH A THEOCRATIC STATE IN HIS COUNTRY AND REJOICE IN ITS SOVEREIGNTY AND INDEPENDENCE.
A FUNDAMENTALIST IS A JIHADIST — AN EXTREMIST. HE DOES NOT BELIEVE IN THE SOVEREIGNTY OF MUSLIM STATES.
THE FUNDAMENTALIST DREAMS OF A UNITED AND INDIVISIBLE UMMA FROM INDONESIA TO MOROCCO WITH THE UNIQUE GOAL OF SUBJUGATING OR DESTROYING THE WEST.
WE ARE NEITHER ISLAMISTS NOR FUNDAMENTALISTS, DOCTOR.
WE ARE THE CHILDREN OF A PEOPLE THAT HAS BEEN DISPOSSESSED AND MALIGNED THAT ARE FIGHTING TO RECOVER THEIR HOMELAND AND THEIR DIGNITY.
NO MORE. NO LESS.

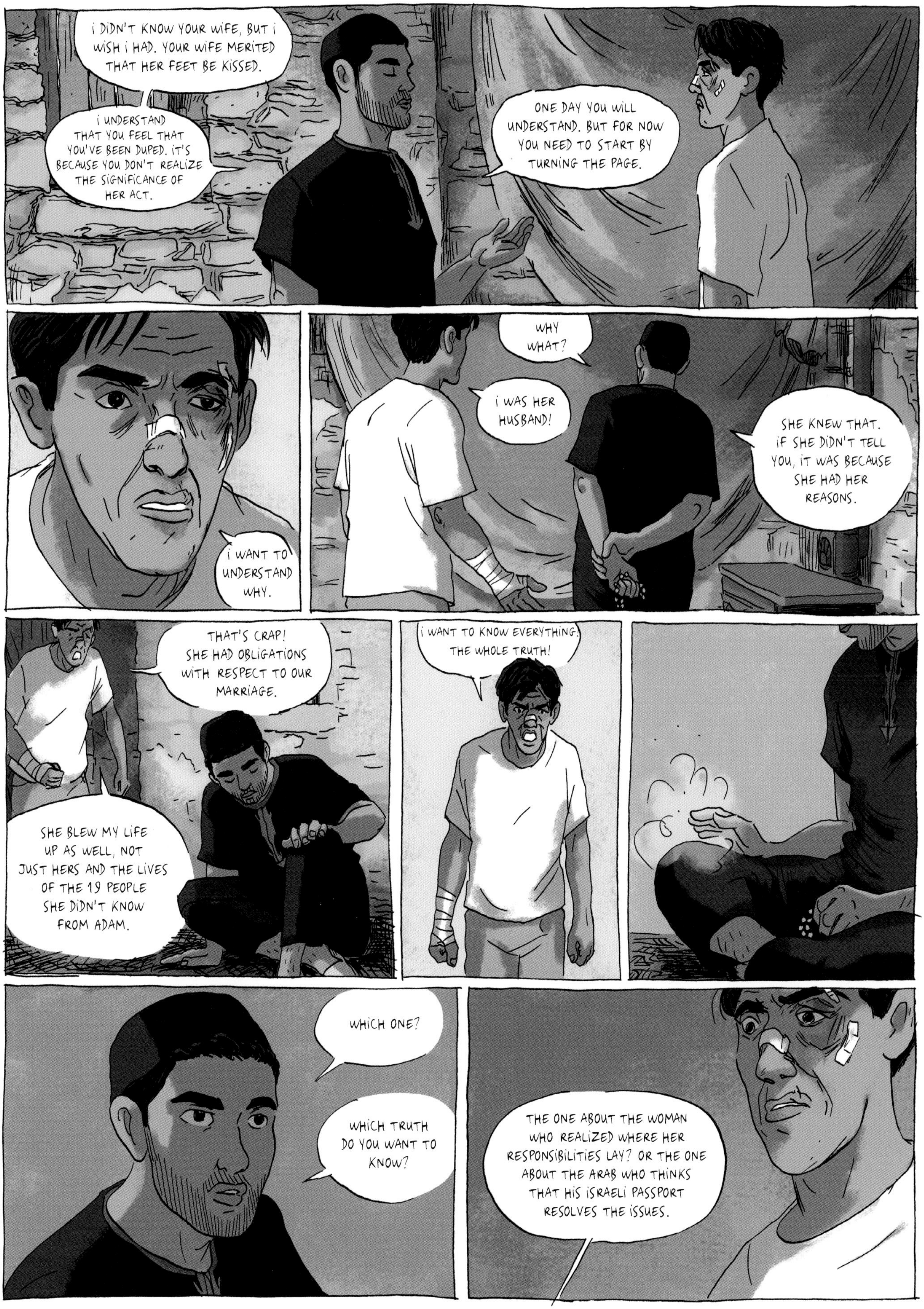
I DIDN'T KNOW YOUR WIFE, BUT I WISH I HAD. YOUR WIFE MERITED THAT HER FEET BE KISSED.
I UNDERSTAND THAT YOU FEEL THAT YOU'VE BEEN DUPED. IT'S BECAUSE YOU DON'T REALIZE THE SIGNIFICANCE OF HER ACT.
ONE DAY YOU WILL UNDERSTAND. BUT FOR NOW YOU NEED TO START BY TURNING THE PAGE.
I WANT TO UNDERSTAND WHY.
WHY WHAT?
I WAS HER HUSBAND!
SHE KNEW THAT. IF SHE DIDN'T TELL YOU, IT WAS BECAUSE SHE HAD HER REASONS.
THAT'S CRAP! SHE HAD OBLIGATIONS WITH RESPECT TO OUR MARRIAGE.
SHE BLEW MY LIFE UP AS WELL, NOT JUST HERS AND THE LIVES OF THE 19 PEOPLE SHE DIDN'T KNOW FROM ADAM.
I WANT TO KNOW EVERYTHING! THE WHOLE TRUTH!
WHICH ONE?
WHICH TRUTH DO YOU WANT TO KNOW?
THE ONE ABOUT THE WOMAN WHO REALIZED WHERE HER RESPONSIBILITIES LAY? OR THE ONE ABOUT THE ARAB WHO THINKS THAT HIS ISRAELI PASSPORT RESOLVES THE ISSUES.

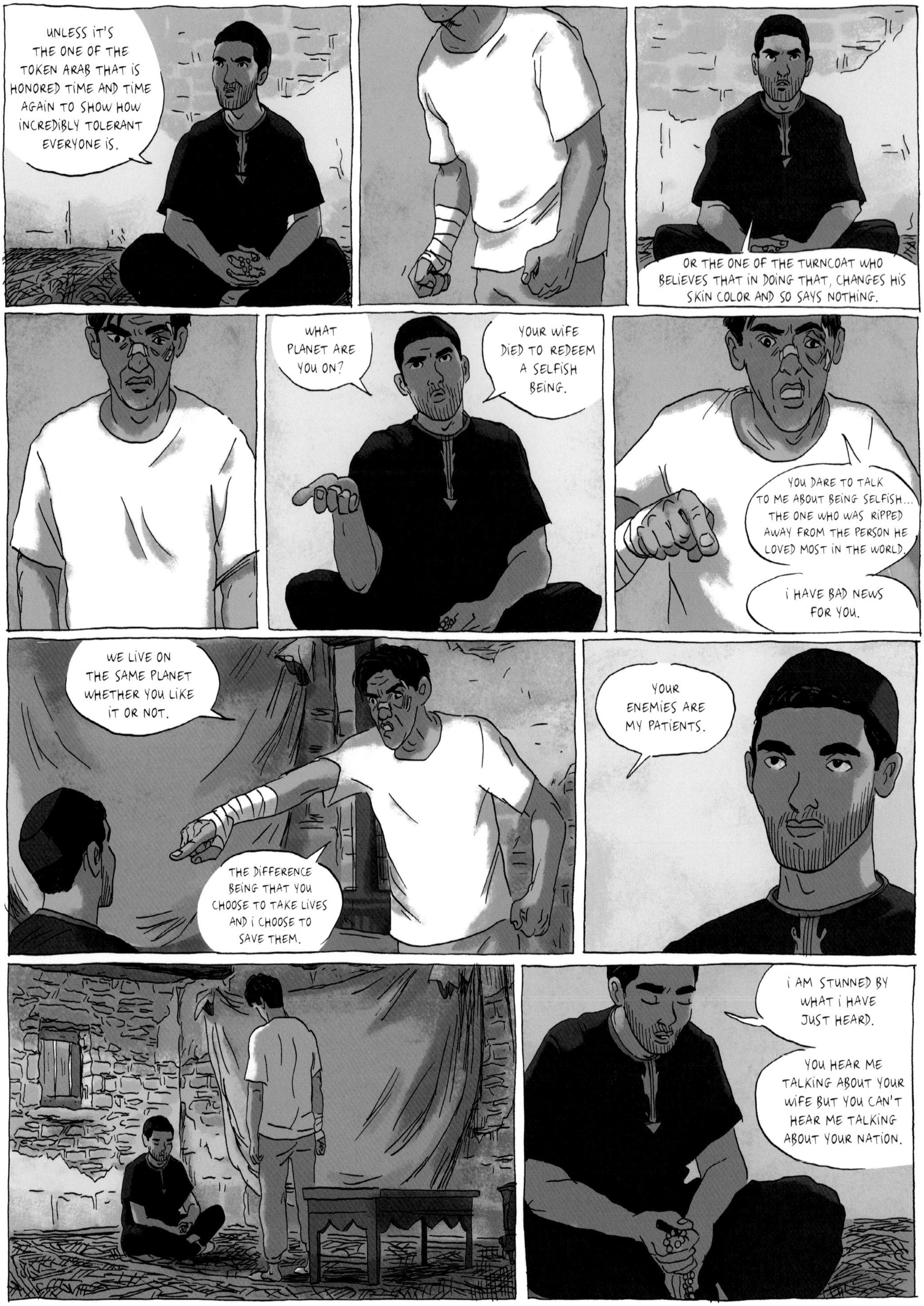
UNLESS IT'S THE ONE OF THE TOKEN ARAB THAT IS HONORED TIME AND TIME AGAIN TO SHOW HOW INCREDIBLY TOLERANT EVERYONE IS.
OR THE ONE OF THE TURNCOAT WHO BELIEVES THAT IN DOING THAT, CHANGES HIS SKIN COLOR AND SO SAYS NOTHING.
WHAT PLANET ARE YOU ON?
YOUR WIFE DIED TO REDEEM A SELFISH BEING.
YOU DARE TO TALK TO ME ABOUT BEING SELFISH... THE ONE WHO WAS RIPPED AWAY FROM THE PERSON HE LOVED MOST IN THE WORLD.
I HAVE BAD NEWS FOR YOU.
WE LIVE ON THE SAME PLANET WHETHER YOU LIKE IT OR NOT.
THE DIFFERENCE BEING THAT YOU CHOOSE TO TAKE LIVES AND I CHOOSE TO SAVE THEM.
YOUR ENEMIES ARE MY PATIENTS.
I AM STUNNED BY WHAT I HAVE JUST HEARD.
YOU HEAR ME TALKING ABOUT YOUR WIFE BUT YOU CAN'T HEAR ME TALKING ABOUT YOUR NATION.

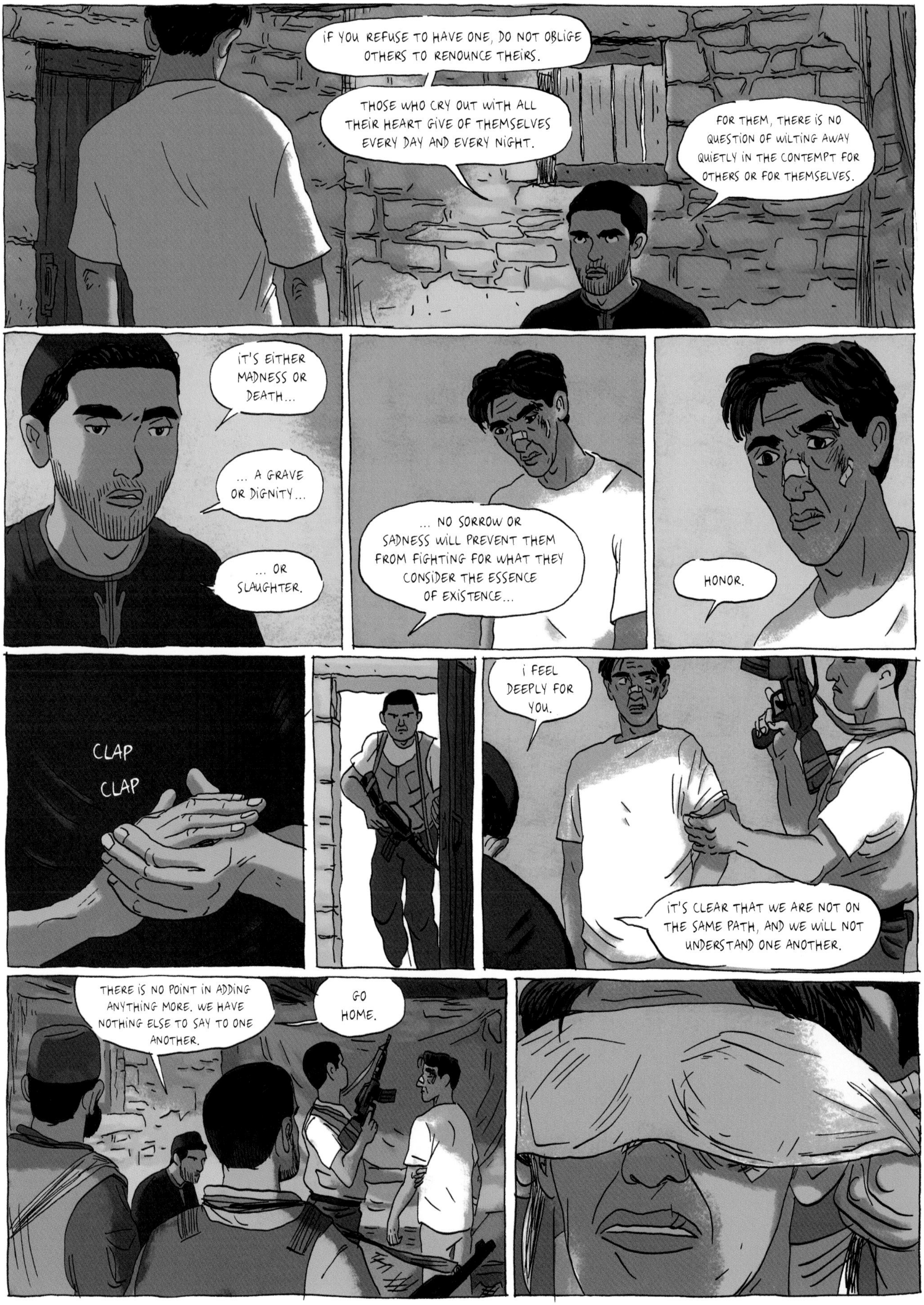

IF YOU REFUSE TO HAVE ONE, DO NOT OBLIGE OTHERS TO RENOUNCE THEIRS.
THOSE WHO CRY OUT WITH ALL THEIR HEART GIVE OF THEMSELVES EVERY DAY AND EVERY NIGHT.
FOR THEM, THERE IS NO QUESTION OF WILTING AWAY QUIETLY IN THE CONTEMPT FOR OTHERS OR FOR THEMSELVES.
IT'S EITHER MADNESS OR DEATH...
... A GRAVE OR DIGNITY...
... OR SLAUGHTER.
... NO SORROW OR SADNESS WILL PREVENT THEM FROM FIGHTING FOR WHAT THEY CONSIDER THE ESSENCE OF EXISTENCE...
HONOR.
CLAP
CLAP
I FEEL DEEPLY FOR YOU.
IT'S CLEAR THAT WE ARE NOT ON THE SAME PATH, AND WE WILL NOT UNDERSTAND ONE ANOTHER.
THERE IS NO POINT IN ADDING ANYTHING MORE. WE HAVE NOTHING ELSE TO SAY TO ONE ANOTHER.
GO HOME.

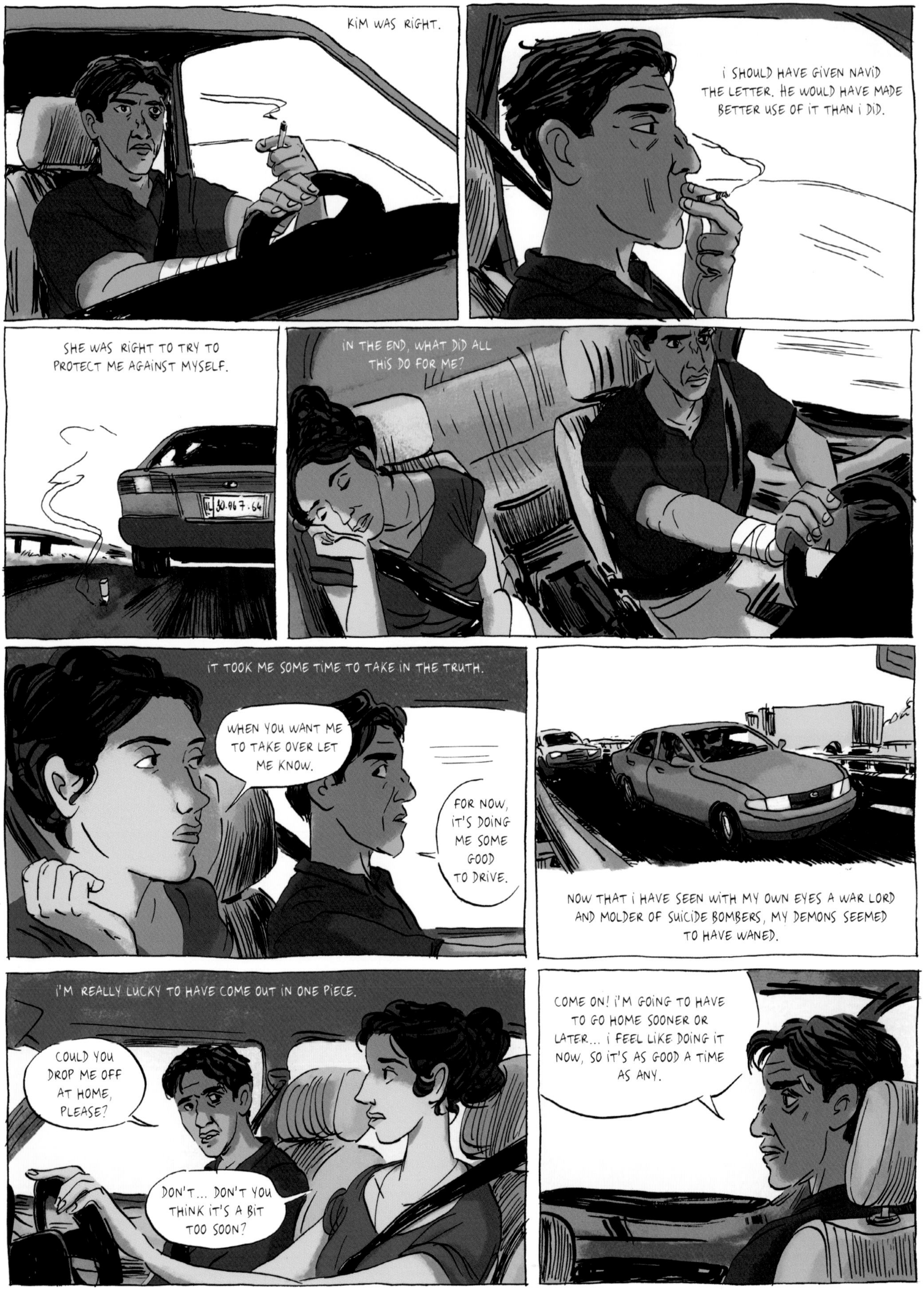
KIM WAS RIGHT.
I SHOULD HAVE GIVEN NAVID THE LETTER. HE WOULD HAVE MADE BETTER USE OF IT THAN I DID.
SHE WAS RIGHT TO TRY TO PROTECT ME AGAINST MYSELF.
IL 30-967.64
IN THE END, WHAT DID ALL THIS DO FOR ME?
IT TOOK ME SOME TIME TO TAKE IN THE TRUTH.
WHEN YOU WANT ME TO TAKE OVER LET ME KNOW.
FOR NOW, IT'S DOING ME SOME GOOD TO DRIVE.
NOW THAT I HAVE SEEN WITH MY OWN EYES A WAR LORD AND MOLDER OF SUICIDE BOMBERS, MY DEMONS SEEMED TO HAVE WANED.
I'M REALLY LUCKY TO HAVE COME OUT IN ONE PIECE.
COULD YOU DROP ME OFF AT HOME, PLEASE?
DON'T... DON'T YOU THINK IT'S A BIT TOO SOON?
COME ON! I'M GOING TO HAVE TO GO HOME SOONER OR LATER... I FEEL LIKE DOING IT NOW, SO IT'S AS GOOD A TIME AS ANY.

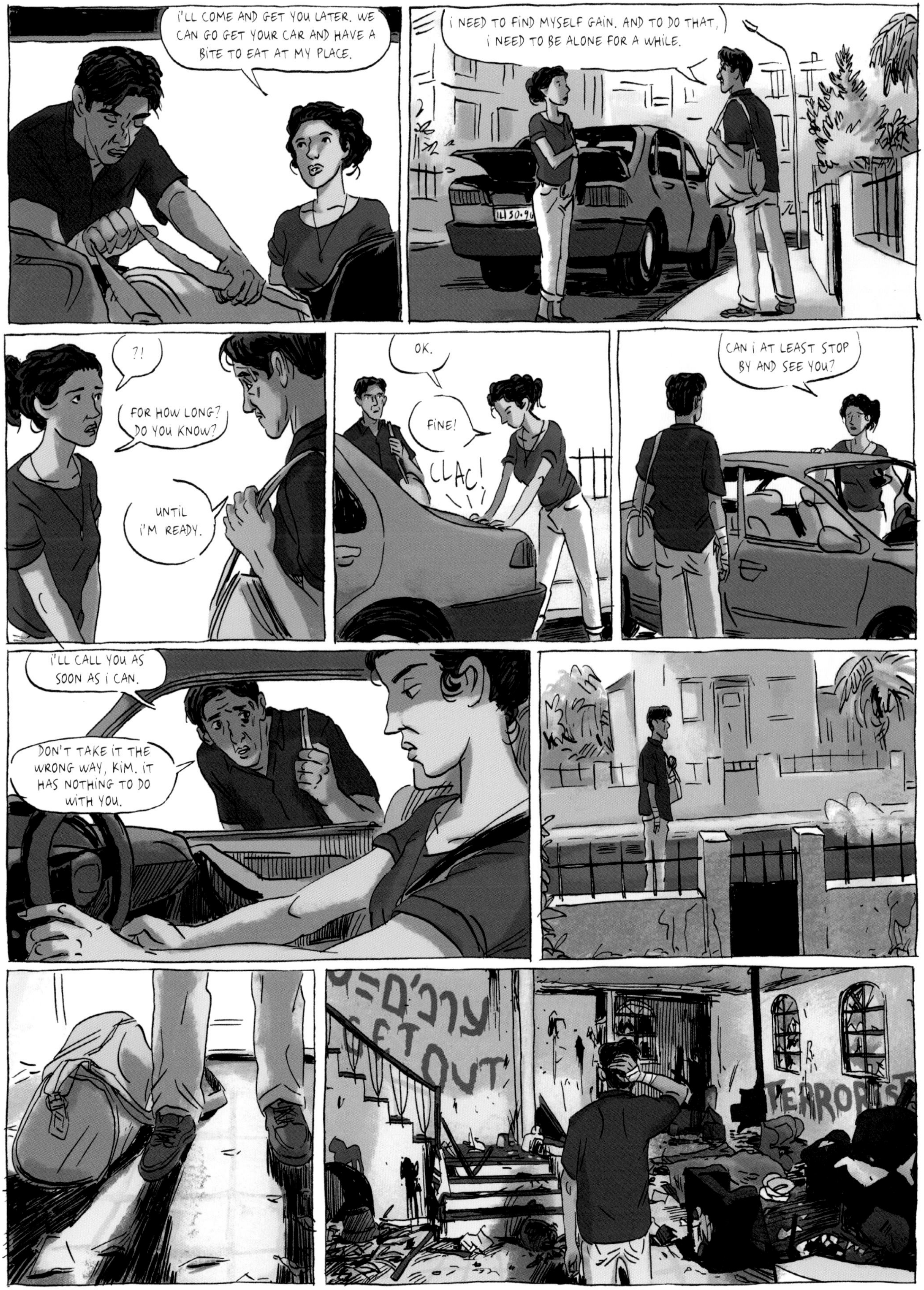
i'LL COME AND GET YOU LATER. WE CAN GO GET YOUR CAR AND HAVE A BiTE TO EAT AT MY PLACE.
i NEED TO FiND MYSELF GAiN. AND TO DO THAT, i NEED TO BE ALONE FOR A WHiLE.
?!
FOR HOW LONG? DO YOU KNOW?
UNTiL i'M READY.
OK.
FiNE!
CLAC!
CAN i AT LEAST STOP BY AND SEE YOU?
i'LL CALL YOU AS SOON AS i CAN.
DON'T TAKE iT THE WRONG WAY, KiM. iT HAS NOTHiNG TO DO WiTH YOU.

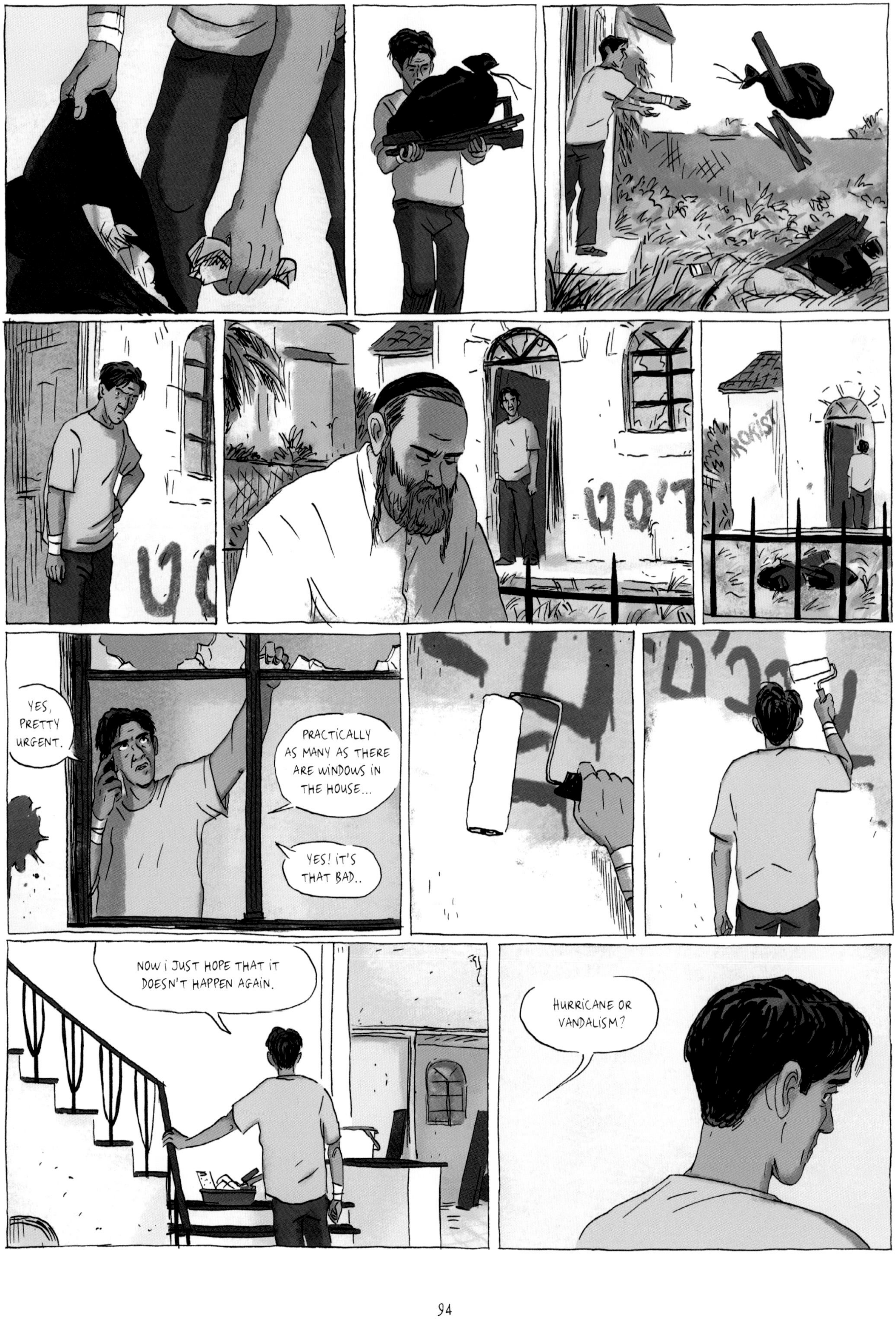
YES, PRETTY URGENT.
PRACTICALLY AS MANY AS THERE ARE WINDOWS IN THE HOUSE...
YES! IT'S THAT BAD..
NOW I JUST HOPE THAT IT DOESN'T HAPPEN AGAIN.
HURRICANE OR VANDALISM?

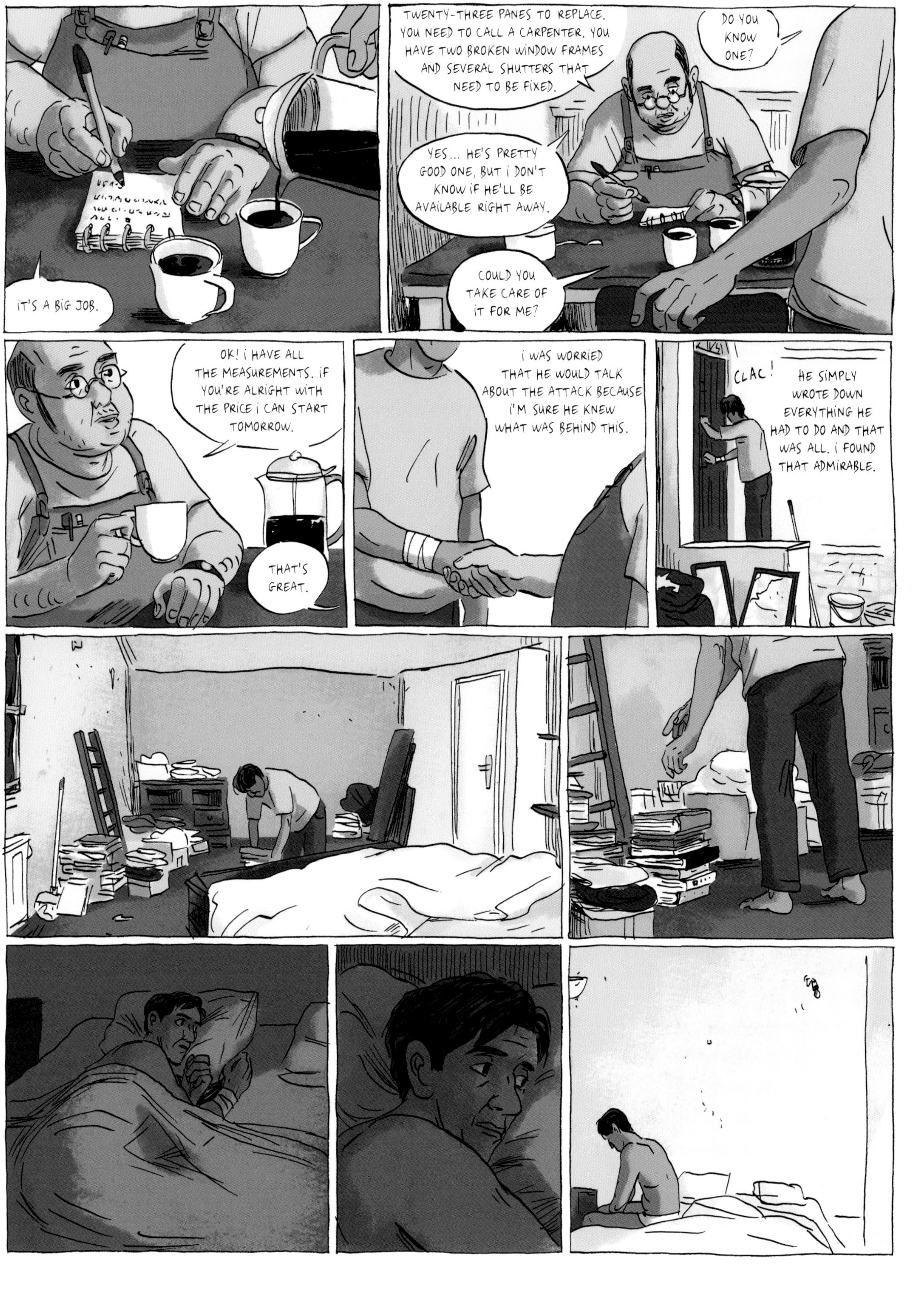
IT'S A BIG JOB.
TWENTY-THREE PANES TO REPLACE. YOU NEED TO CALL A CARPENTER. YOU HAVE TWO BROKEN WINDOW FRAMES AND SEVERAL SHUTTERS THAT NEED TO BE FIXED.
DO YOU KNOW ONE?
YES... HE'S PRETTY GOOD ONE, BUT I DON'T KNOW IF HE'LL BE AVAILABLE RIGHT AWAY.
COULD YOU TAKE CARE OF IT FOR ME?
OK! I HAVE ALL THE MEASUREMENTS. IF YOU'RE ALRIGHT WITH THE PRICE I CAN START TOMORROW.
THAT'S GREAT.
I WAS WORRIED THAT HE WOULD TALK ABOUT THE ATTACK BECAUSE I'M SURE HE KNEW WHAT WAS BEHIND THIS.
CLAC!
HE SIMPLY WROTE DOWN EVERYTHING HE HAD TO DO AND THAT WAS ALL. I FOUND THAT ADMIRABLE.

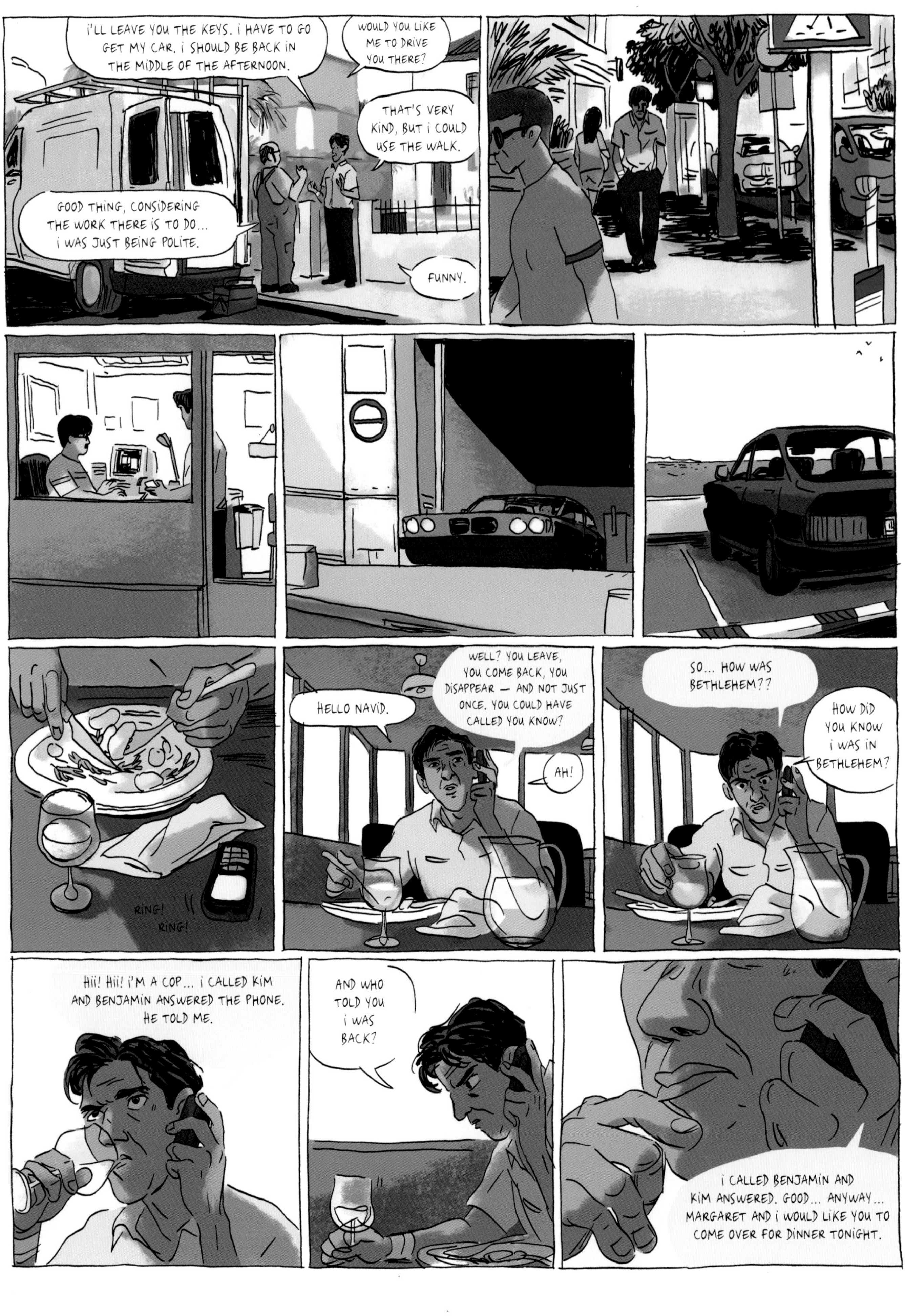
i'LL LEAVE YOU THE KEYS. i HAVE TO GO GET MY CAR. i SHOULD BE BACK IN THE MIDDLE OF THE AFTERNOON.
WOULD YOU LIKE ME TO DRIVE YOU THERE?
THAT'S VERY KIND, BUT i COULD USE THE WALK.
GOOD THING, CONSIDERING THE WORK THERE IS TO DO... i WAS JUST BEING POLITE.
FUNNY.
RING! RING!
HELLO NAVID.
WELL? YOU LEAVE, YOU COME BACK, YOU DISAPPEAR — AND NOT JUST ONCE. YOU COULD HAVE CALLED YOU KNOW?
AH!
SO... HOW WAS BETHLEHEM??
HOW DID YOU KNOW i WAS IN BETHLEHEM?
Hii! Hii! i'M A COP... i CALLED KiM AND BENJAMIN ANSWERED THE PHONE. HE TOLD ME.
AND WHO TOLD YOU i WAS BACK?
i CALLED BENJAMIN AND KiM ANSWERED. GOOD... ANYWAY... MARGARET AND i WOULD LIKE YOU TO COME OVER FOR DINNER TONIGHT.

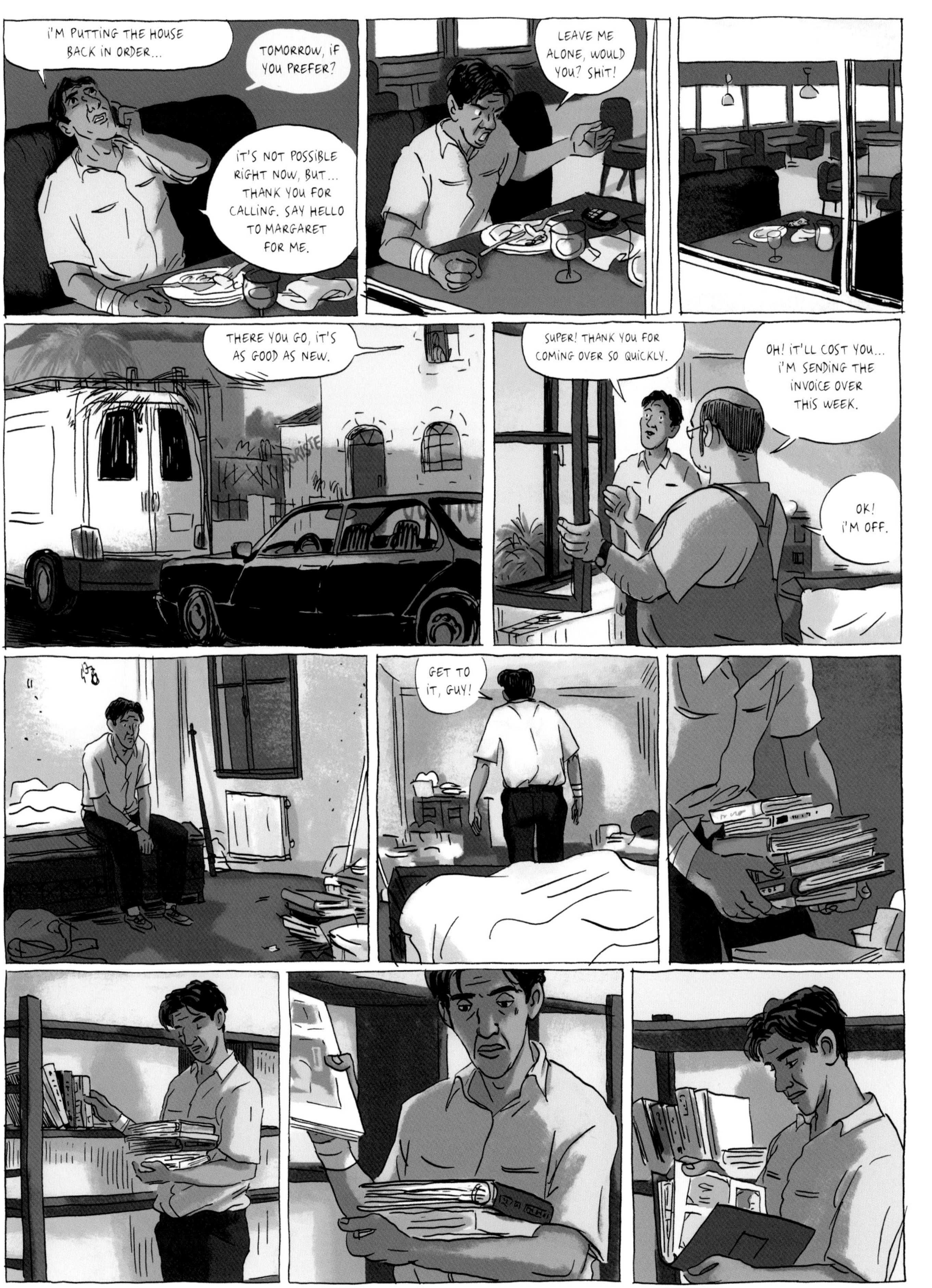
I'M PUTTING THE HOUSE BACK IN ORDER...
TOMORROW, IF YOU PREFER?
IT'S NOT POSSIBLE RIGHT NOW, BUT... THANK YOU FOR CALLING. SAY HELLO TO MARGARET FOR ME.
LEAVE ME ALONE, WOULD YOU? SHIT!
THERE YOU GO, IT'S AS GOOD AS NEW.
SUPER! THANK YOU FOR COMING OVER SO QUICKLY.
OH! IT'LL COST YOU... I'M SENDING THE INVOICE OVER THIS WEEK.
OK! I'M OFF.
GET TO IT, GUY!

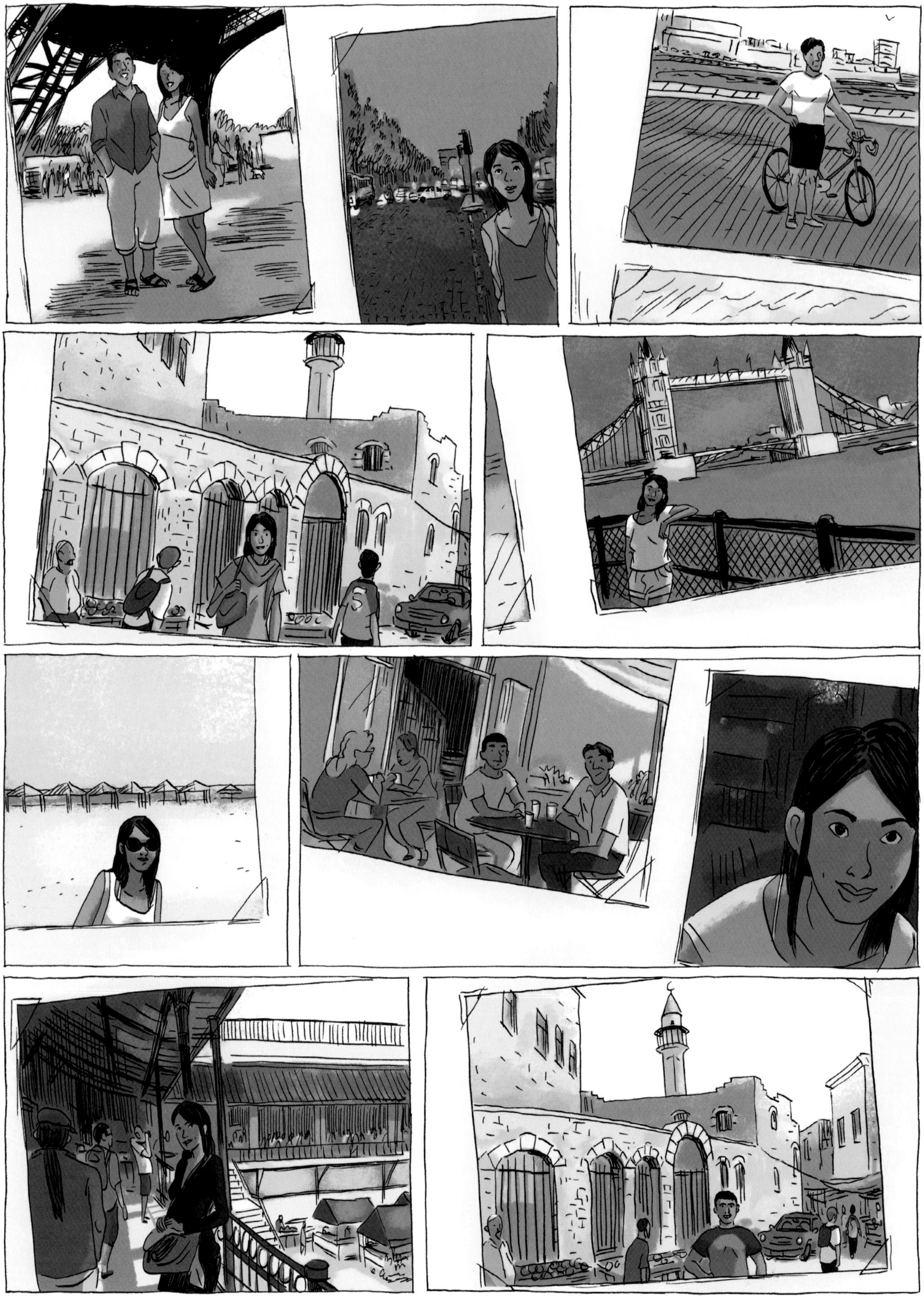

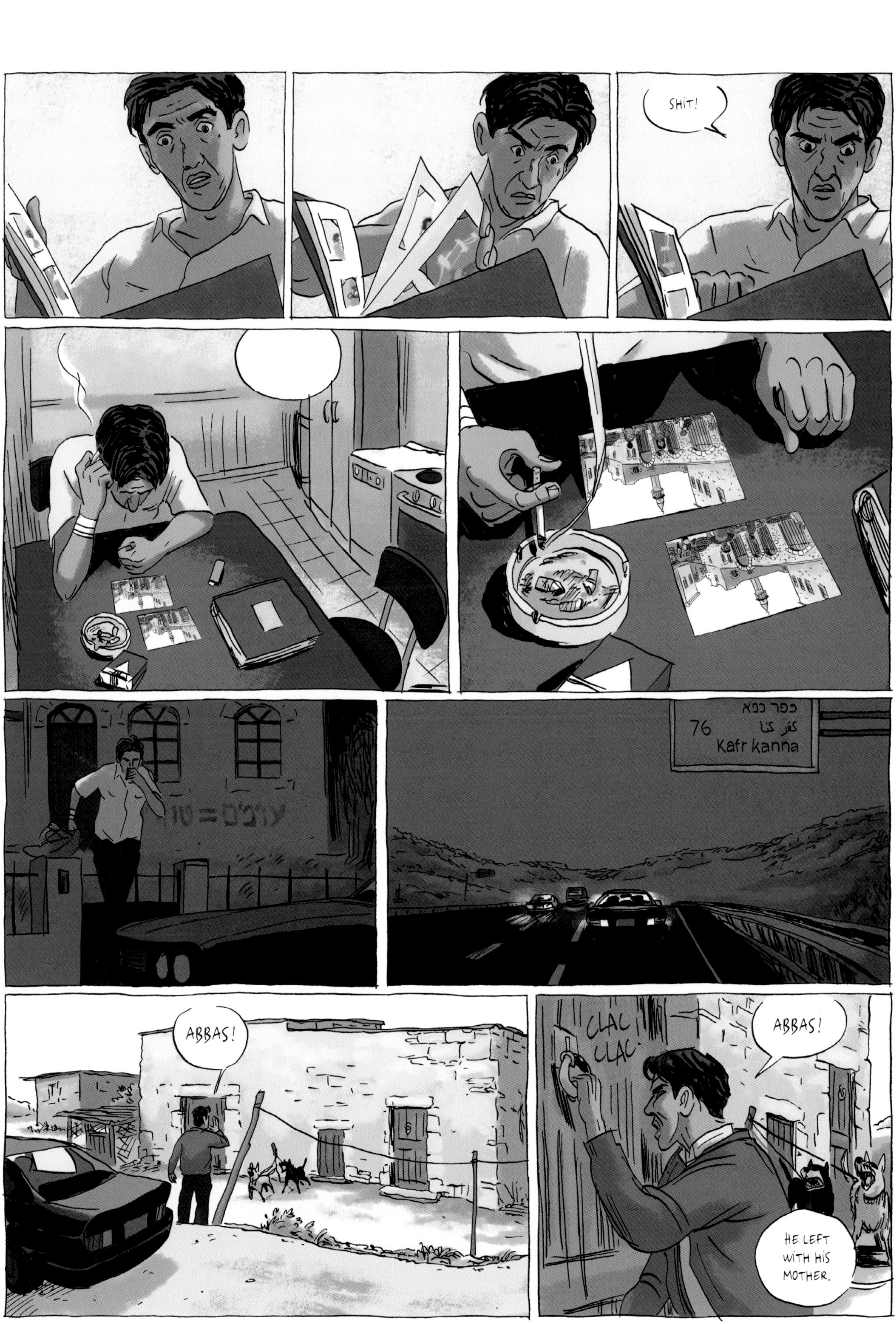
SHIT!
כפר כנא
كفر كنا
76
Kafr kanna
ABBAS!
CLAC
CLAC
ABBAS!
HE LEFT WITH HIS MOTHER.

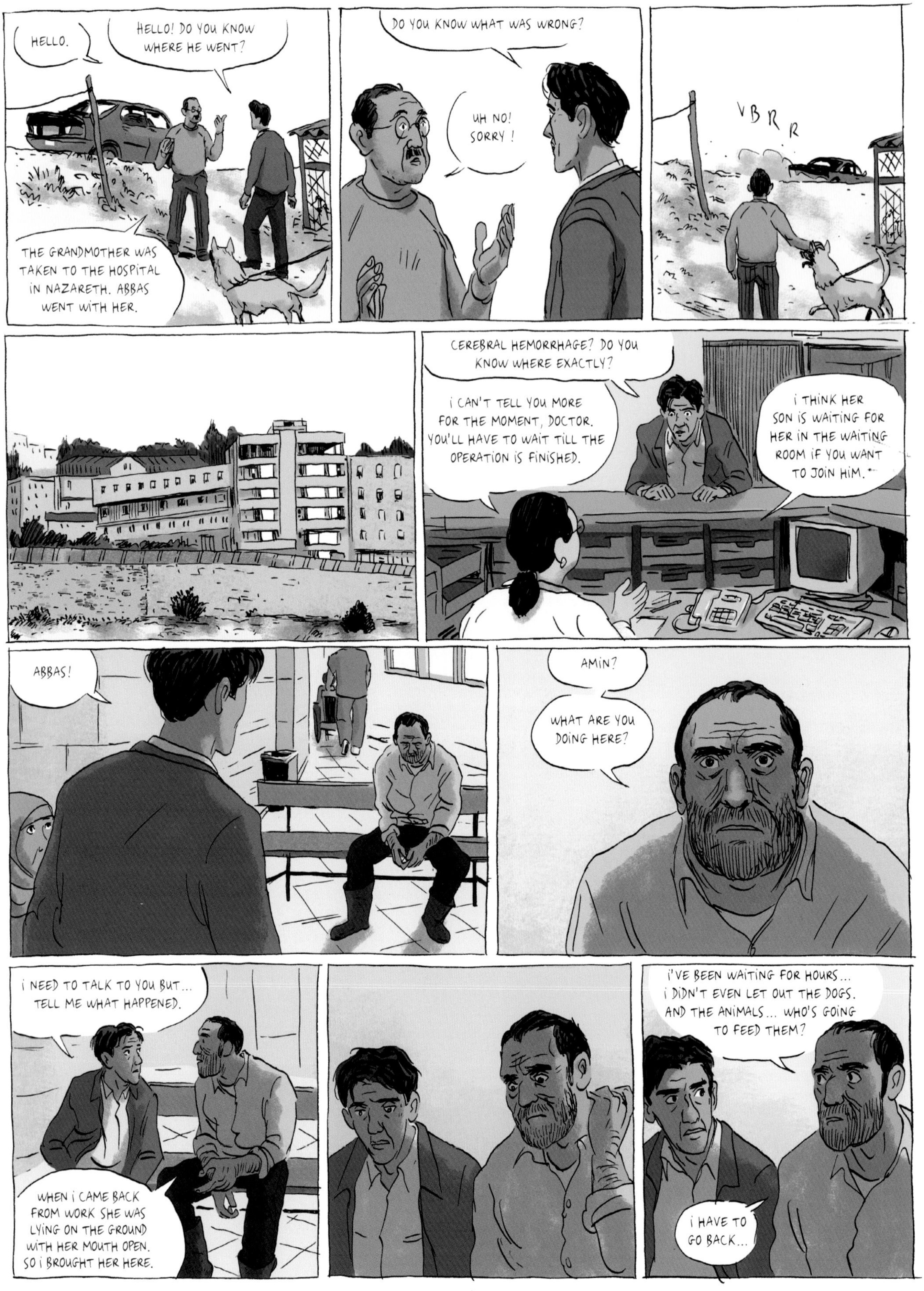
HELLO.
HELLO! DO YOU KNOW WHERE HE WENT?
THE GRANDMOTHER WAS TAKEN TO THE HOSPITAL IN NAZARETH. ABBAS WENT WITH HER.
DO YOU KNOW WHAT WAS WRONG?
UH NO! SORRY!
VBRR
CEREBRAL HEMORRHAGE? DO YOU KNOW WHERE EXACTLY?
I CAN'T TELL YOU MORE FOR THE MOMENT, DOCTOR. YOU'LL HAVE TO WAIT TILL THE OPERATION IS FINISHED.
I THINK HER SON IS WAITING FOR HER IN THE WAITING ROOM IF YOU WANT TO JOIN HIM.
ABBAS!
AMIN?
WHAT ARE YOU DOING HERE?
I NEED TO TALK TO YOU BUT... TELL ME WHAT HAPPENED.
WHEN I CAME BACK FROM WORK SHE WAS LYING ON THE GROUND WITH HER MOUTH OPEN. SO I BROUGHT HER HERE.
I'VE BEEN WAITING FOR HOURS... I DIDN'T EVEN LET OUT THE DOGS. AND THE ANIMALS... WHO'S GOING TO FEED THEM?
I HAVE TO GO BACK...

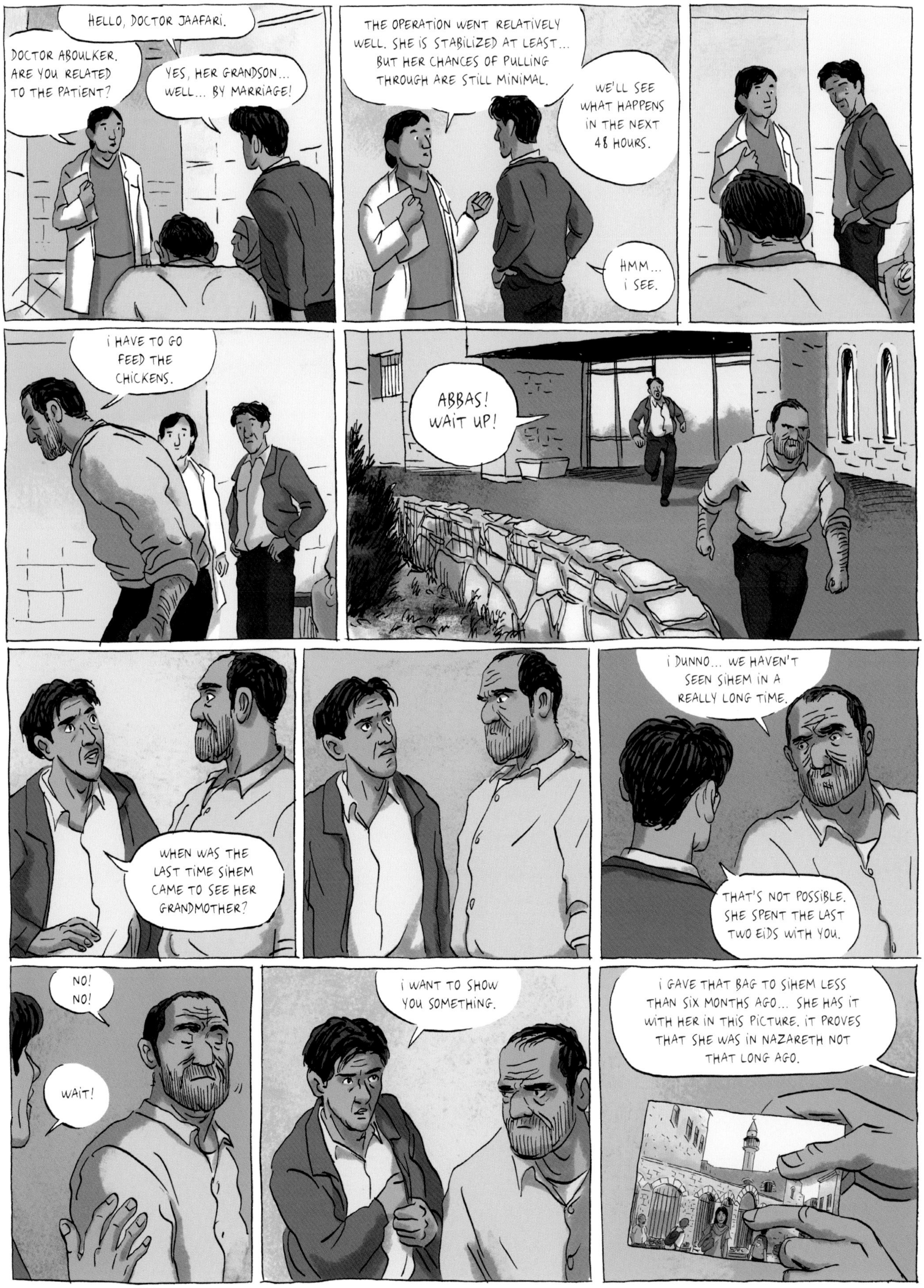
HELLO, DOCTOR JAAFARI.
DOCTOR ABOULKER. ARE YOU RELATED TO THE PATIENT?
YES, HER GRANDSON... WELL... BY MARRIAGE!
THE OPERATION WENT RELATIVELY WELL. SHE IS STABILIZED AT LEAST... BUT HER CHANCES OF PULLING THROUGH ARE STILL MINIMAL.
WE'LL SEE WHAT HAPPENS IN THE NEXT 48 HOURS.
HMM... I SEE.
I HAVE TO GO FEED THE CHICKENS.
ABBAS! WAIT UP!
WHEN WAS THE LAST TIME SIHEM CAME TO SEE HER GRANDMOTHER?
I DUNNO... WE HAVEN'T SEEN SIHEM IN A REALLY LONG TIME.
THAT'S NOT POSSIBLE. SHE SPENT THE LAST TWO EIDS WITH YOU.
NO! NO!
WAIT!
I WANT TO SHOW YOU SOMETHING.
I GAVE THAT BAG TO SIHEM LESS THAN SIX MONTHS AGO... SHE HAS IT WITH HER IN THIS PICTURE. IT PROVES THAT SHE WAS IN NAZARETH NOT THAT LONG AGO.

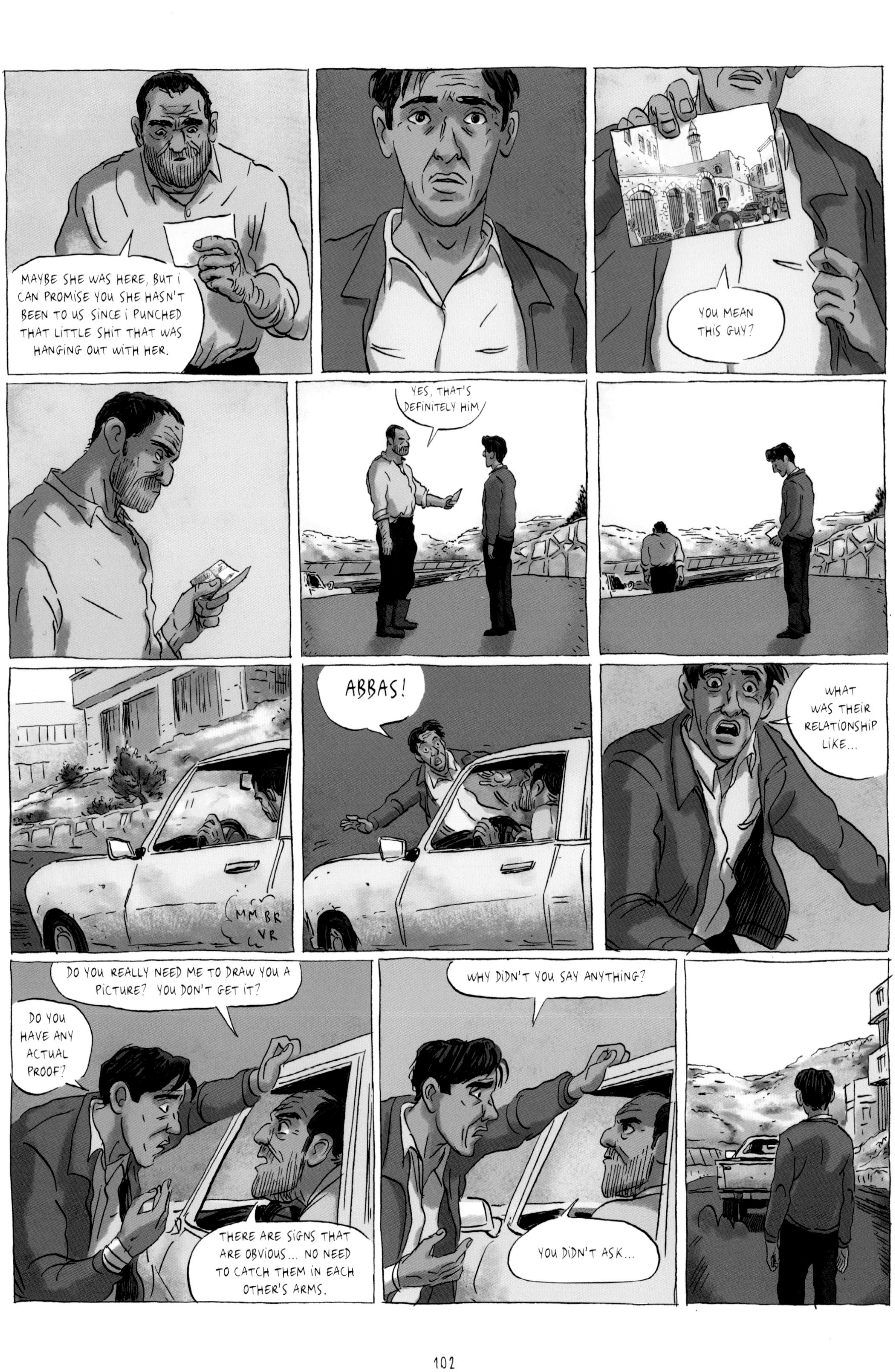
MAYBE SHE WAS HERE, BUT I CAN PROMISE YOU SHE HASN'T BEEN TO US SINCE I PUNCHED THAT LITTLE SHIT THAT WAS HANGING OUT WITH HER.
YOU MEAN THIS GUY?
YES, THAT'S DEFINITELY HIM
ABBAS!
WHAT WAS THEIR RELATIONSHIP LIKE...
MM BR VR
DO YOU REALLY NEED ME TO DRAW YOU A PICTURE? YOU DON'T GET IT?
DO YOU HAVE ANY ACTUAL PROOF?
THERE ARE SIGNS THAT ARE OBVIOUS... NO NEED TO CATCH THEM IN EACH OTHER'S ARMS.
WHY DIDN'T YOU SAY ANYTHING?
YOU DIDN'T ASK...

... AND ME... i MIND
MY OWN BUSINESS.

MR. JAAFARI!

MR. JAAFARI!

MR. JAAFARI!

MR. JAAFARI!

COME AND HELP ME! WE'RE GOING TO SIT HIM UP.

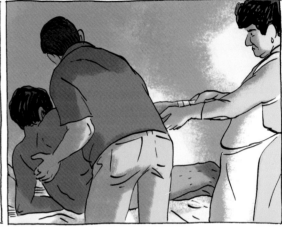

LET GO OF ME!

WHAT'S GOING ON?

I THINK THAT YOU'RE IN PAIN, MR. JAAFARI...

WHO ARE YOU?

I'M THE HOTEL MANAGER, SIR.

YOU CAME TWO DAYS AGO AND SHUT YOURSELF UP IN THIS ROOM. WE WERE WORRIED AND WE...

I'M PERFECTLY FINE. JUST LEAVE ME ALONE.

WE HAVE A REALLY GOOD DOCTOR.

I AM A DOCTOR! SO LEAVE ME ALONE! I TOLD YOU I'M FINE.

CHBOUM

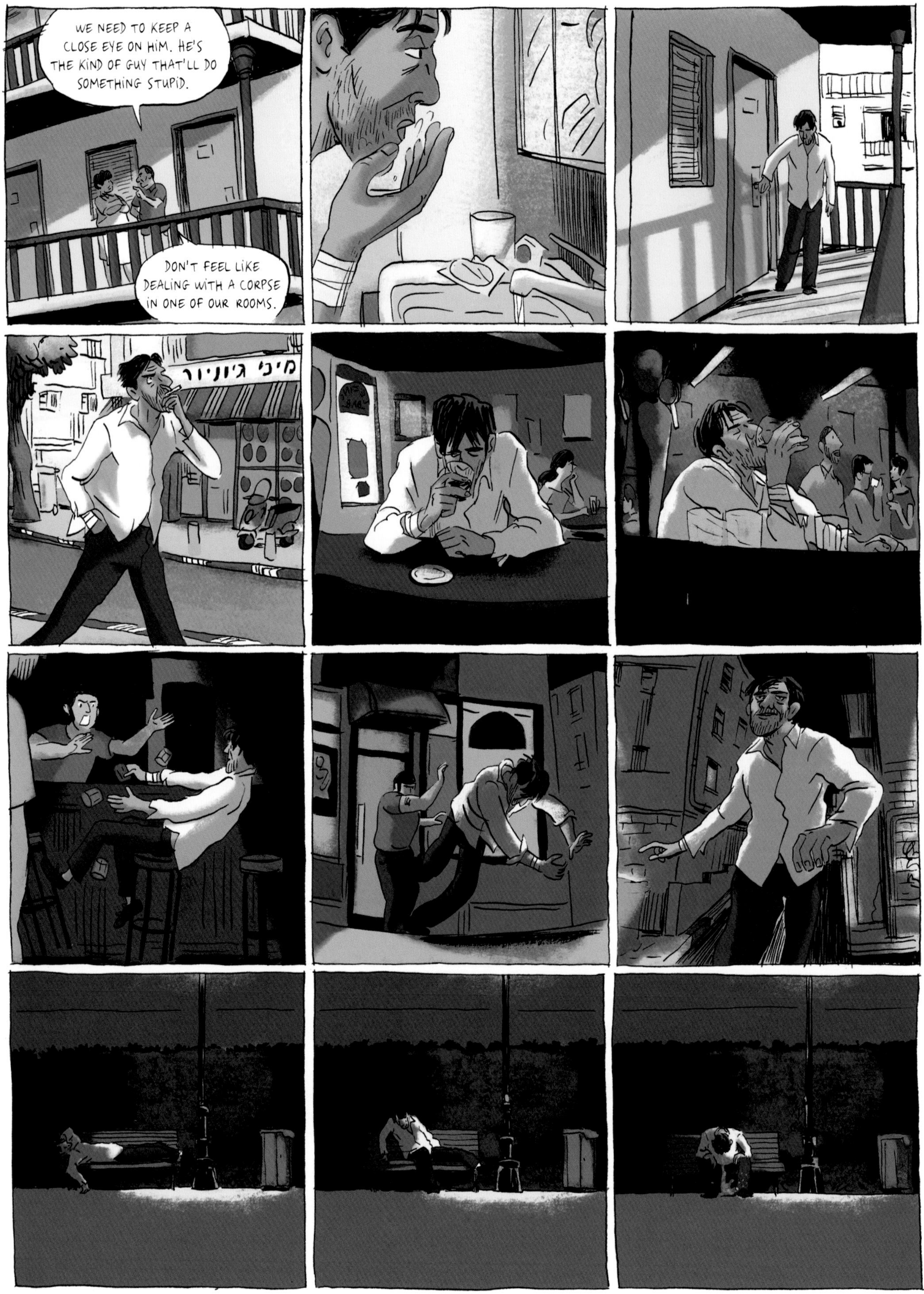
WE NEED TO KEEP A CLOSE EYE ON HIM. HE'S THE KIND OF GUY THAT'LL DO SOMETHING STUPID.
DON'T FEEL LIKE DEALING WITH A CORPSE IN ONE OF OUR ROOMS.

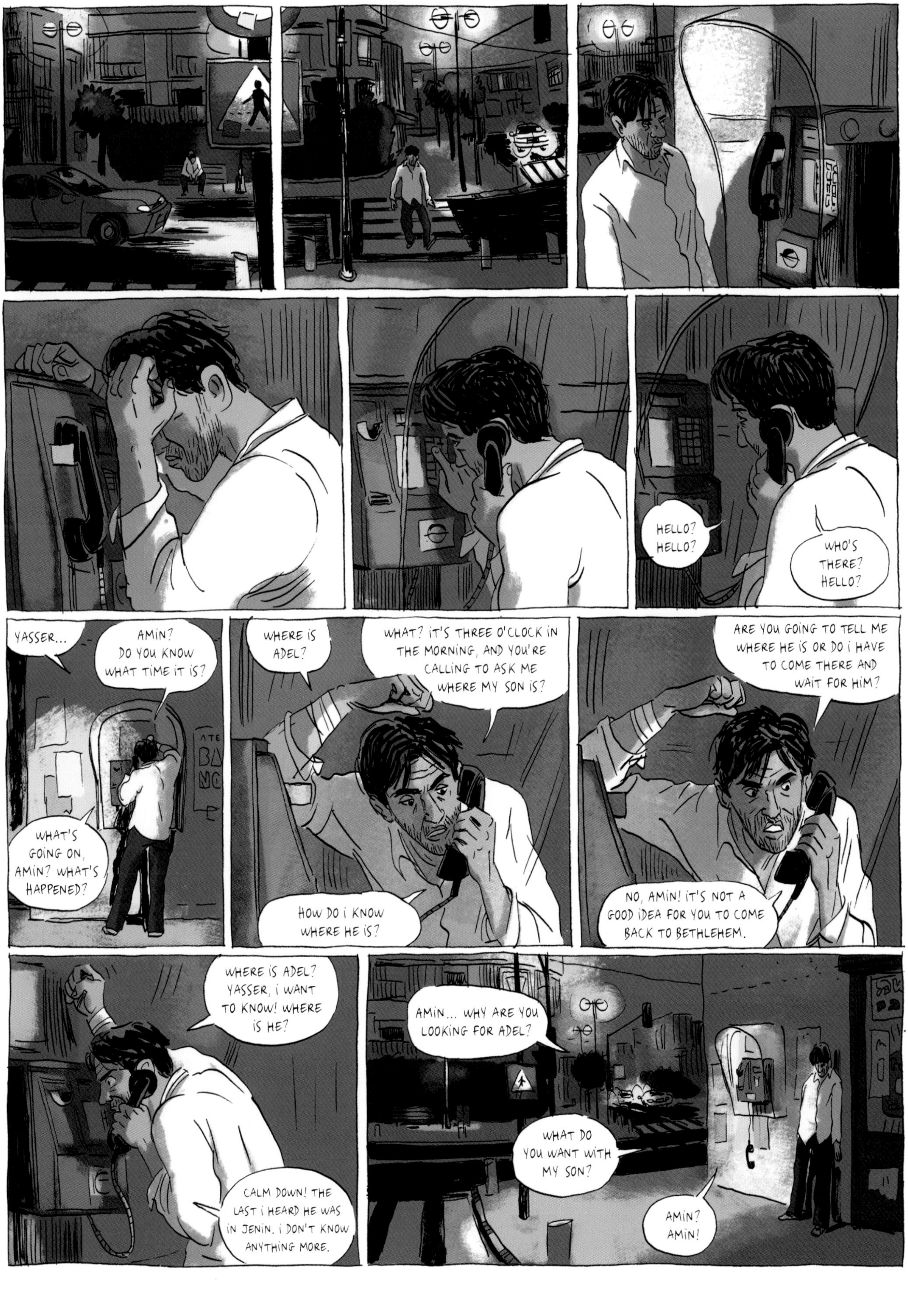
HELLO? HELLO?
WHO'S THERE? HELLO?
YASSER...
AMIN? DO YOU KNOW WHAT TIME IT IS?
WHAT'S GOING ON, AMIN? WHAT'S HAPPENED?
WHERE IS ADEL?
WHAT? IT'S THREE O'CLOCK IN THE MORNING, AND YOU'RE CALLING TO ASK ME WHERE MY SON IS?
HOW DO I KNOW WHERE HE IS?
ARE YOU GOING TO TELL ME WHERE HE IS OR DO I HAVE TO COME THERE AND WAIT FOR HIM?
NO, AMIN! IT'S NOT A GOOD IDEA FOR YOU TO COME BACK TO BETHLEHEM.
WHERE IS ADEL? YASSER, I WANT TO KNOW! WHERE IS HE?
CALM DOWN! THE LAST I HEARD HE WAS IN JENIN. I DON'T KNOW ANYTHING MORE.
AMIN... WHY ARE YOU LOOKING FOR ADEL?
WHAT DO YOU WANT WITH MY SON?
AMIN? AMIN!

BUURP!

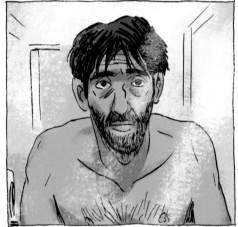

GOOD EVENING, SIR.

NO.

ARE YOU ALONE OR ARE YOU WAITING FOR SOMEONE?

I'LL TAKE THE GRILLED LIVER.

I'M SORRY BUT WE'RE OUT OF IT. HOW ABOUT...

THAT'S NOT MY PROBLEM. IT'S ON THE MENU.

YES, SIR. BUT...

SO, I WANT THE GRILLED LIVER!

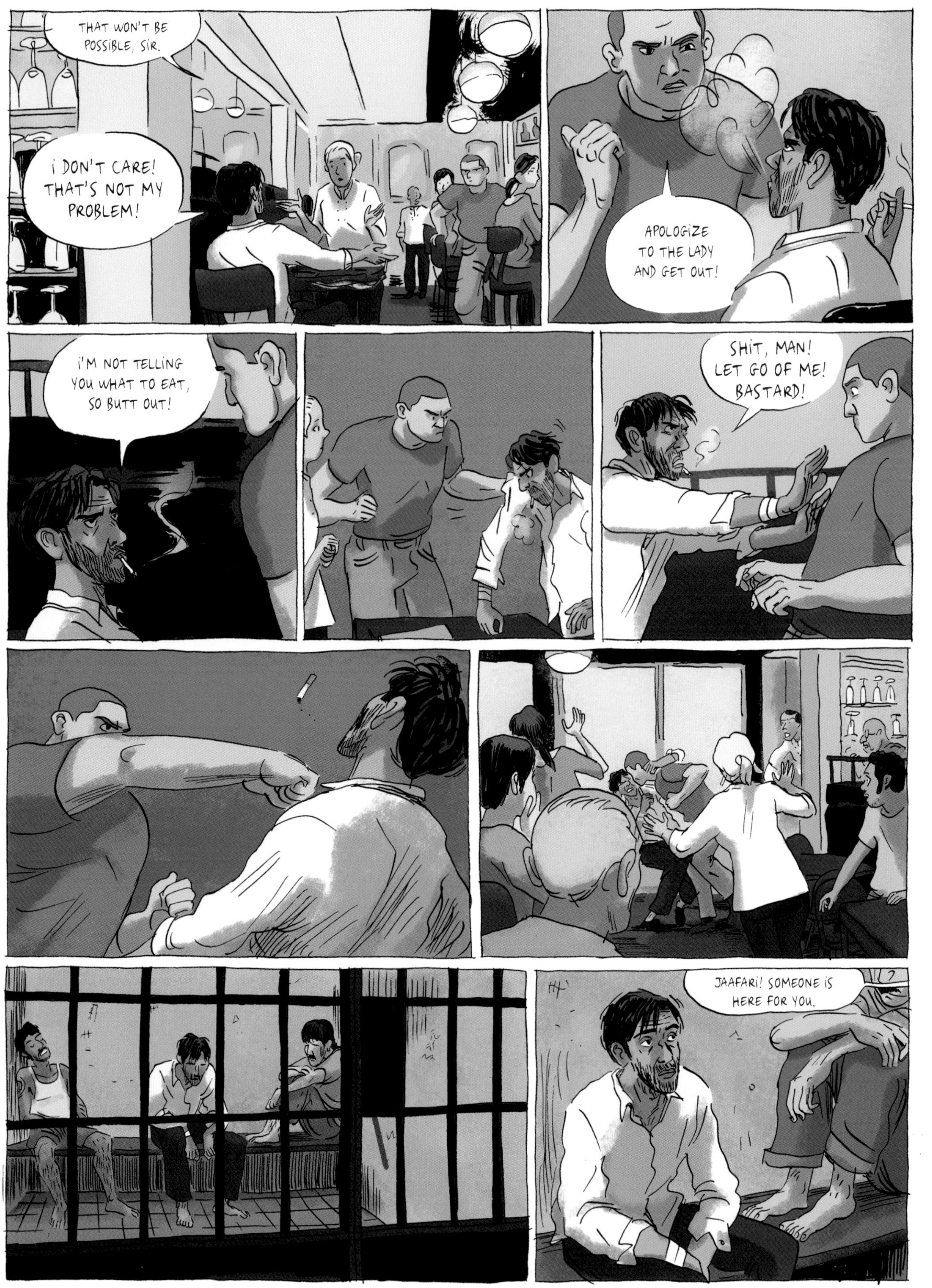
THAT WON'T BE POSSIBLE, SIR.
I DON'T CARE! THAT'S NOT MY PROBLEM!
APOLOGIZE TO THE LADY AND GET OUT!
I'M NOT TELLING YOU WHAT TO EAT, SO BUTT OUT!
SHIT, MAN! LET GO OF ME! BASTARD!
JAAFARI! SOMEONE IS HERE FOR YOU.

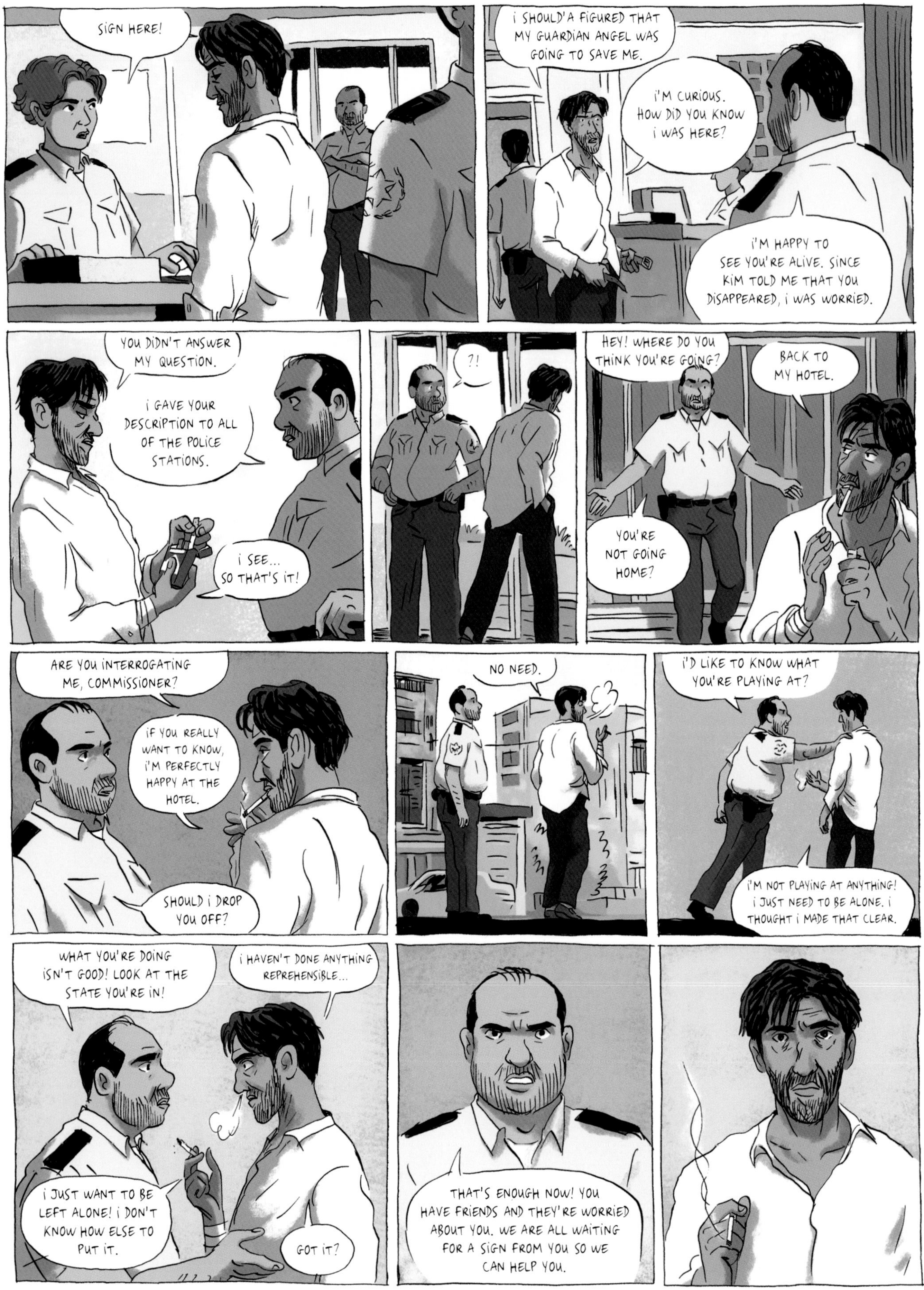
SIGN HERE!
I SHOULD'A FIGURED THAT MY GUARDIAN ANGEL WAS GOING TO SAVE ME.
I'M CURIOUS. HOW DID YOU KNOW I WAS HERE?
I'M HAPPY TO SEE YOU'RE ALIVE. SINCE KIM TOLD ME THAT YOU DISAPPEARED, I WAS WORRIED.
YOU DIDN'T ANSWER MY QUESTION.
I GAVE YOUR DESCRIPTION TO ALL OF THE POLICE STATIONS.
I SEE... SO THAT'S IT!
?!
HEY! WHERE DO YOU THINK YOU'RE GOING?
BACK TO MY HOTEL.
YOU'RE NOT GOING HOME?
ARE YOU INTERROGATING ME, COMMISSIONER?
IF YOU REALLY WANT TO KNOW, I'M PERFECTLY HAPPY AT THE HOTEL.
SHOULD I DROP YOU OFF?
NO NEED.
I'D LIKE TO KNOW WHAT YOU'RE PLAYING AT?
I'M NOT PLAYING AT ANYTHING! I JUST NEED TO BE ALONE. I THOUGHT I MADE THAT CLEAR.
WHAT YOU'RE DOING ISN'T GOOD! LOOK AT THE STATE YOU'RE IN!
I HAVEN'T DONE ANYTHING REPREHENSIBLE...
I JUST WANT TO BE LEFT ALONE! I DON'T KNOW HOW ELSE TO PUT IT.
GOT IT?
THAT'S ENOUGH NOW! YOU HAVE FRIENDS AND THEY'RE WORRIED ABOUT YOU. WE ARE ALL WAITING FOR A SIGN FROM YOU SO WE CAN HELP YOU.

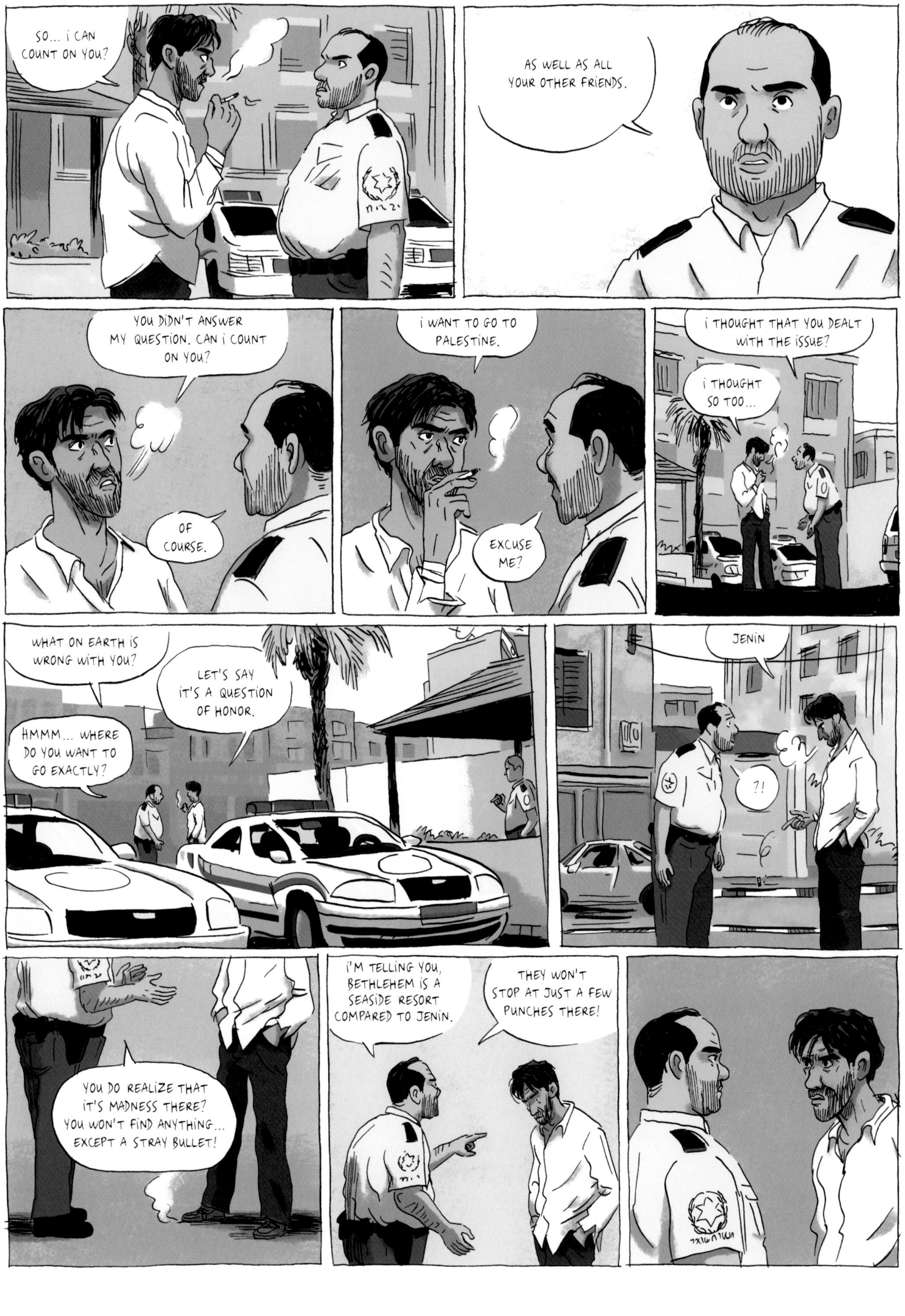
SO... I CAN COUNT ON YOU?
AS WELL AS ALL YOUR OTHER FRIENDS.
YOU DIDN'T ANSWER MY QUESTION. CAN I COUNT ON YOU?
OF COURSE.
I WANT TO GO TO PALESTINE.
EXCUSE ME?
I THOUGHT THAT YOU DEALT WITH THE ISSUE?
I THOUGHT SO TOO...
WHAT ON EARTH IS WRONG WITH YOU?
LET'S SAY IT'S A QUESTION OF HONOR.
HMMM... WHERE DO YOU WANT TO GO EXACTLY?
JENIN
?!
YOU DO REALIZE THAT IT'S MADNESS THERE? YOU WON'T FIND ANYTHING... EXCEPT A STRAY BULLET!
I'M TELLING YOU, BETHLEHEM IS A SEASIDE RESORT COMPARED TO JENIN.
THEY WON'T STOP AT JUST A FEW PUNCHES THERE!

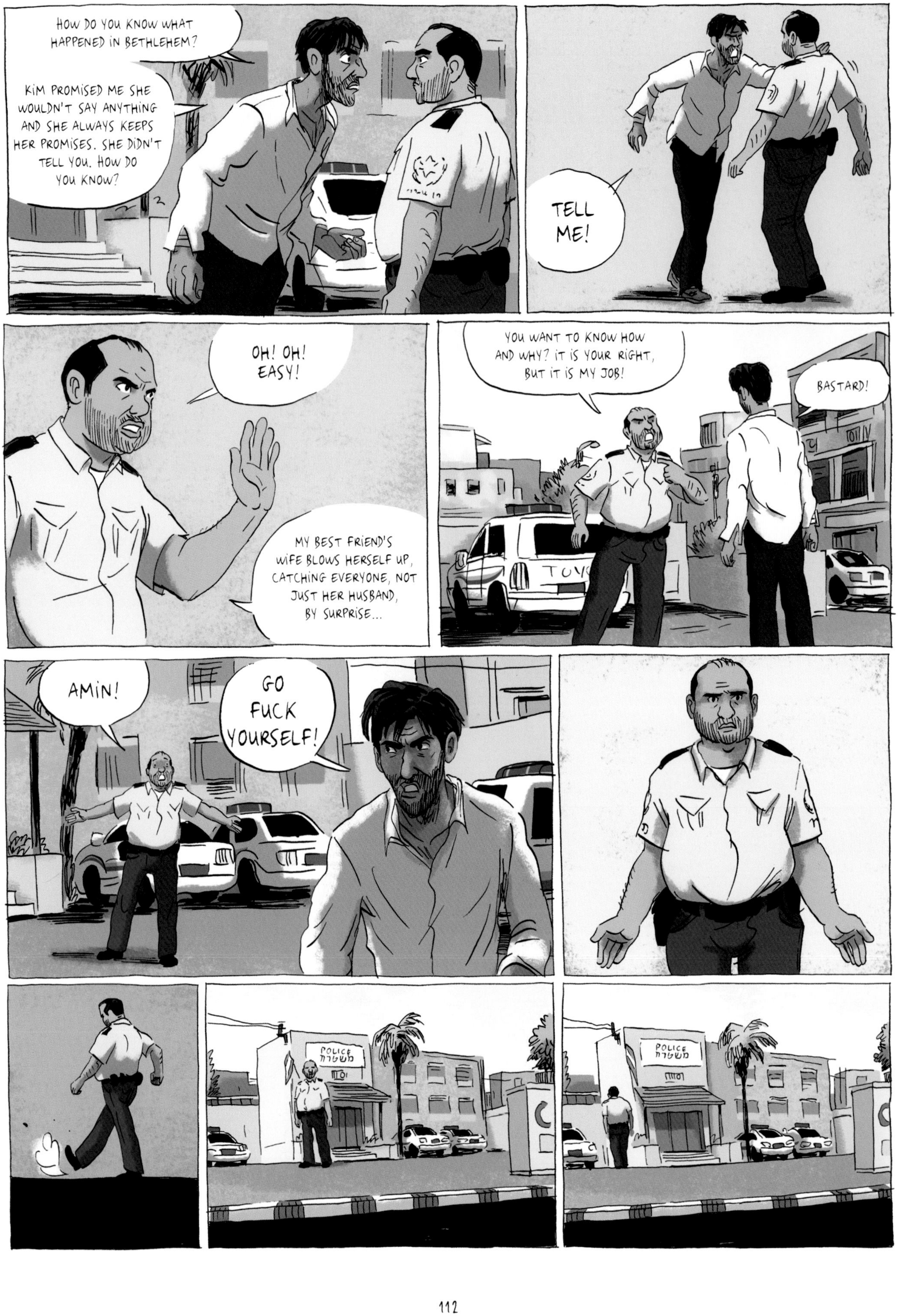
HOW DO YOU KNOW WHAT HAPPENED IN BETHLEHEM?
KIM PROMISED ME SHE WOULDN'T SAY ANYTHING AND SHE ALWAYS KEEPS HER PROMISES. SHE DIDN'T TELL YOU. HOW DO YOU KNOW?
TELL ME!
OH! OH! EASY!
MY BEST FRIEND'S WIFE BLOWS HERSELF UP, CATCHING EVERYONE, NOT JUST HER HUSBAND, BY SURPRISE...
YOU WANT TO KNOW HOW AND WHY? IT IS YOUR RIGHT, BUT IT IS MY JOB!
BASTARD!
AMIN!
GO FUCK YOURSELF!
POLICE
משטרה
POLICE
משטרה

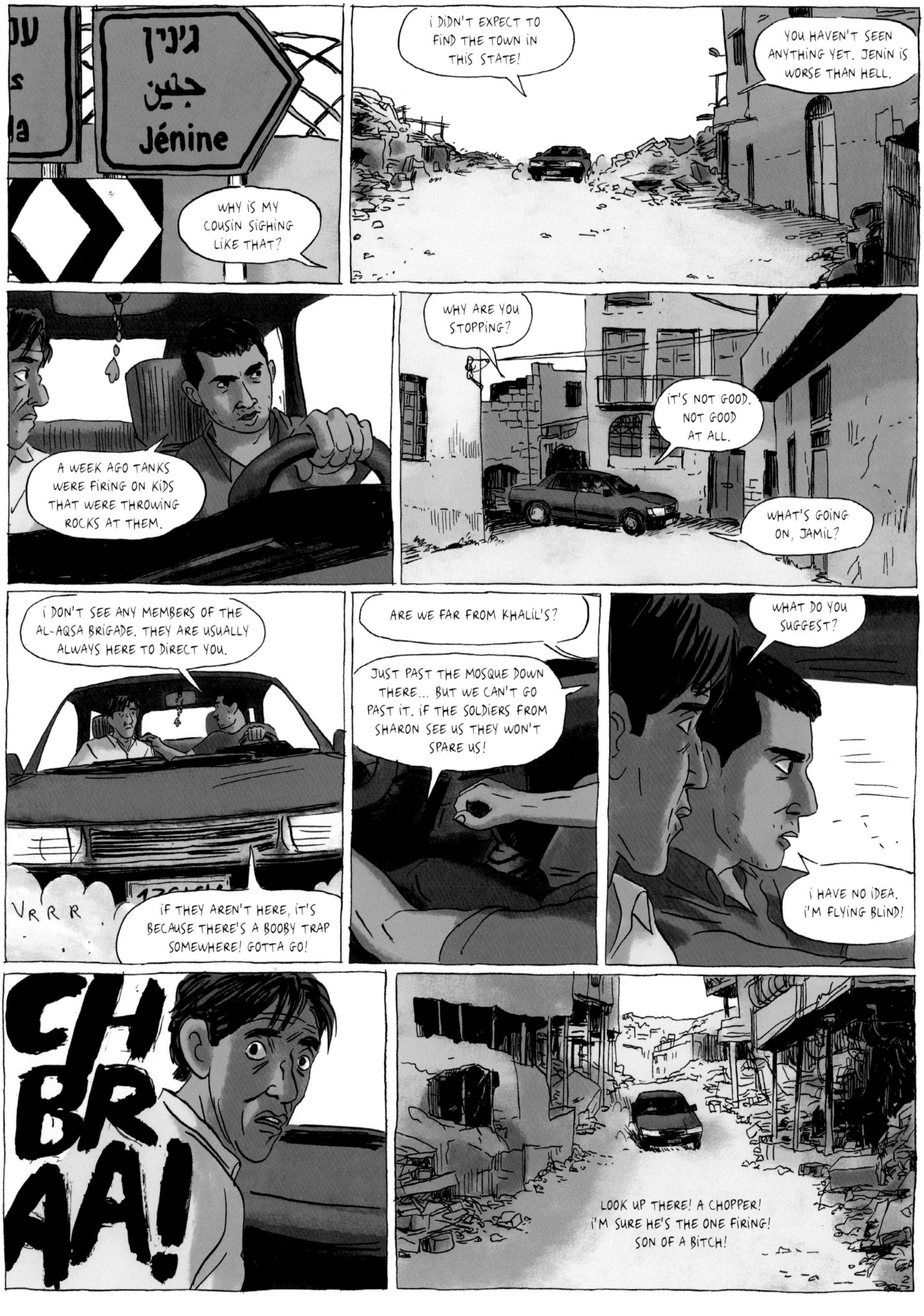
ג'נין
جنين
Jénine
WHY IS MY COUSIN SIGHING LIKE THAT?
I DIDN'T EXPECT TO FIND THE TOWN IN THIS STATE!
YOU HAVEN'T SEEN ANYTHING YET. JENIN IS WORSE THAN HELL.
A WEEK AGO TANKS WERE FIRING ON KIDS THAT WERE THROWING ROCKS AT THEM.
WHY ARE YOU STOPPING?
IT'S NOT GOOD. NOT GOOD AT ALL.
WHAT'S GOING ON, JAMIL?
I DON'T SEE ANY MEMBERS OF THE AL-AQSA BRIGADE. THEY ARE USUALLY ALWAYS HERE TO DIRECT YOU.
VRRR
IF THEY AREN'T HERE, IT'S BECAUSE THERE'S A BOOBY TRAP SOMEWHERE! GOTTA GO!
ARE WE FAR FROM KHALIL'S?
JUST PAST THE MOSQUE DOWN THERE... BUT WE CAN'T GO PAST IT. IF THE SOLDIERS FROM SHARON SEE US THEY WON'T SPARE US!
WHAT DO YOU SUGGEST?
I HAVE NO IDEA. I'M FLYING BLIND!
CHBRAA!
LOOK UP THERE! A CHOPPER! I'M SURE HE'S THE ONE FIRING! SON OF A BITCH!

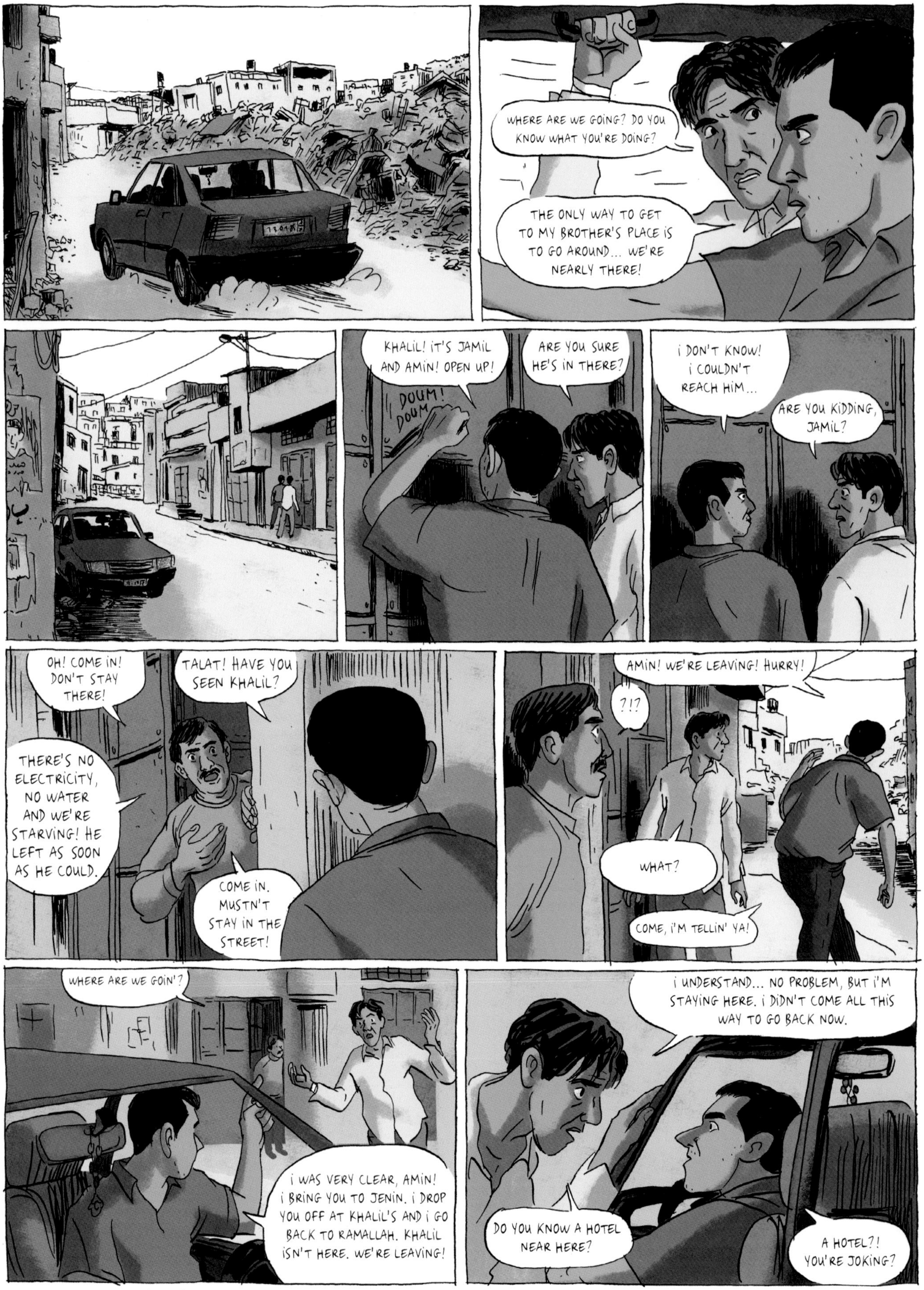
WHERE ARE WE GOING? DO YOU KNOW WHAT YOU'RE DOING?
THE ONLY WAY TO GET TO MY BROTHER'S PLACE IS TO GO AROUND... WE'RE NEARLY THERE!
KHALIL! IT'S JAMIL AND AMIN! OPEN UP!
DOUM! DOUM
ARE YOU SURE HE'S IN THERE?
I DON'T KNOW! I COULDN'T REACH HIM...
ARE YOU KIDDING, JAMIL?
OH! COME IN! DON'T STAY THERE!
TALAT! HAVE YOU SEEN KHALIL?
THERE'S NO ELECTRICITY, NO WATER AND WE'RE STARVING! HE LEFT AS SOON AS HE COULD.
COME IN. MUSTN'T STAY IN THE STREET!
AMIN! WE'RE LEAVING! HURRY!
?!?
WHAT?
COME, I'M TELLIN' YA!
WHERE ARE WE GOIN'?
I WAS VERY CLEAR, AMIN! I BRING YOU TO JENIN. I DROP YOU OFF AT KHALIL'S AND I GO BACK TO RAMALLAH. KHALIL ISN'T HERE. WE'RE LEAVING!
I UNDERSTAND... NO PROBLEM, BUT I'M STAYING HERE. I DIDN'T COME ALL THIS WAY TO GO BACK NOW.
DO YOU KNOW A HOTEL NEAR HERE?
A HOTEL?! YOU'RE JOKING?

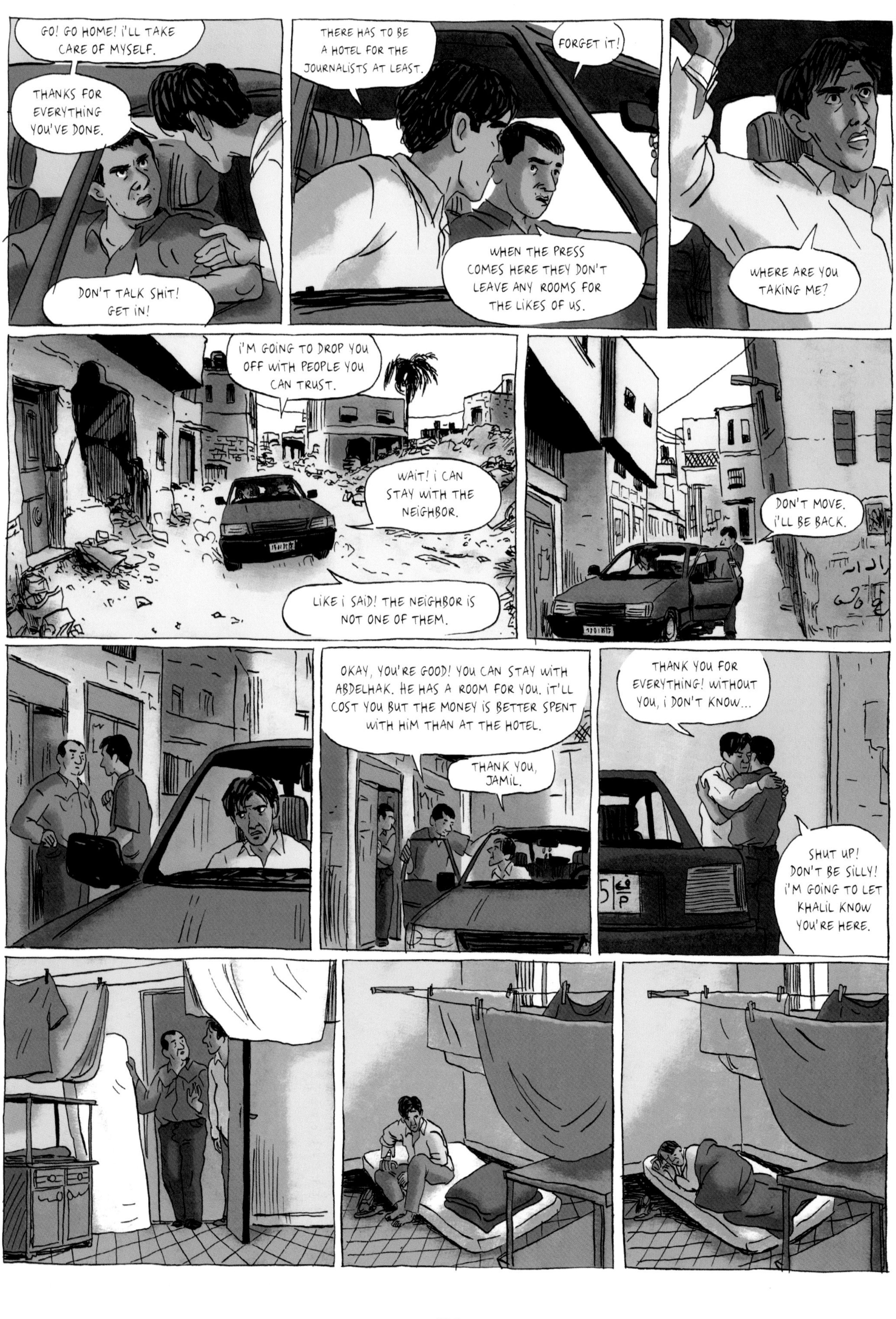
GO! GO HOME! I'LL TAKE CARE OF MYSELF.
THANKS FOR EVERYTHING YOU'VE DONE.
DON'T TALK SHIT! GET IN!
THERE HAS TO BE A HOTEL FOR THE JOURNALISTS AT LEAST.
FORGET IT!
WHEN THE PRESS COMES HERE THEY DON'T LEAVE ANY ROOMS FOR THE LIKES OF US.
WHERE ARE YOU TAKING ME?
I'M GOING TO DROP YOU OFF WITH PEOPLE YOU CAN TRUST.
WAIT! I CAN STAY WITH THE NEIGHBOR.
LIKE I SAID! THE NEIGHBOR IS NOT ONE OF THEM.
DON'T MOVE. I'LL BE BACK.
OKAY, YOU'RE GOOD! YOU CAN STAY WITH ABDELHAK. HE HAS A ROOM FOR YOU. IT'LL COST YOU BUT THE MONEY IS BETTER SPENT WITH HIM THAN AT THE HOTEL.
THANK YOU, JAMIL.
THANK YOU FOR EVERYTHING! WITHOUT YOU, I DON'T KNOW...
SHUT UP! DON'T BE SILLY! I'M GOING TO LET KHALIL KNOW YOU'RE HERE.

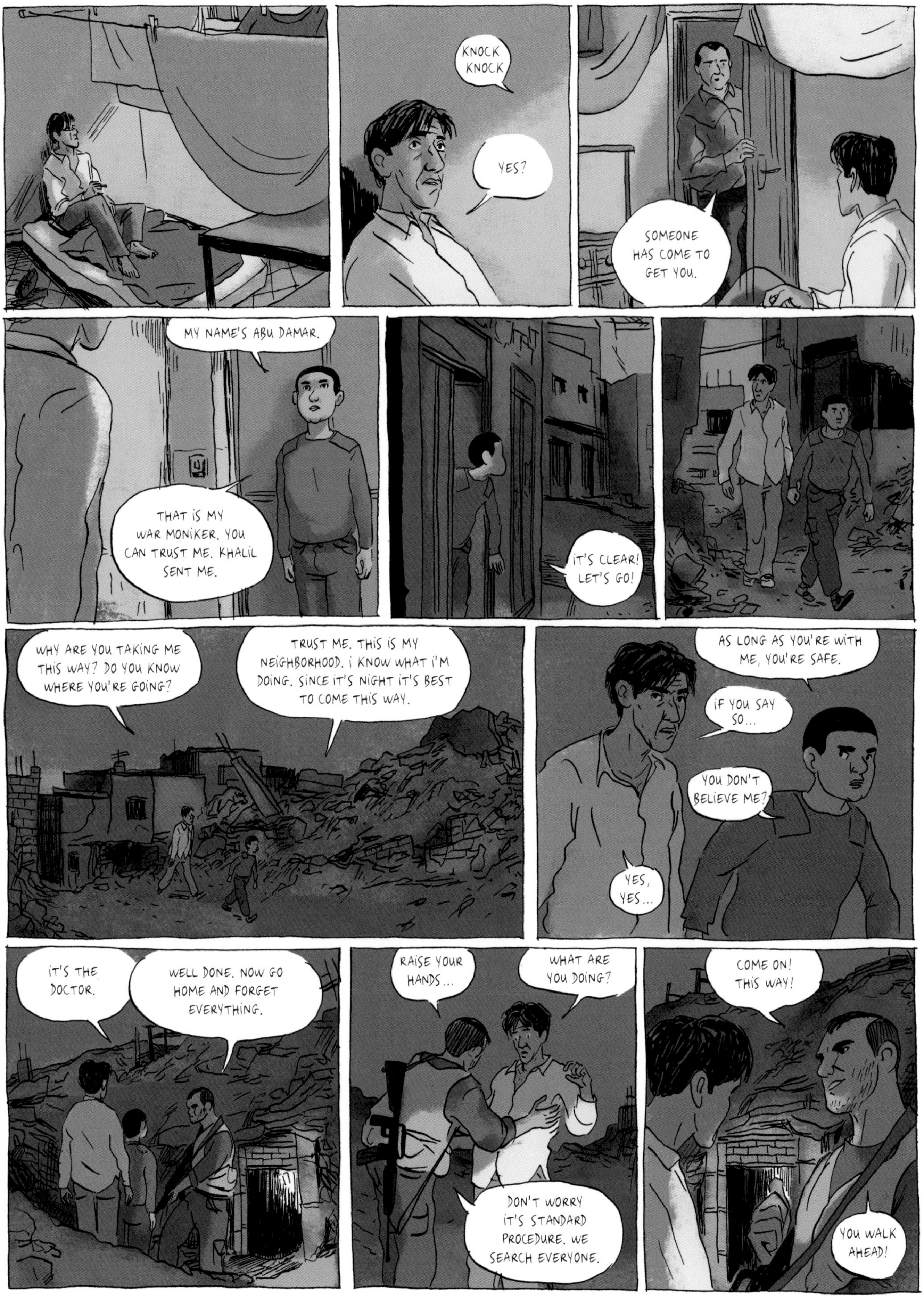
KNOCK KNOCK
YES?
SOMEONE HAS COME TO GET YOU.
MY NAME'S ABU DAMAR.
THAT IS MY WAR MONIKER. YOU CAN TRUST ME. KHALIL SENT ME.
IT'S CLEAR! LET'S GO!
WHY ARE YOU TAKING ME THIS WAY? DO YOU KNOW WHERE YOU'RE GOING?
TRUST ME. THIS IS MY NEIGHBORHOOD. I KNOW WHAT I'M DOING. SINCE IT'S NIGHT IT'S BEST TO COME THIS WAY.
AS LONG AS YOU'RE WITH ME, YOU'RE SAFE.
IF YOU SAY SO...
YOU DON'T BELIEVE ME?
YES, YES...
IT'S THE DOCTOR.
WELL DONE. NOW GO HOME AND FORGET EVERYTHING.
RAISE YOUR HANDS...
WHAT ARE YOU DOING?
DON'T WORRY IT'S STANDARD PROCEDURE. WE SEARCH EVERYONE.
COME ON! THIS WAY!
YOU WALK AHEAD!

SO DOCTOR, YOU WANT YOUR REVENGE?

?

YOU UNDERSTOOD WHAT I SAID.

SHIN BET SENT YOU TO POKE THE HORNETS' NEST, TO FORCE US OUT OF HIDING AND GET SHOT BY THE DRONES.

YOU'RE WRONG.

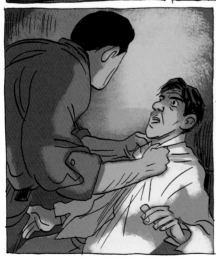

DON'T TAKE ME FOR A FOOL!

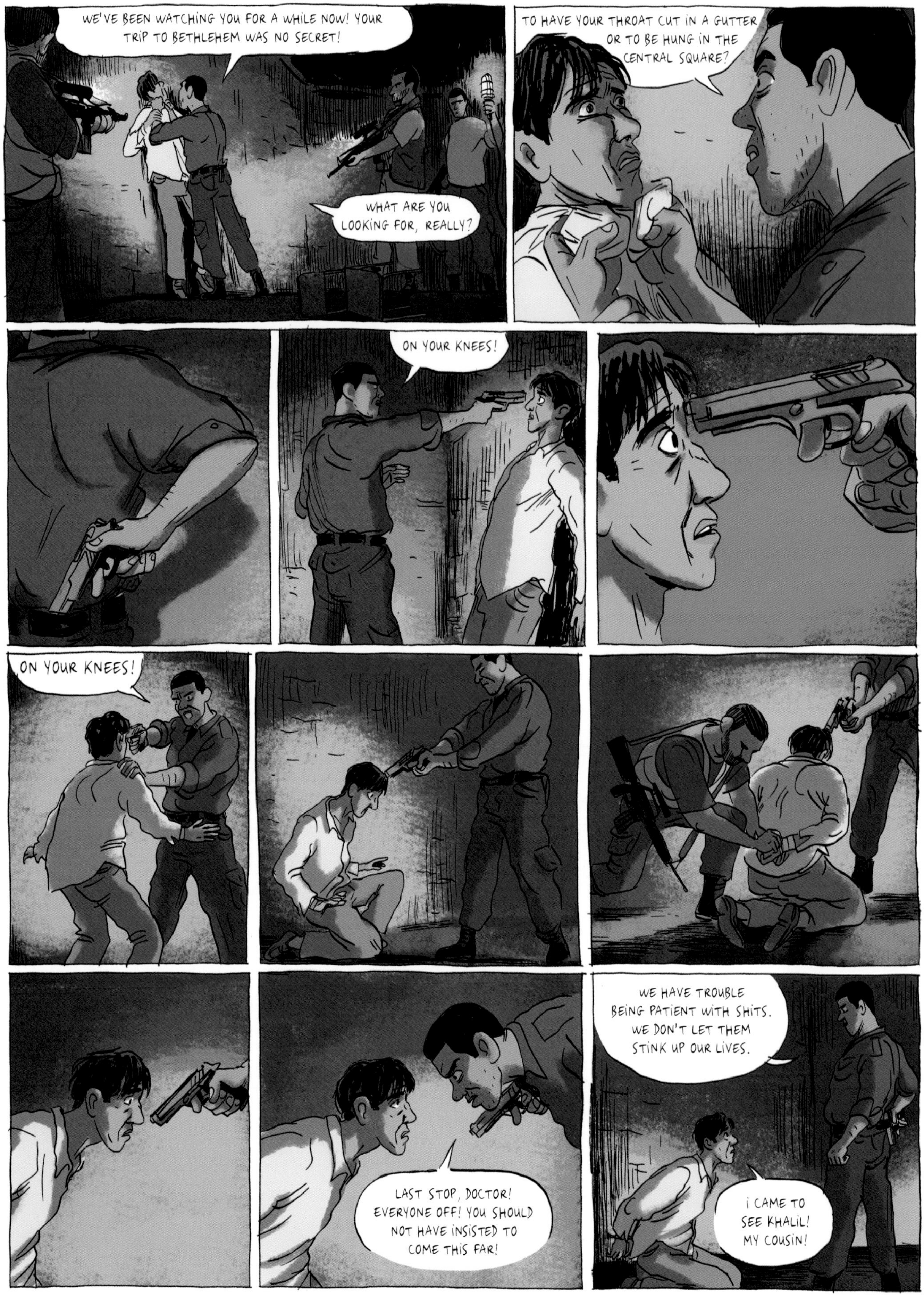
WE'VE BEEN WATCHING YOU FOR A WHILE NOW! YOUR TRIP TO BETHLEHEM WAS NO SECRET!
WHAT ARE YOU LOOKING FOR, REALLY?
TO HAVE YOUR THROAT CUT IN A GUTTER OR TO BE HUNG IN THE CENTRAL SQUARE?
ON YOUR KNEES!
ON YOUR KNEES!
LAST STOP, DOCTOR! EVERYONE OFF! YOU SHOULD NOT HAVE INSISTED TO COME THIS FAR!
WE HAVE TROUBLE BEING PATIENT WITH SHITS. WE DON'T LET THEM STINK UP OUR LIVES.
I CAME TO SEE KHALIL! MY COUSIN!

KHALIL PISSED OFF AS SOON AS HE HEARD YOU WERE COMING! DO YOU REALIZE THE SHIT STORM YOU CAUSED IN BETHLEHEM?

BECAUSE OF YOU, THE IMAM FROM THE BIG MOSQUE HAD TO MOVE AWAY.

WE WERE OBLIGATED TO SUSPEND ALL OUR ACTIVITIES THERE AND MAKE SURE OUR NETWORKS WERE NOT COMPROMISED!

I DON'T KNOW WHY ABOU MOUKAOUM AGREED TO SEE YOU, BUT IT WAS A VERY BAD IDEA. HE HAD TO MOVE AS WELL.

AND NOW YOU COME TO JENIN. EXPLAIN THAT?

I AM NOT BEING MANIPULATED!

REALLY... THEY ARREST YOU AFTER YOUR WIFE'S ATTACK AND THEN THREE DAYS LATER THEY LET YOU GO... JUST LIKE THAT... WITHOUT BEING ACCUSED OF ANYTHING. NO TRIAL.

DO YOU THINK WE'RE STUPID?

THAT DOESN'T HAPPEN. SHIN BET DOES NOT LET ANYONE GO UNLESS THEY SOLD THEIR SOUL TO THE DEVIL!

I WONDER IF THEY DIDN'T APOLOGIZE FOR THE INCONVENIENCE THEY CAUSED YOU!

YOU'RE WRONG...

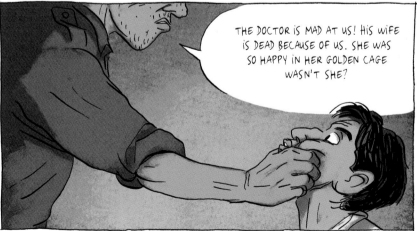

THE DOCTOR IS MAD AT US! HIS WIFE IS DEAD BECAUSE OF US. SHE WAS SO HAPPY IN HER GOLDEN CAGE WASN'T SHE?

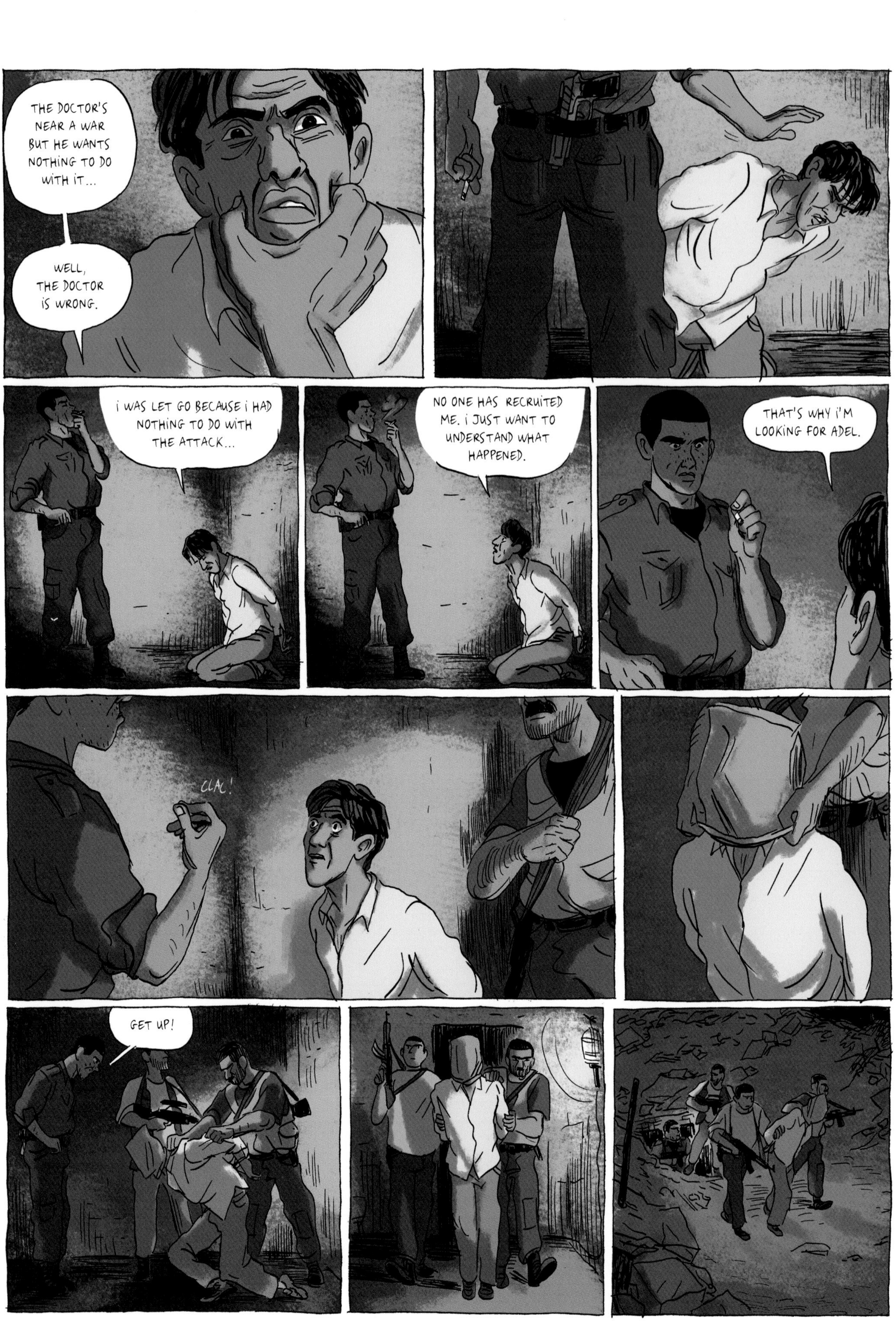
THE DOCTOR'S NEAR A WAR BUT HE WANTS NOTHING TO DO WITH IT...
WELL, THE DOCTOR IS WRONG.
I WAS LET GO BECAUSE I HAD NOTHING TO DO WITH THE ATTACK...
NO ONE HAS RECRUITED ME. I JUST WANT TO UNDERSTAND WHAT HAPPENED.
THAT'S WHY I'M LOOKING FOR ADEL.
CLAC!
GET UP!

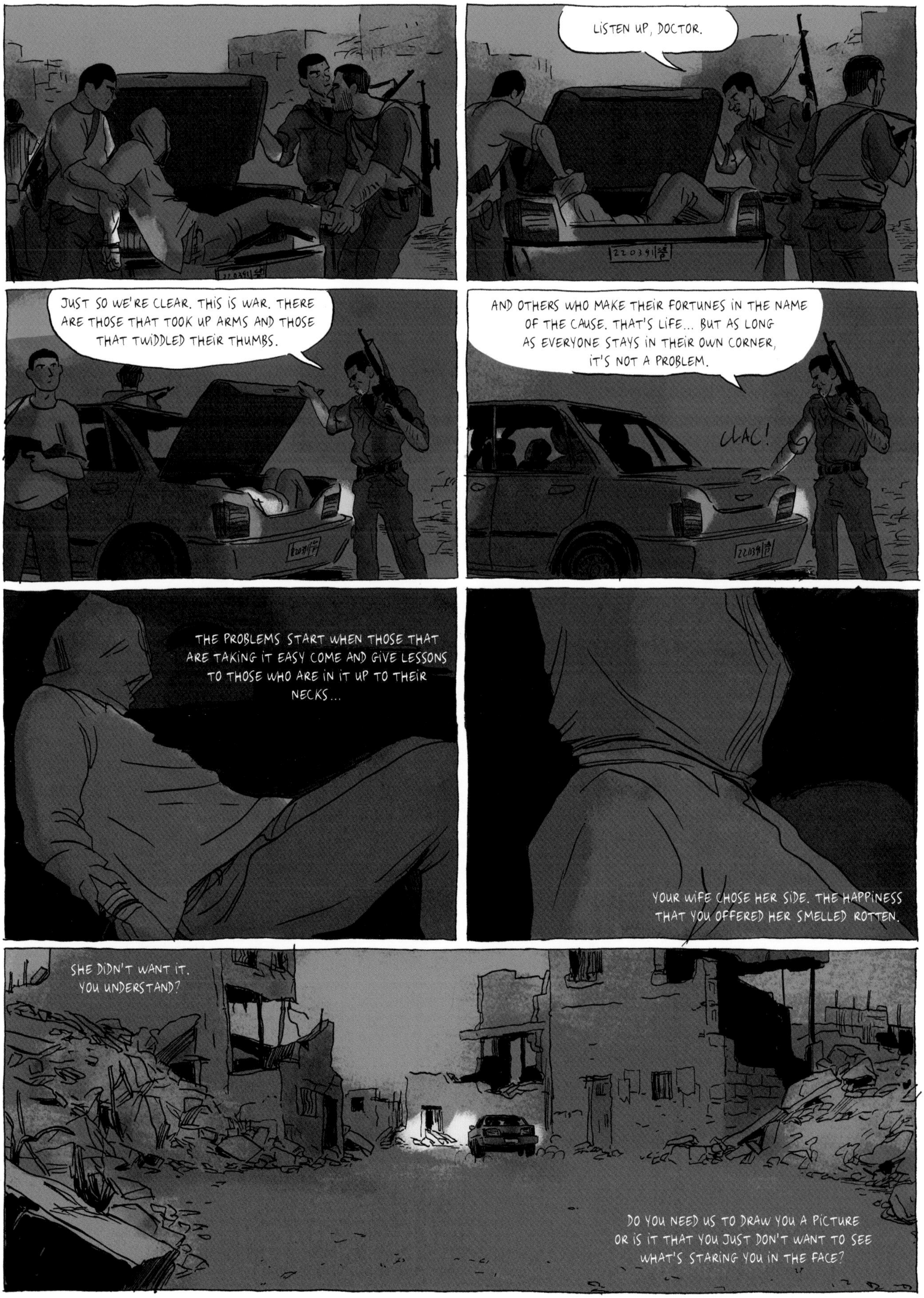
LISTEN UP, DOCTOR.
JUST SO WE'RE CLEAR. THIS IS WAR. THERE ARE THOSE THAT TOOK UP ARMS AND THOSE THAT TWIDDLED THEIR THUMBS.
AND OTHERS WHO MAKE THEIR FORTUNES IN THE NAME OF THE CAUSE. THAT'S LIFE... BUT AS LONG AS EVERYONE STAYS IN THEIR OWN CORNER, IT'S NOT A PROBLEM.
CLAC!
THE PROBLEMS START WHEN THOSE THAT ARE TAKING IT EASY COME AND GIVE LESSONS TO THOSE WHO ARE IN IT UP TO THEIR NECKS...
YOUR WIFE CHOSE HER SIDE. THE HAPPINESS THAT YOU OFFERED HER SMELLED ROTTEN.
SHE DIDN'T WANT IT. YOU UNDERSTAND?
DO YOU NEED US TO DRAW YOU A PICTURE OR IS IT THAT YOU JUST DON'T WANT TO SEE WHAT'S STARING YOU IN THE FACE?

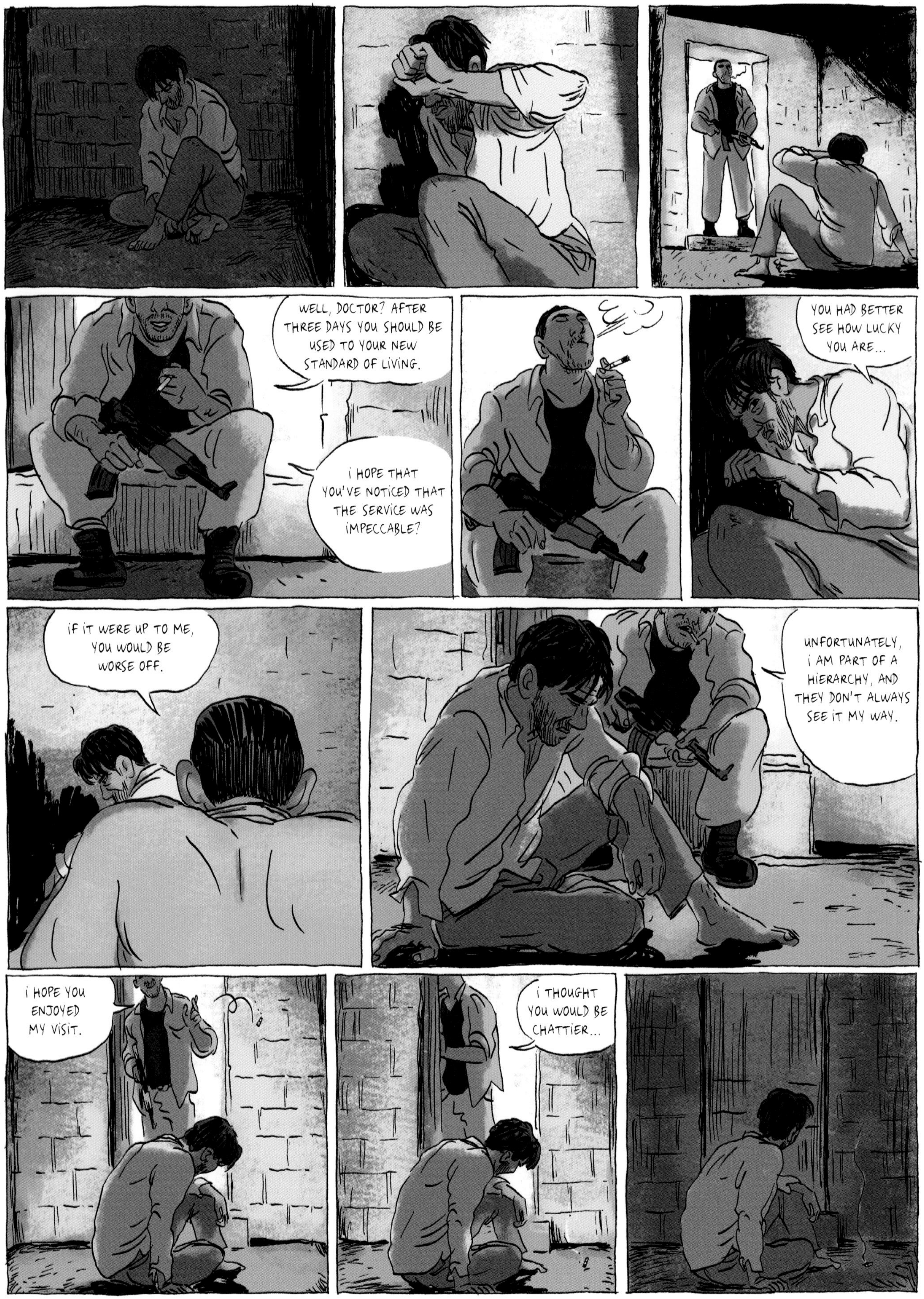
WELL, DOCTOR? AFTER THREE DAYS YOU SHOULD BE USED TO YOUR NEW STANDARD OF LIVING.
I HOPE THAT YOU'VE NOTICED THAT THE SERVICE WAS IMPECCABLE?
YOU HAD BETTER SEE HOW LUCKY YOU ARE...
IF IT WERE UP TO ME, YOU WOULD BE WORSE OFF.
UNFORTUNATELY, I AM PART OF A HIERARCHY, AND THEY DON'T ALWAYS SEE IT MY WAY.
I HOPE YOU ENJOYED MY VISIT.
I THOUGHT YOU WOULD BE CHATTIER...

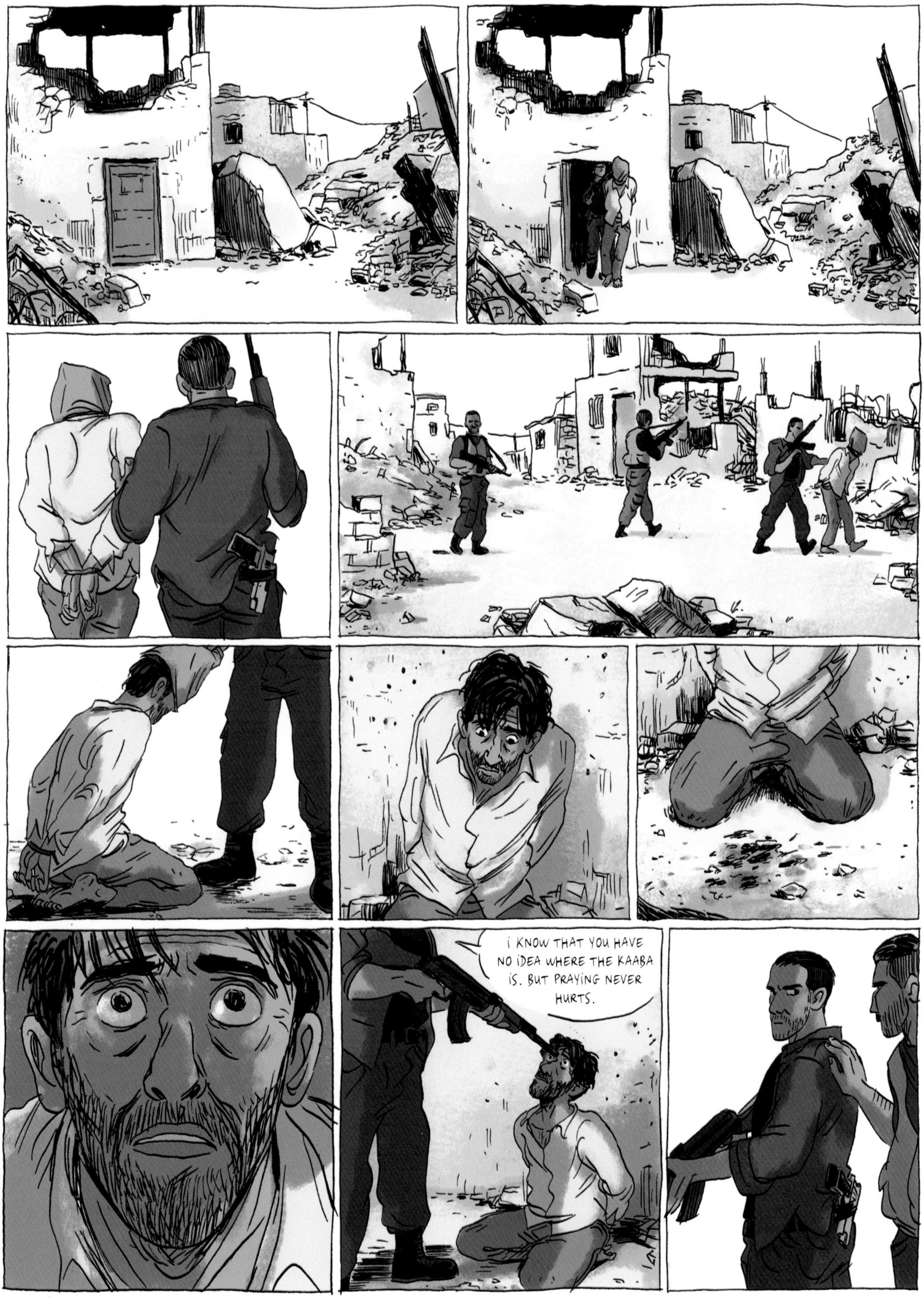
I KNOW THAT YOU HAVE NO IDEA WHERE THE KAABA IS. BUT PRAYING NEVER HURTS.

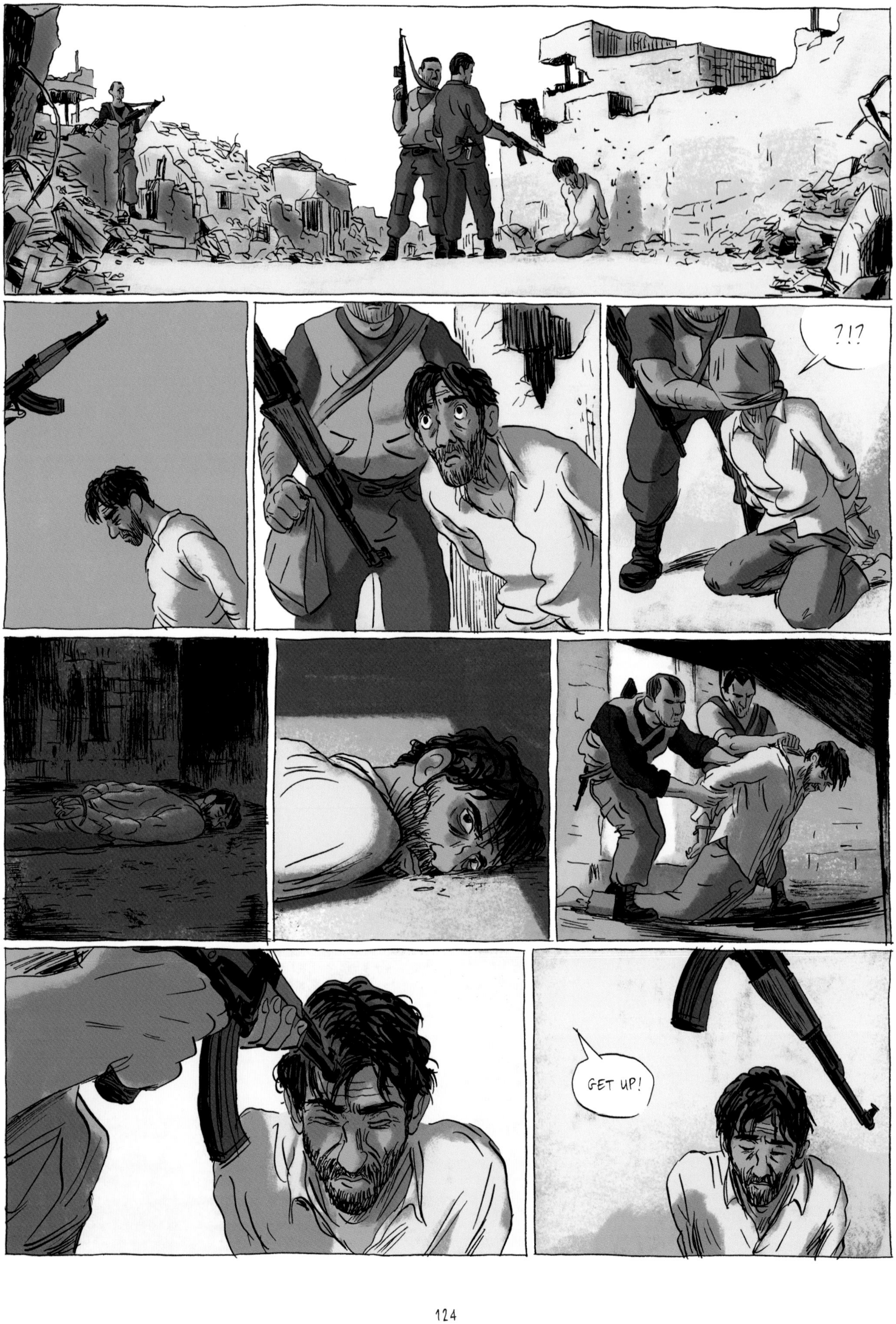
?!?
GET UP!

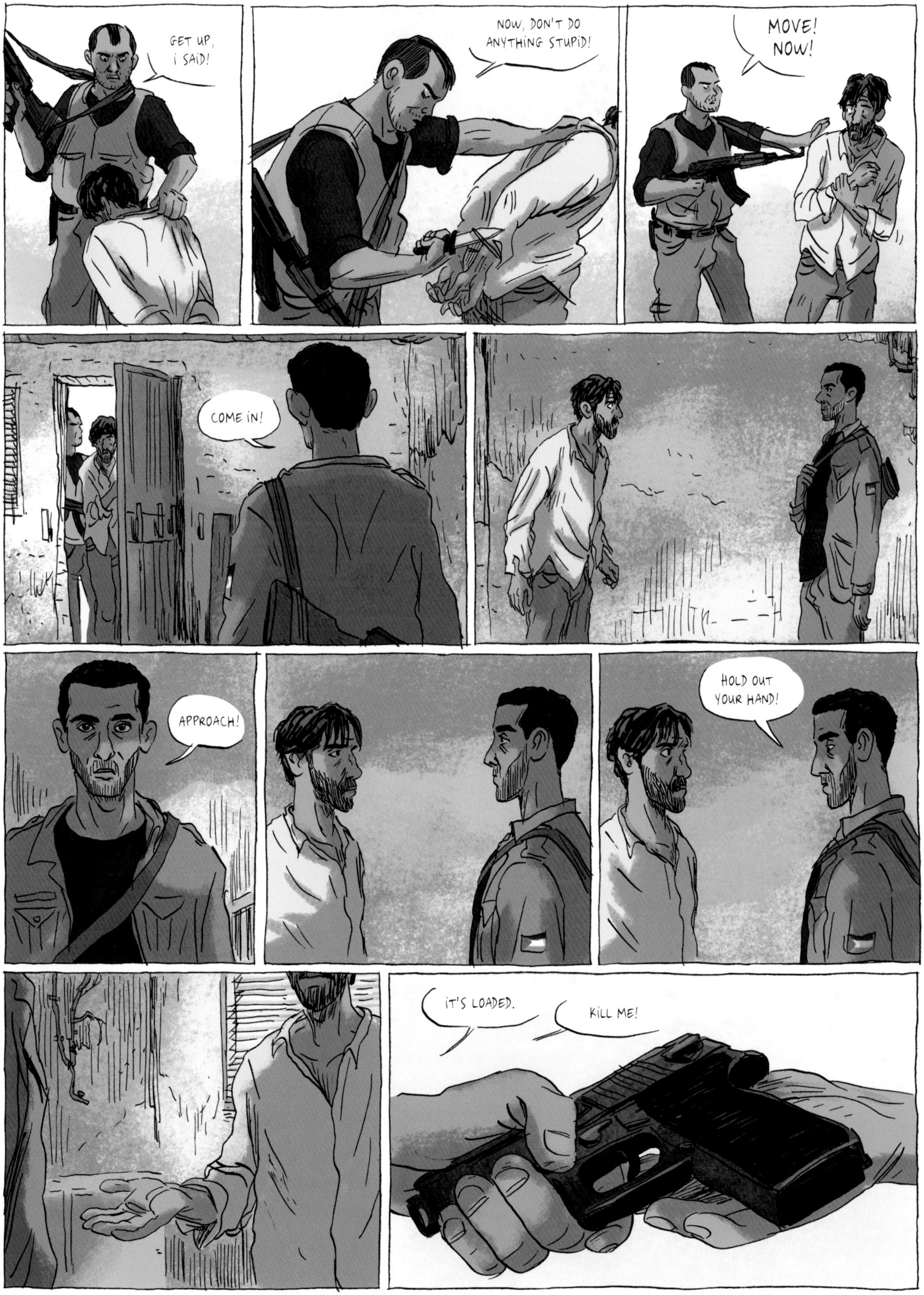
GET UP, i SAiD!
NOW, DON'T DO ANYTHING STUPiD!
MOVE! NOW!
COME iN!
APPROACH!
HOLD OUT YOUR HAND!
iT'S LOADED.
KiLL ME!

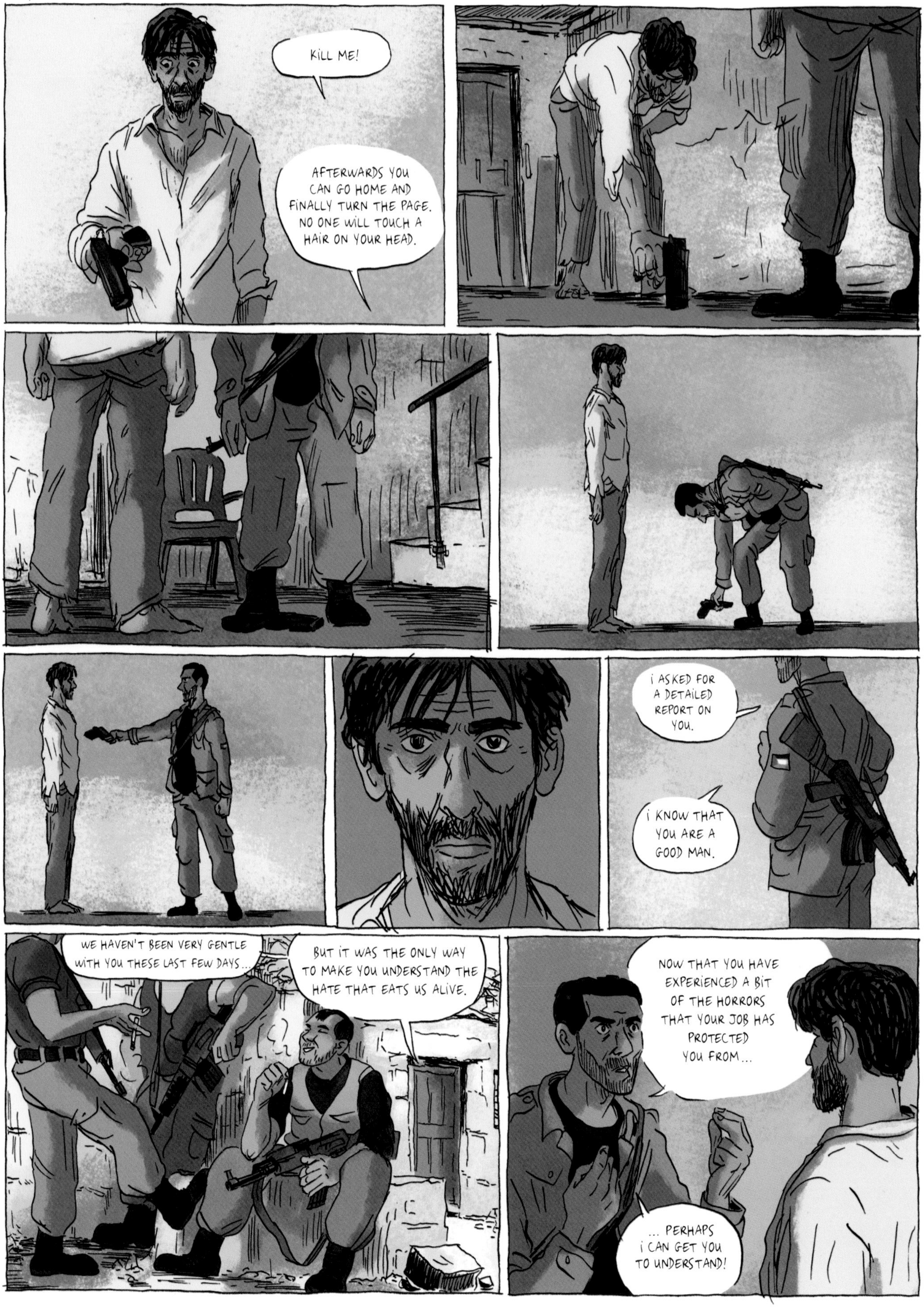
KILL ME!
AFTERWARDS YOU CAN GO HOME AND FINALLY TURN THE PAGE. NO ONE WILL TOUCH A HAIR ON YOUR HEAD.
I ASKED FOR A DETAILED REPORT ON YOU.
I KNOW THAT YOU ARE A GOOD MAN.
WE HAVEN'T BEEN VERY GENTLE WITH YOU THESE LAST FEW DAYS...
BUT IT WAS THE ONLY WAY TO MAKE YOU UNDERSTAND THE HATE THAT EATS US ALIVE.
NOW THAT YOU HAVE EXPERIENCED A BIT OF THE HORRORS THAT YOUR JOB HAS PROTECTED YOU FROM...
... PERHAPS I CAN GET YOU TO UNDERSTAND!

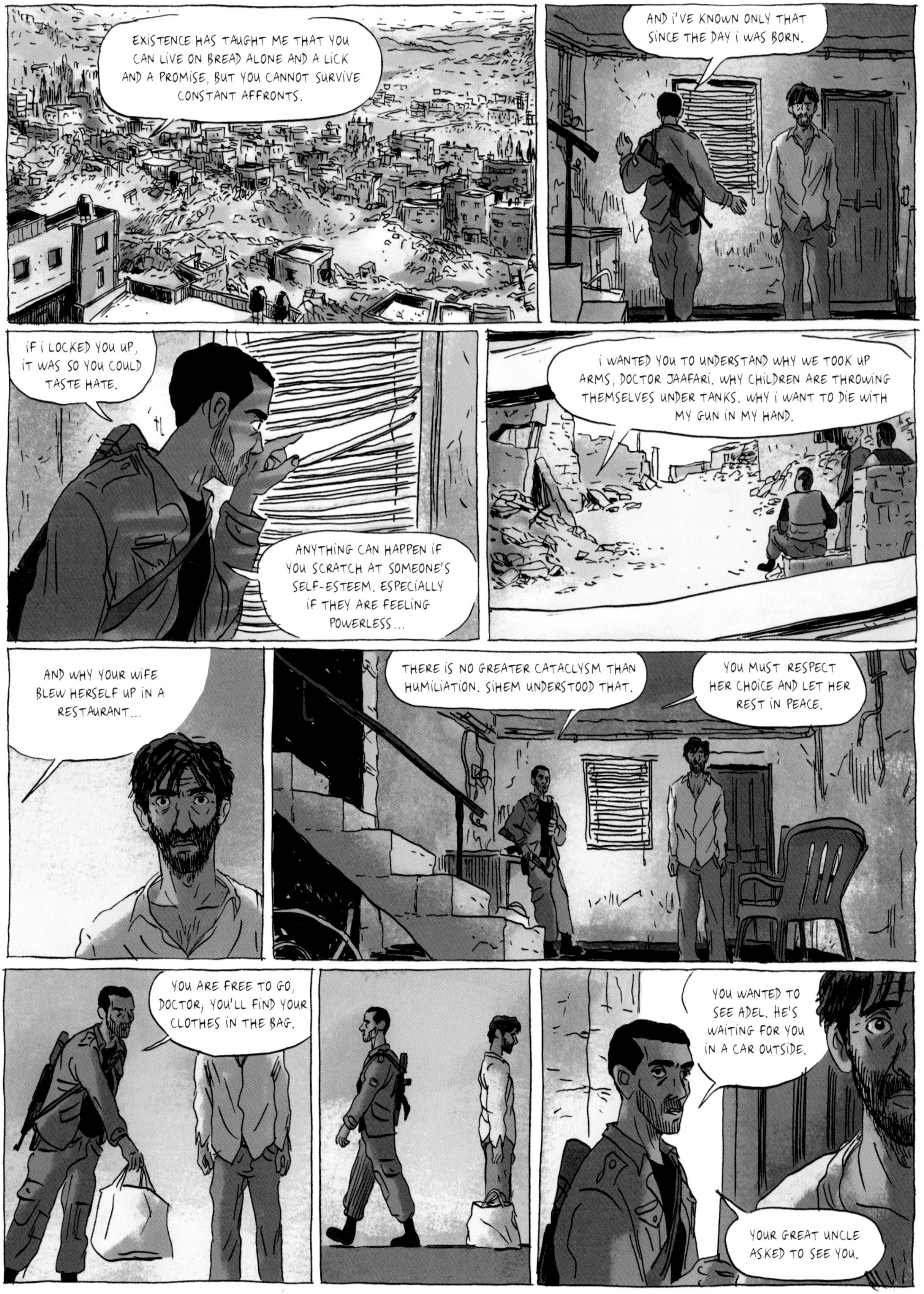
EXISTENCE HAS TAUGHT ME THAT YOU CAN LIVE ON BREAD ALONE AND A LICK AND A PROMISE, BUT YOU CANNOT SURVIVE CONSTANT AFFRONTS.
AND I'VE KNOWN ONLY THAT SINCE THE DAY I WAS BORN.
IF I LOCKED YOU UP, IT WAS SO YOU COULD TASTE HATE.
ANYTHING CAN HAPPEN IF YOU SCRATCH AT SOMEONE'S SELF-ESTEEM. ESPECIALLY IF THEY ARE FEELING POWERLESS...
I WANTED YOU TO UNDERSTAND WHY WE TOOK UP ARMS, DOCTOR JAAFARI. WHY CHILDREN ARE THROWING THEMSELVES UNDER TANKS. WHY I WANT TO DIE WITH MY GUN IN MY HAND.
AND WHY YOUR WIFE BLEW HERSELF UP IN A RESTAURANT...
THERE IS NO GREATER CATACLYSM THAN HUMILIATION. SIHEM UNDERSTOOD THAT.
YOU MUST RESPECT HER CHOICE AND LET HER REST IN PEACE.
YOU ARE FREE TO GO, DOCTOR; YOU'LL FIND YOUR CLOTHES IN THE BAG.
YOU WANTED TO SEE ADEL. HE'S WAITING FOR YOU IN A CAR OUTSIDE.
YOUR GREAT UNCLE ASKED TO SEE YOU.

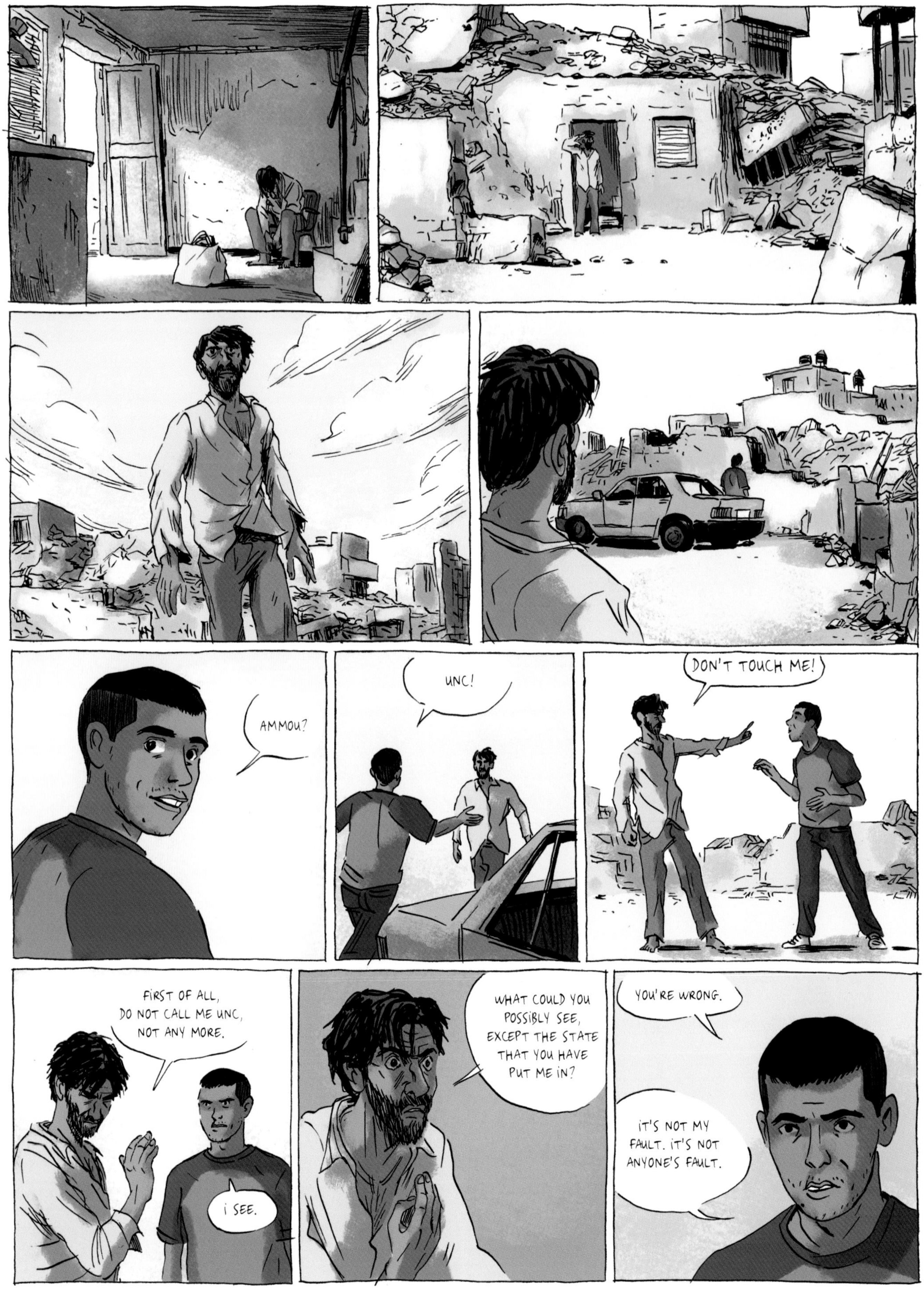
AMMOU?
UNC!
DON'T TOUCH ME!
FIRST OF ALL, DO NOT CALL ME UNC, NOT ANY MORE.
I SEE.
WHAT COULD YOU POSSIBLY SEE, EXCEPT THE STATE THAT YOU HAVE PUT ME IN?
YOU'RE WRONG.
IT'S NOT MY FAULT. IT'S NOT ANYONE'S FAULT.

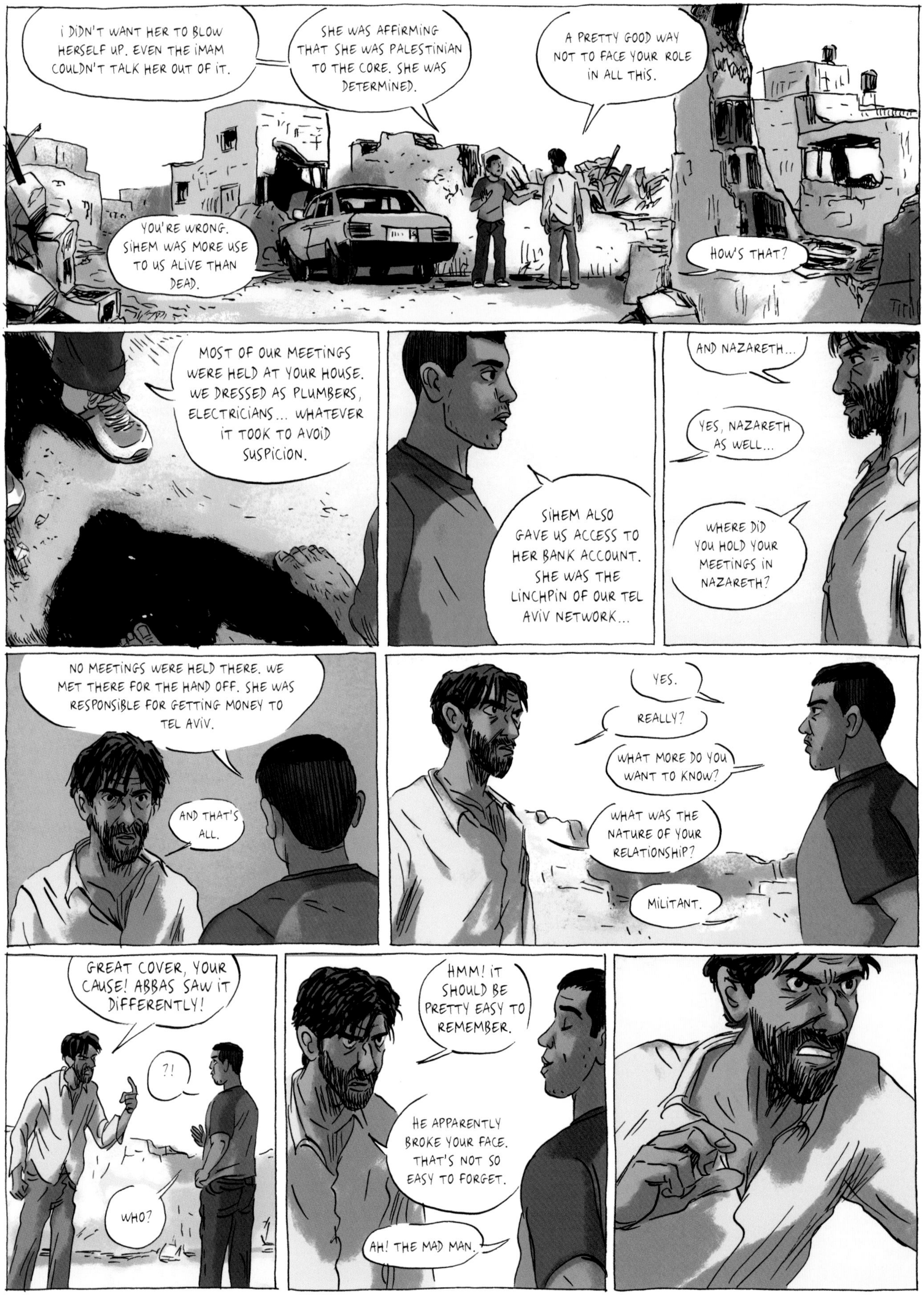
I DIDN'T WANT HER TO BLOW HERSELF UP. EVEN THE IMAM COULDN'T TALK HER OUT OF IT.
SHE WAS AFFIRMING THAT SHE WAS PALESTINIAN TO THE CORE. SHE WAS DETERMINED.
A PRETTY GOOD WAY NOT TO FACE YOUR ROLE IN ALL THIS.
YOU'RE WRONG. SIHEM WAS MORE USE TO US ALIVE THAN DEAD.
HOW'S THAT?
MOST OF OUR MEETINGS WERE HELD AT YOUR HOUSE. WE DRESSED AS PLUMBERS, ELECTRICIANS... WHATEVER IT TOOK TO AVOID SUSPICION.
SIHEM ALSO GAVE US ACCESS TO HER BANK ACCOUNT. SHE WAS THE LINCHPIN OF OUR TEL AVIV NETWORK...
AND NAZARETH...
YES, NAZARETH AS WELL...
WHERE DID YOU HOLD YOUR MEETINGS IN NAZARETH?
NO MEETINGS WERE HELD THERE. WE MET THERE FOR THE HAND OFF. SHE WAS RESPONSIBLE FOR GETTING MONEY TO TEL AVIV.
AND THAT'S ALL.
YES.
REALLY?
WHAT MORE DO YOU WANT TO KNOW?
WHAT WAS THE NATURE OF YOUR RELATIONSHIP?
MILITANT.
GREAT COVER, YOUR CAUSE! ABBAS SAW IT DIFFERENTLY!
?!
WHO?
HMM! IT SHOULD BE PRETTY EASY TO REMEMBER.
HE APPARENTLY BROKE YOUR FACE. THAT'S NOT SO EASY TO FORGET.
AH! THE MAD MAN.

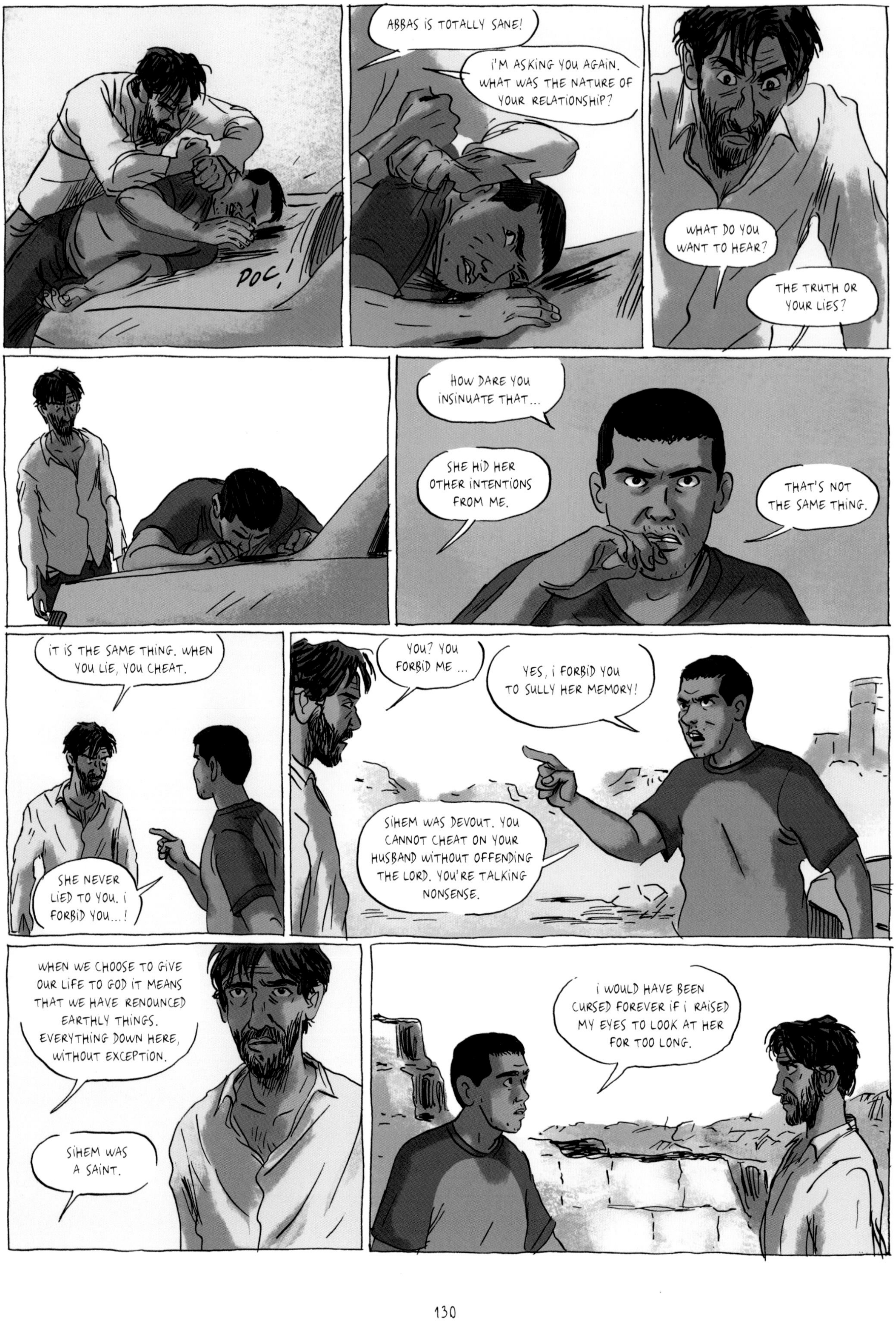
POC!
ABBAS IS TOTALLY SANE!
I'M ASKING YOU AGAIN. WHAT WAS THE NATURE OF YOUR RELATIONSHIP?
WHAT DO YOU WANT TO HEAR?
THE TRUTH OR YOUR LIES?
HOW DARE YOU INSINUATE THAT...
SHE HID HER OTHER INTENTIONS FROM ME.
THAT'S NOT THE SAME THING.
IT IS THE SAME THING. WHEN YOU LIE, YOU CHEAT.
SHE NEVER LIED TO YOU. I FORBID YOU...!
YOU? YOU FORBID ME ...
YES, I FORBID YOU TO SULLY HER MEMORY!
SIHEM WAS DEVOUT. YOU CANNOT CHEAT ON YOUR HUSBAND WITHOUT OFFENDING THE LORD. YOU'RE TALKING NONSENSE.
WHEN WE CHOOSE TO GIVE OUR LIFE TO GOD IT MEANS THAT WE HAVE RENOUNCED EARTHLY THINGS. EVERYTHING DOWN HERE, WITHOUT EXCEPTION.
SIHEM WAS A SAINT.
I WOULD HAVE BEEN CURSED FOREVER IF I RAISED MY EYES TO LOOK AT HER FOR TOO LONG.

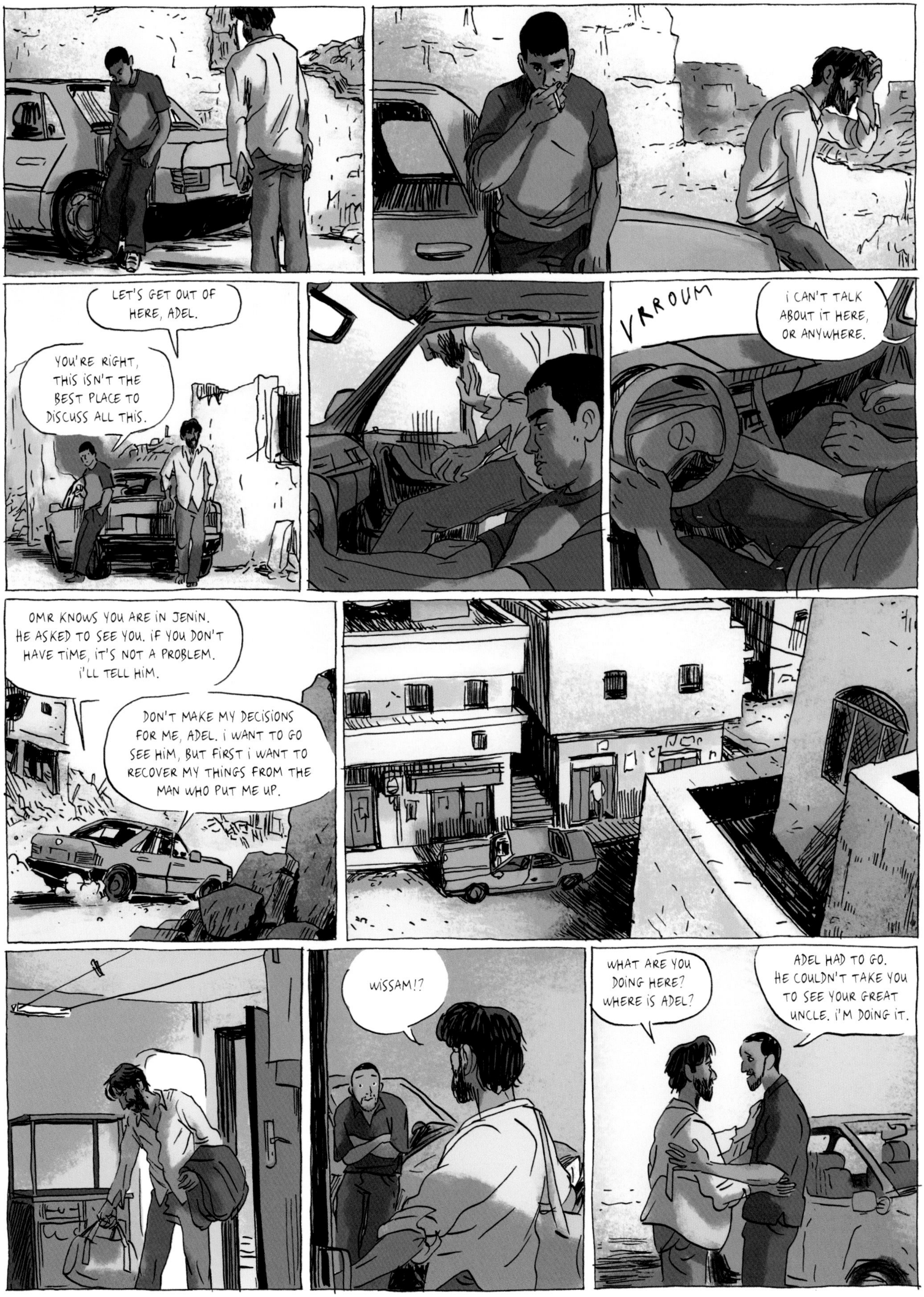

LET'S GET OUT OF HERE, ADEL.
YOU'RE RIGHT, THIS ISN'T THE BEST PLACE TO DISCUSS ALL THIS.
VRROUM
I CAN'T TALK ABOUT IT HERE, OR ANYWHERE.
OMR KNOWS YOU ARE IN JENIN. HE ASKED TO SEE YOU. IF YOU DON'T HAVE TIME, IT'S NOT A PROBLEM. I'LL TELL HIM.
DON'T MAKE MY DECISIONS FOR ME, ADEL. I WANT TO GO SEE HIM, BUT FIRST I WANT TO RECOVER MY THINGS FROM THE MAN WHO PUT ME UP.
WISSAM!?
WHAT ARE YOU DOING HERE? WHERE IS ADEL?
ADEL HAD TO GO. HE COULDN'T TAKE YOU TO SEE YOUR GREAT UNCLE. I'M DOING IT.

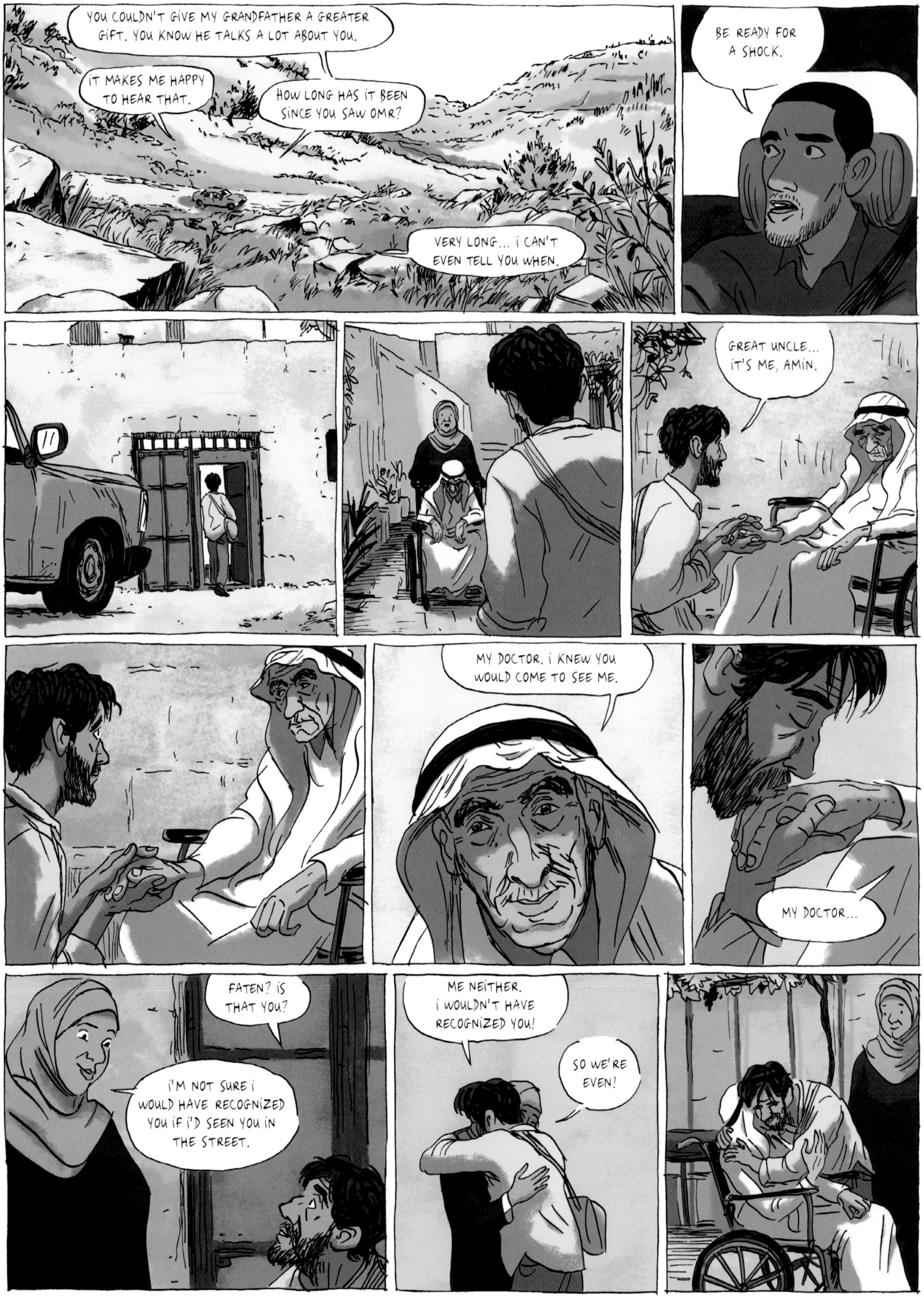
YOU COULDN'T GIVE MY GRANDFATHER A GREATER GIFT. YOU KNOW HE TALKS A LOT ABOUT YOU.
IT MAKES ME HAPPY TO HEAR THAT.
HOW LONG HAS IT BEEN SINCE YOU SAW OMR?
VERY LONG... I CAN'T EVEN TELL YOU WHEN.
BE READY FOR A SHOCK.
GREAT UNCLE... IT'S ME, AMIN.
MY DOCTOR. I KNEW YOU WOULD COME TO SEE ME.
MY DOCTOR...
FATEN? IS THAT YOU?
I'M NOT SURE I WOULD HAVE RECOGNIZED YOU IF I'D SEEN YOU IN THE STREET.
ME NEITHER. I WOULDN'T HAVE RECOGNIZED YOU!
SO WE'RE EVEN!

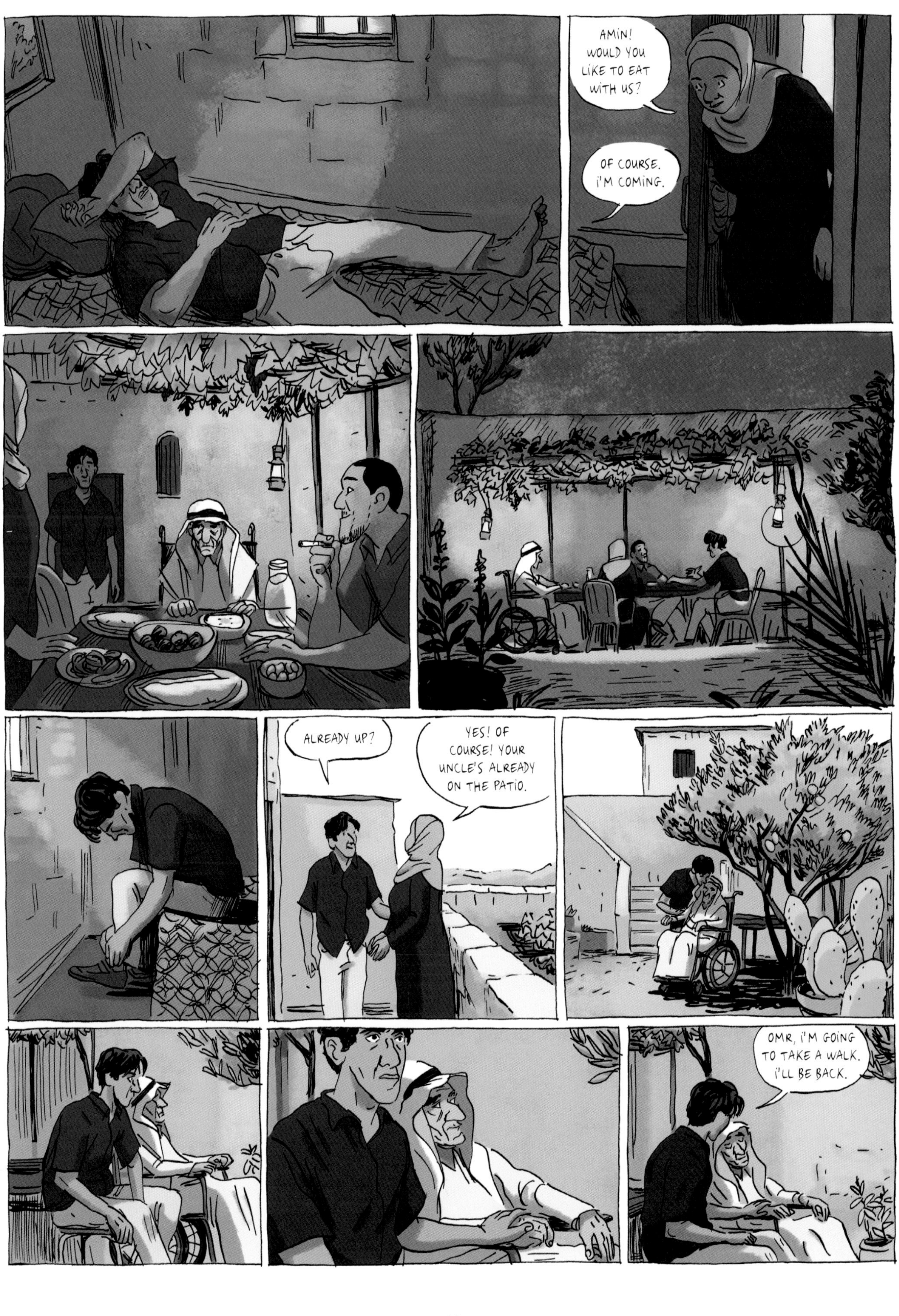
AMIN! WOULD YOU LIKE TO EAT WITH US?
OF COURSE. I'M COMING.
ALREADY UP?
YES! OF COURSE! YOUR UNCLE'S ALREADY ON THE PATIO.
OMR, I'M GOING TO TAKE A WALK. I'LL BE BACK.

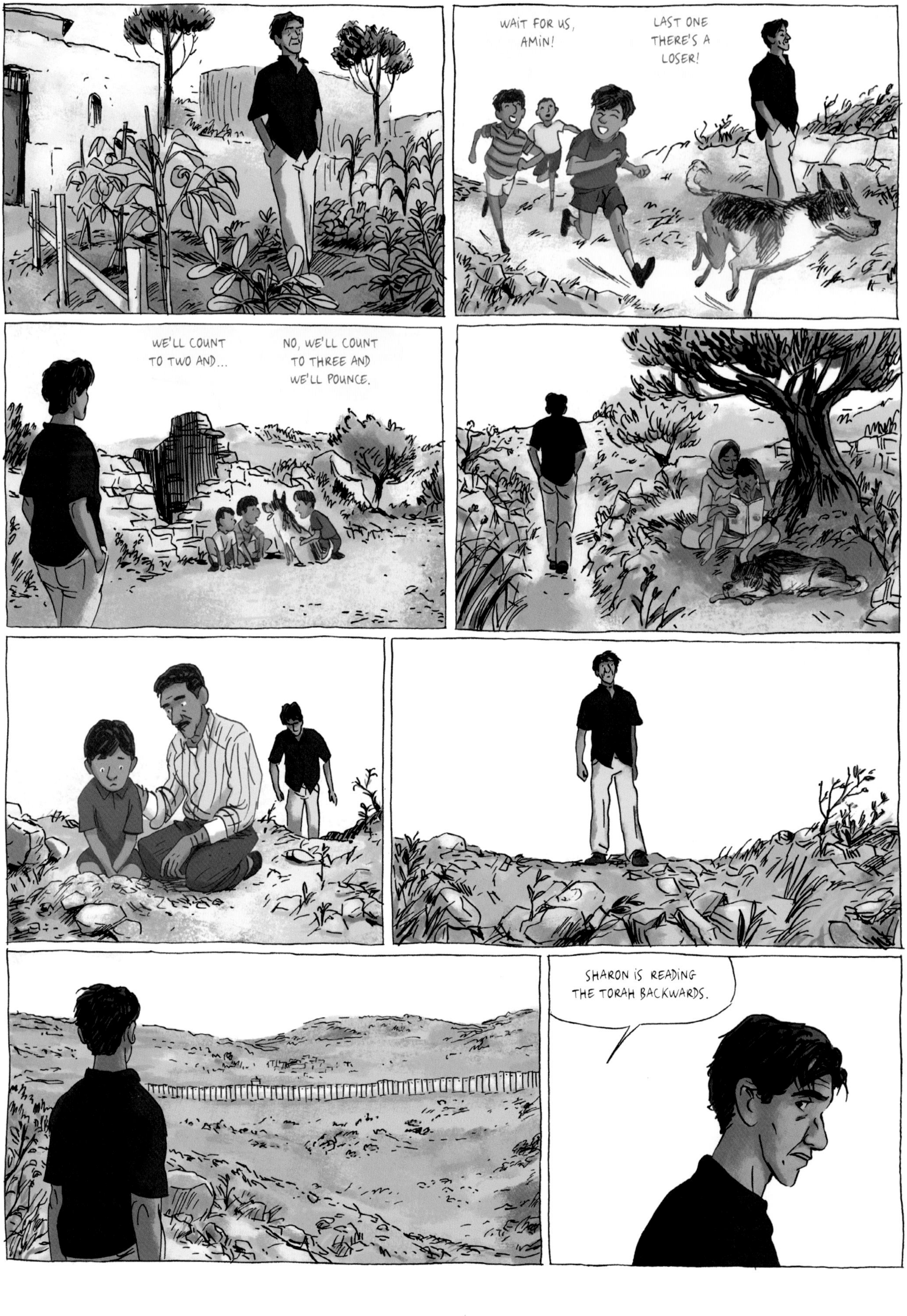
WAIT FOR US, AMIN!
LAST ONE THERE'S A LOSER!
WE'LL COUNT TO TWO AND...
NO, WE'LL COUNT TO THREE AND WE'LL POUNCE.
SHARON IS READING THE TORAH BACKWARDS.

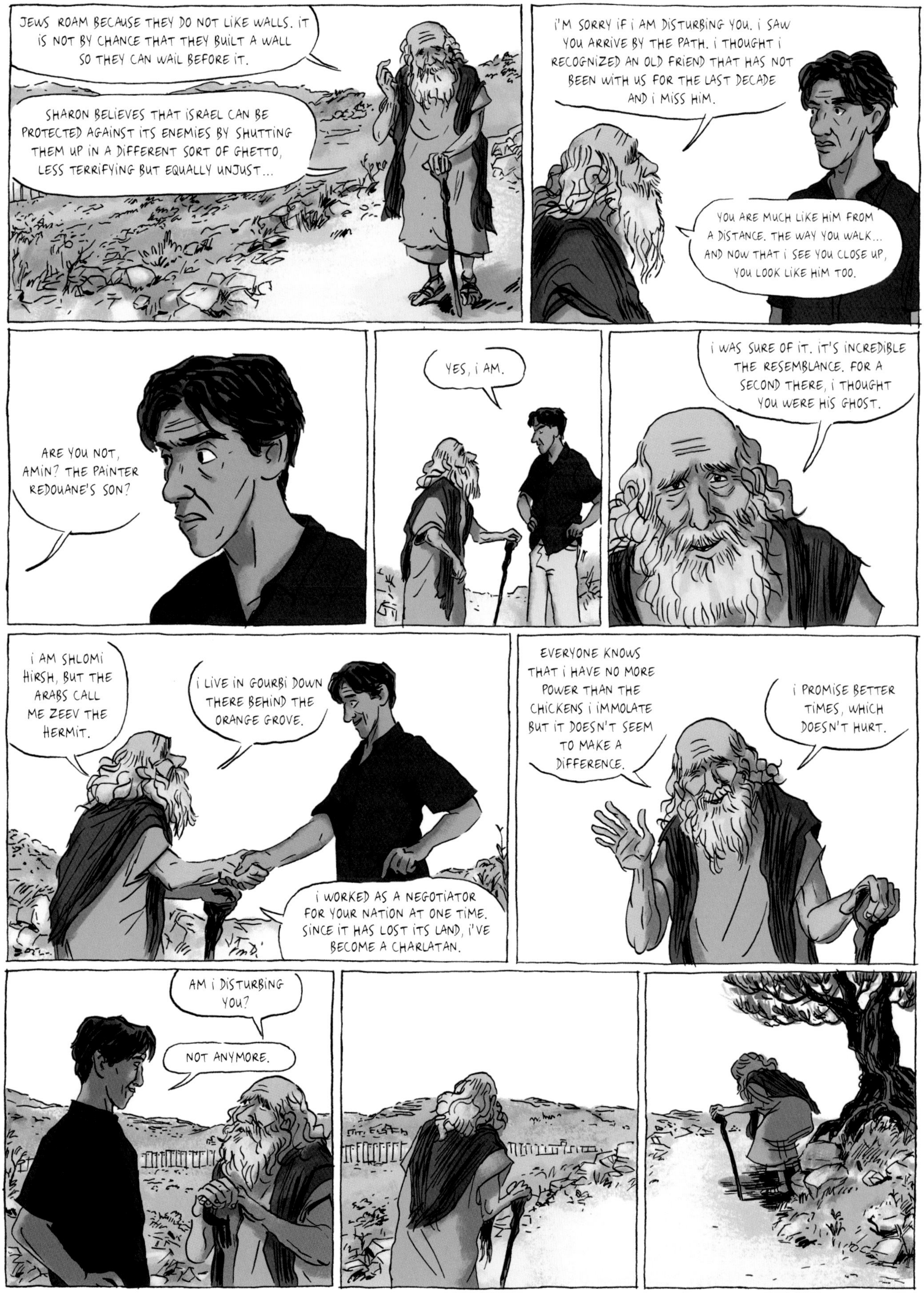
JEWS ROAM BECAUSE THEY DO NOT LIKE WALLS. IT IS NOT BY CHANCE THAT THEY BUILT A WALL SO THEY CAN WAIL BEFORE IT.
SHARON BELIEVES THAT ISRAEL CAN BE PROTECTED AGAINST ITS ENEMIES BY SHUTTING THEM UP IN A DIFFERENT SORT OF GHETTO, LESS TERRIFYING BUT EQUALLY UNJUST...
I'M SORRY IF I AM DISTURBING YOU. I SAW YOU ARRIVE BY THE PATH. I THOUGHT I RECOGNIZED AN OLD FRIEND THAT HAS NOT BEEN WITH US FOR THE LAST DECADE AND I MISS HIM.
YOU ARE MUCH LIKE HIM FROM A DISTANCE. THE WAY YOU WALK... AND NOW THAT I SEE YOU CLOSE UP, YOU LOOK LIKE HIM TOO.
ARE YOU NOT, AMIN? THE PAINTER REDOUANE'S SON?
YES, I AM.
I WAS SURE OF IT. IT'S INCREDIBLE THE RESEMBLANCE. FOR A SECOND THERE, I THOUGHT YOU WERE HIS GHOST.
I AM SHLOMI HIRSH, BUT THE ARABS CALL ME ZEEV THE HERMIT.
I LIVE IN GOURBI DOWN THERE BEHIND THE ORANGE GROVE.
I WORKED AS A NEGOTIATOR FOR YOUR NATION AT ONE TIME. SINCE IT HAS LOST ITS LAND, I'VE BECOME A CHARLATAN.
EVERYONE KNOWS THAT I HAVE NO MORE POWER THAN THE CHICKENS I IMMOLATE BUT IT DOESN'T SEEM TO MAKE A DIFFERENCE.
I PROMISE BETTER TIMES, WHICH DOESN'T HURT.
AM I DISTURBING YOU?
NOT ANYMORE.

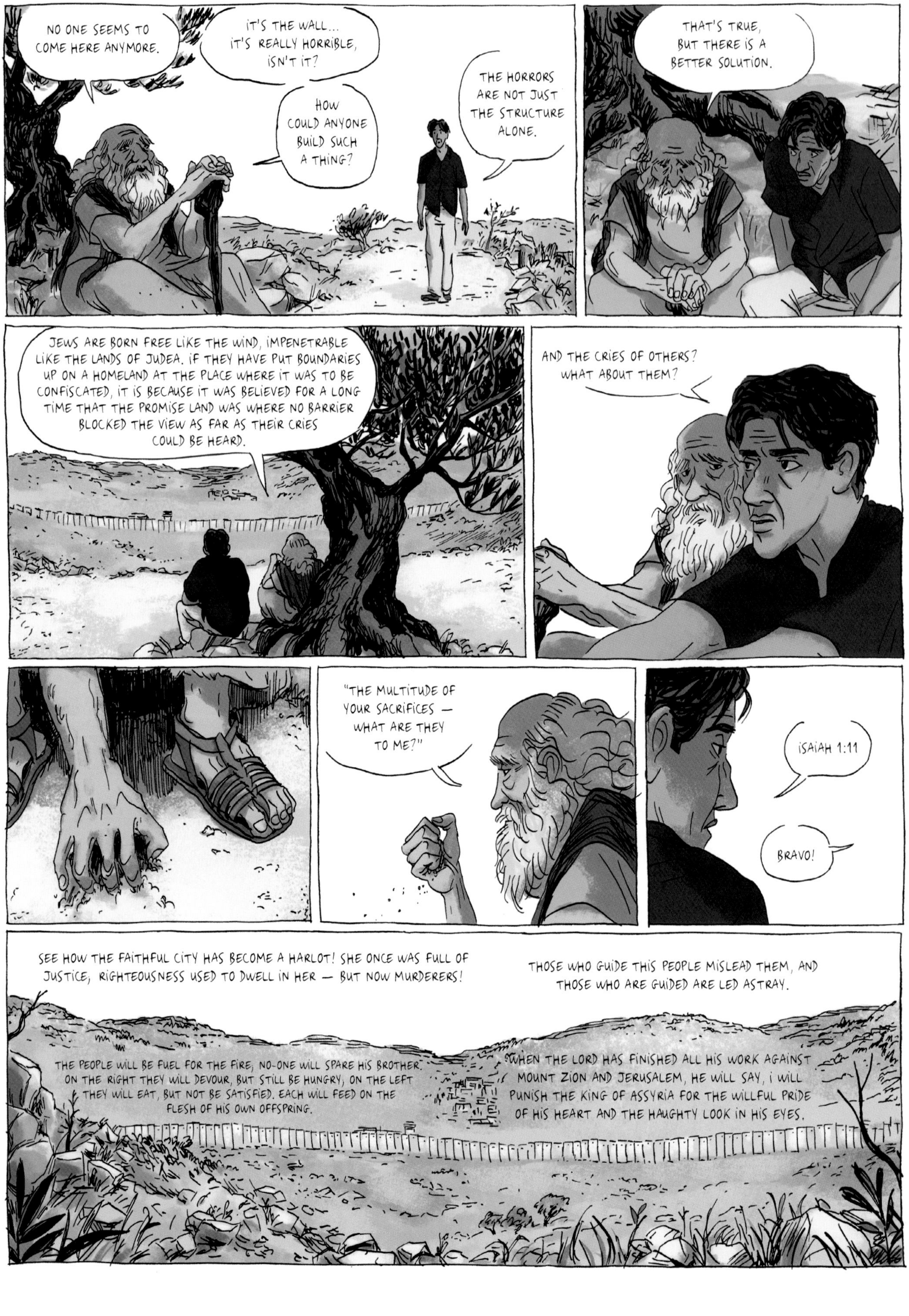
NO ONE SEEMS TO COME HERE ANYMORE.
IT'S THE WALL... IT'S REALLY HORRIBLE, ISN'T IT?
HOW COULD ANYONE BUILD SUCH A THING?
THE HORRORS ARE NOT JUST THE STRUCTURE ALONE.
THAT'S TRUE, BUT THERE IS A BETTER SOLUTION.
JEWS ARE BORN FREE LIKE THE WIND, IMPENETRABLE LIKE THE LANDS OF JUDEA. IF THEY HAVE PUT BOUNDARIES UP ON A HOMELAND AT THE PLACE WHERE IT WAS TO BE CONFISCATED, IT IS BECAUSE IT WAS BELIEVED FOR A LONG TIME THAT THE PROMISE LAND WAS WHERE NO BARRIER BLOCKED THE VIEW AS FAR AS THEIR CRIES COULD BE HEARD.
AND THE CRIES OF OTHERS? WHAT ABOUT THEM?
"THE MULTITUDE OF YOUR SACRIFICES — WHAT ARE THEY TO ME?"
ISAIAH 1:11
BRAVO!
SEE HOW THE FAITHFUL CITY HAS BECOME A HARLOT! SHE ONCE WAS FULL OF JUSTICE, RIGHTEOUSNESS USED TO DWELL IN HER — BUT NOW MURDERERS!
THOSE WHO GUIDE THIS PEOPLE MISLEAD THEM, AND THOSE WHO ARE GUIDED ARE LED ASTRAY.
THE PEOPLE WILL BE FUEL FOR THE FIRE; NO-ONE WILL SPARE HIS BROTHER. ON THE RIGHT THEY WILL DEVOUR, BUT STILL BE HUNGRY; ON THE LEFT THEY WILL EAT, BUT NOT BE SATISFIED. EACH WILL FEED ON THE FLESH OF HIS OWN OFFSPRING.
WHEN THE LORD HAS FINISHED ALL HIS WORK AGAINST MOUNT ZION AND JERUSALEM, HE WILL SAY, I WILL PUNISH THE KING OF ASSYRIA FOR THE WILLFUL PRIDE OF HIS HEART AND THE HAUGHTY LOOK IN HIS EYES.

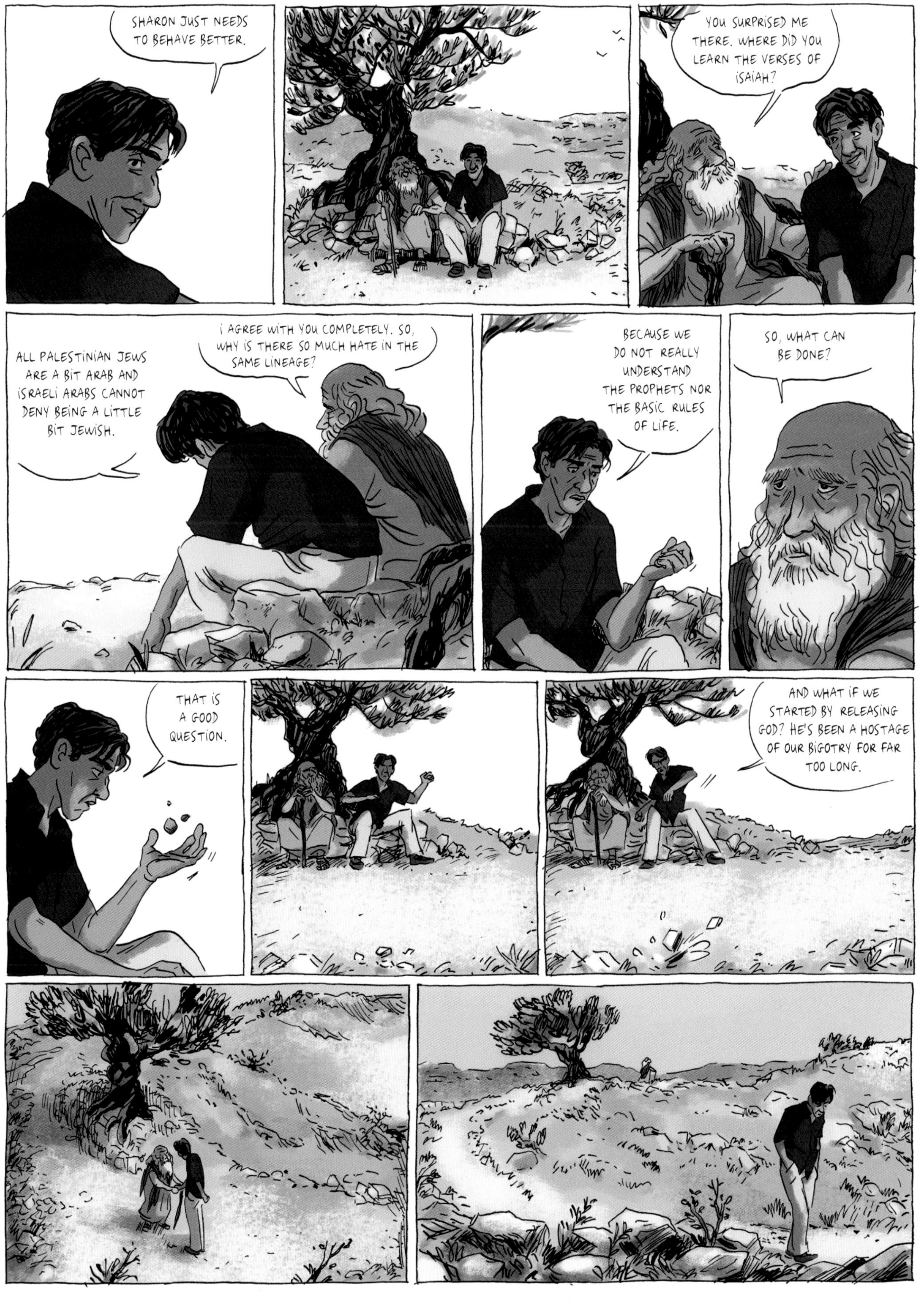
SHARON JUST NEEDS TO BEHAVE BETTER.
YOU SURPRISED ME THERE. WHERE DID YOU LEARN THE VERSES OF ISAIAH?
ALL PALESTINIAN JEWS ARE A BIT ARAB AND ISRAELI ARABS CANNOT DENY BEING A LITTLE BIT JEWISH.
I AGREE WITH YOU COMPLETELY. SO, WHY IS THERE SO MUCH HATE IN THE SAME LINEAGE?
BECAUSE WE DO NOT REALLY UNDERSTAND THE PROPHETS NOR THE BASIC RULES OF LIFE.
SO, WHAT CAN BE DONE?
THAT IS A GOOD QUESTION.
AND WHAT IF WE STARTED BY RELEASING GOD? HE'S BEEN A HOSTAGE OF OUR BIGOTRY FOR FAR TOO LONG.

AMIN! WHERE YA BEEN? COME ON!

WHAT'S GOING ON?

THE NEWS THAT YOU CAME BACK HAS SPREAD QUICKLY. THE FAMILY HAS COME TO SEE YOU.

COME ON!

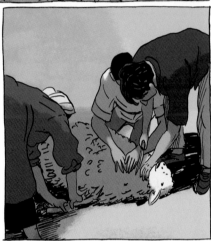

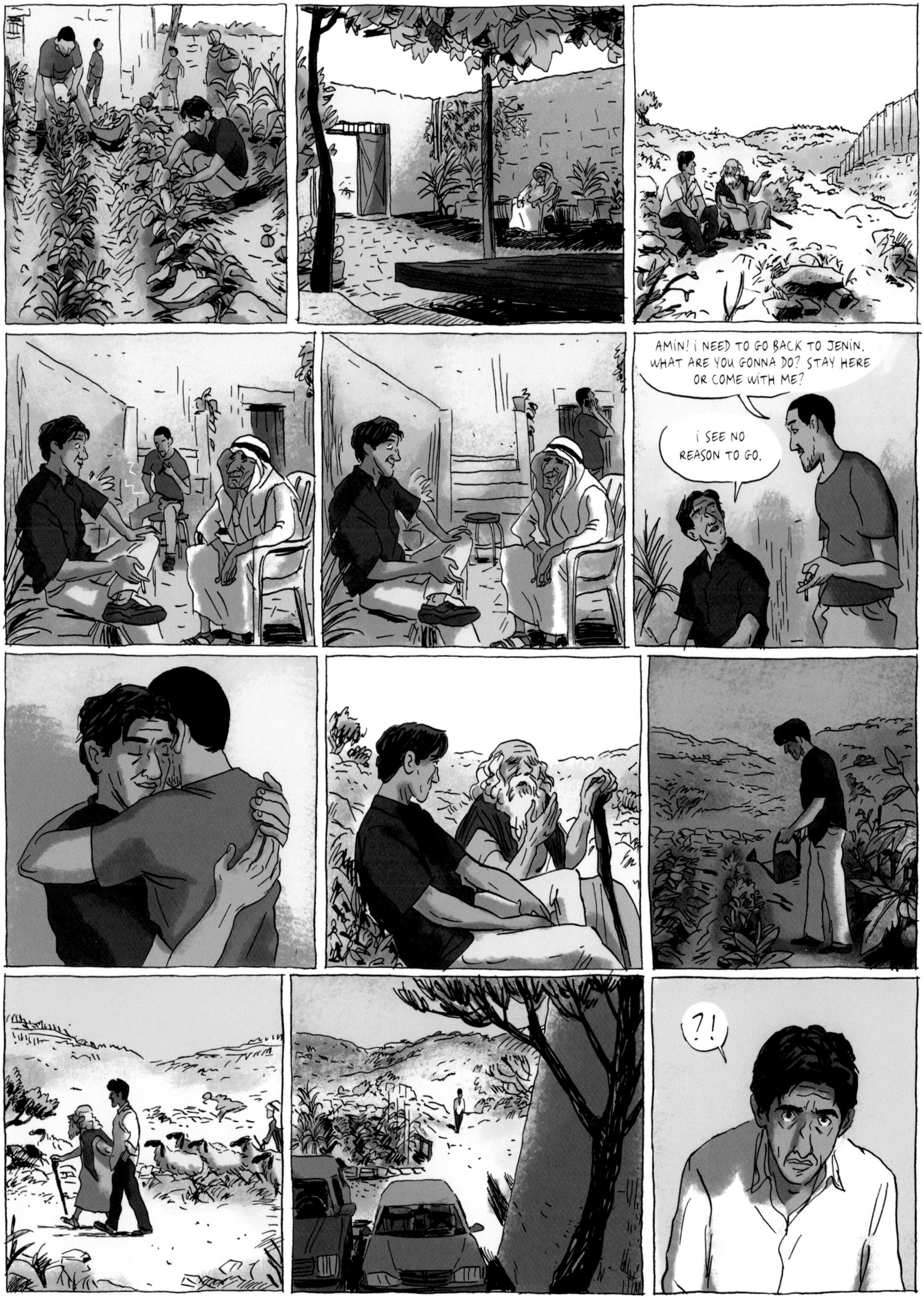
AMIN! I NEED TO GO BACK TO JENIN. WHAT ARE YOU GONNA DO? STAY HERE OR COME WITH ME?
I SEE NO REASON TO GO.
?!

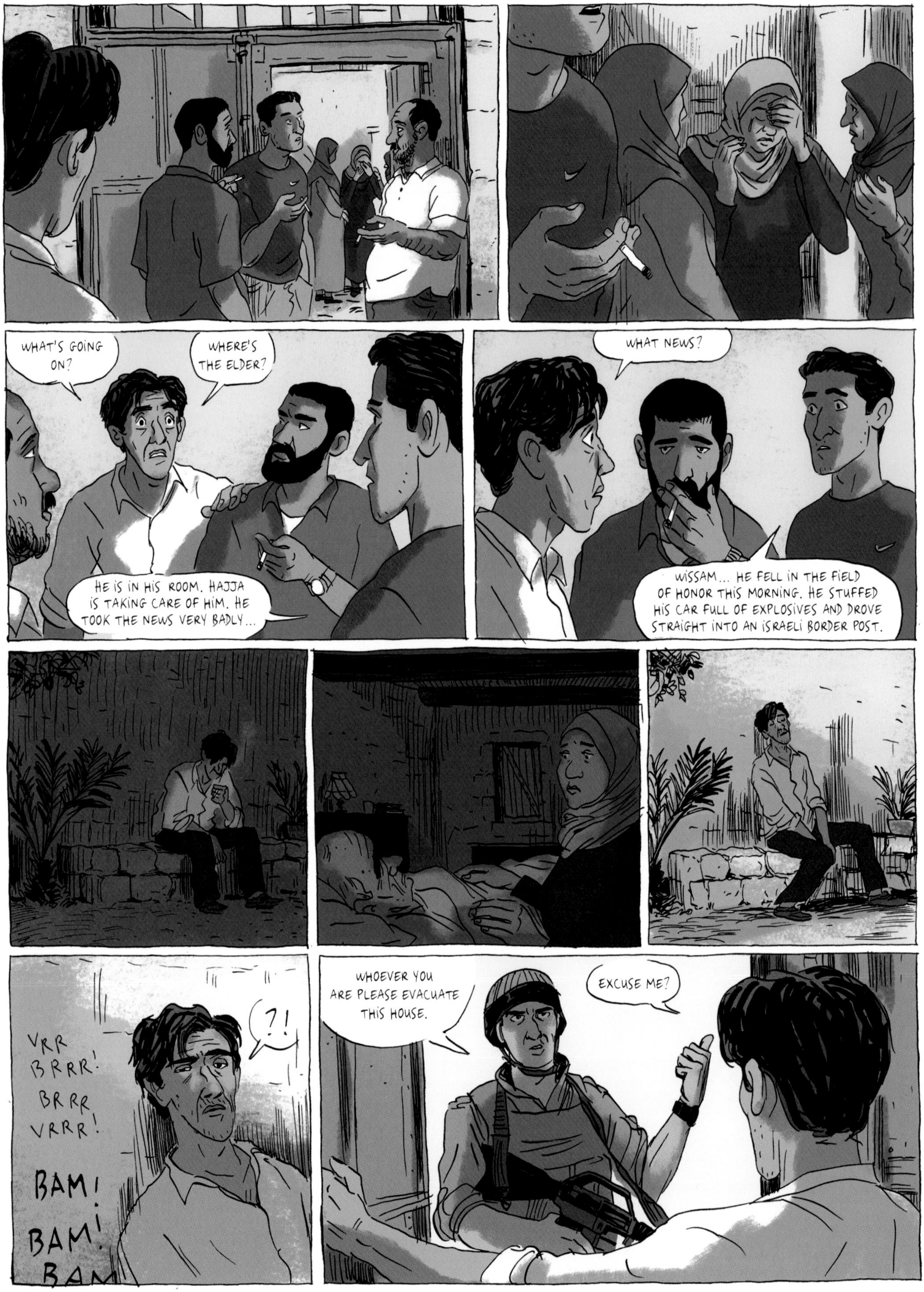
WHAT'S GOING ON?
WHERE'S THE ELDER?
HE IS IN HIS ROOM. HAJJA IS TAKING CARE OF HIM. HE TOOK THE NEWS VERY BADLY...
WHAT NEWS?
WISSAM... HE FELL IN THE FIELD OF HONOR THIS MORNING. HE STUFFED HIS CAR FULL OF EXPLOSIVES AND DROVE STRAIGHT INTO AN ISRAELI BORDER POST.
VRR BRRR! BRRR VRRR!
BAM! BAM! BAM
?!
WHOEVER YOU ARE PLEASE EVACUATE THIS HOUSE.
EXCUSE ME?

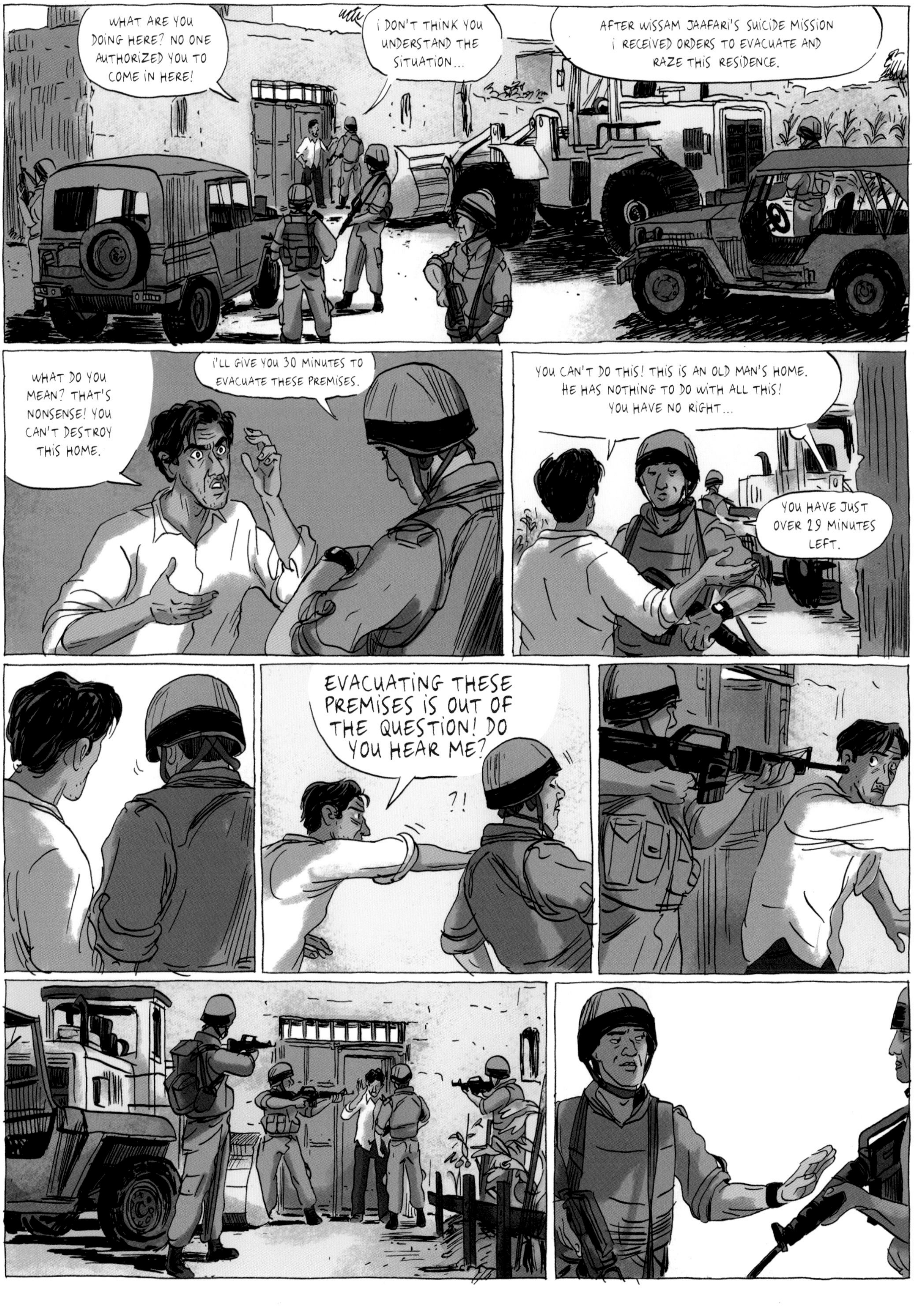
WHAT ARE YOU DOING HERE? NO ONE AUTHORIZED YOU TO COME IN HERE!
I DON'T THINK YOU UNDERSTAND THE SITUATION...
AFTER WISSAM JAAFARI'S SUICIDE MISSION I RECEIVED ORDERS TO EVACUATE AND RAZE THIS RESIDENCE.
WHAT DO YOU MEAN? THAT'S NONSENSE! YOU CAN'T DESTROY THIS HOME.
I'LL GIVE YOU 30 MINUTES TO EVACUATE THESE PREMISES.
YOU CAN'T DO THIS! THIS IS AN OLD MAN'S HOME. HE HAS NOTHING TO DO WITH ALL THIS! YOU HAVE NO RIGHT...
YOU HAVE JUST OVER 29 MINUTES LEFT.
EVACUATING THESE PREMISES IS OUT OF THE QUESTION! DO YOU HEAR ME?
?!

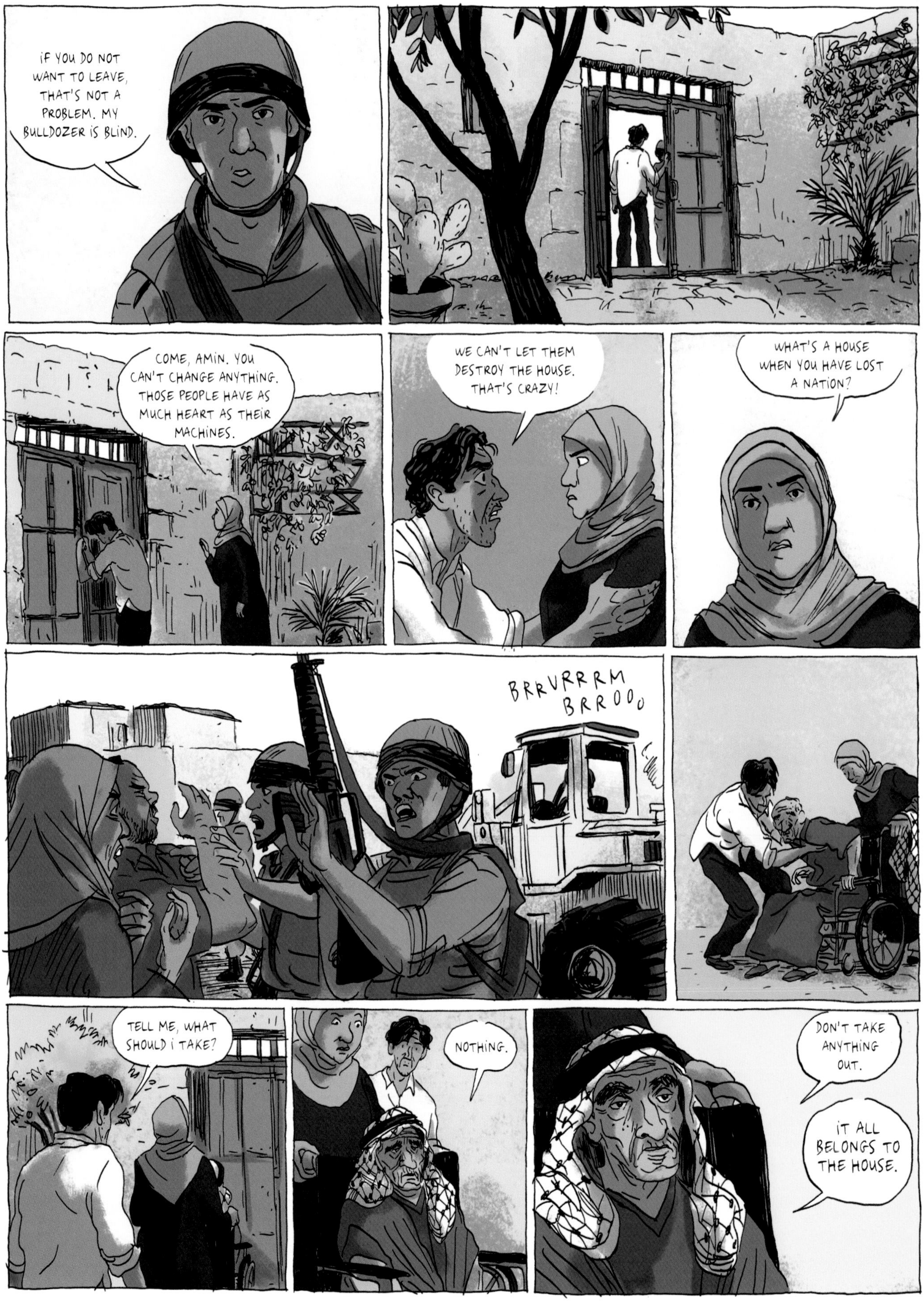
IF YOU DO NOT WANT TO LEAVE, THAT'S NOT A PROBLEM. MY BULLDOZER IS BLIND.
COME, AMIN. YOU CAN'T CHANGE ANYTHING. THOSE PEOPLE HAVE AS MUCH HEART AS THEIR MACHINES.
WE CAN'T LET THEM DESTROY THE HOUSE. THAT'S CRAZY!
WHAT'S A HOUSE WHEN YOU HAVE LOST A NATION?
BRRURRRM BRROOO
TELL ME, WHAT SHOULD I TAKE?
NOTHING.
DON'T TAKE ANYTHING OUT.
IT ALL BELONGS TO THE HOUSE.

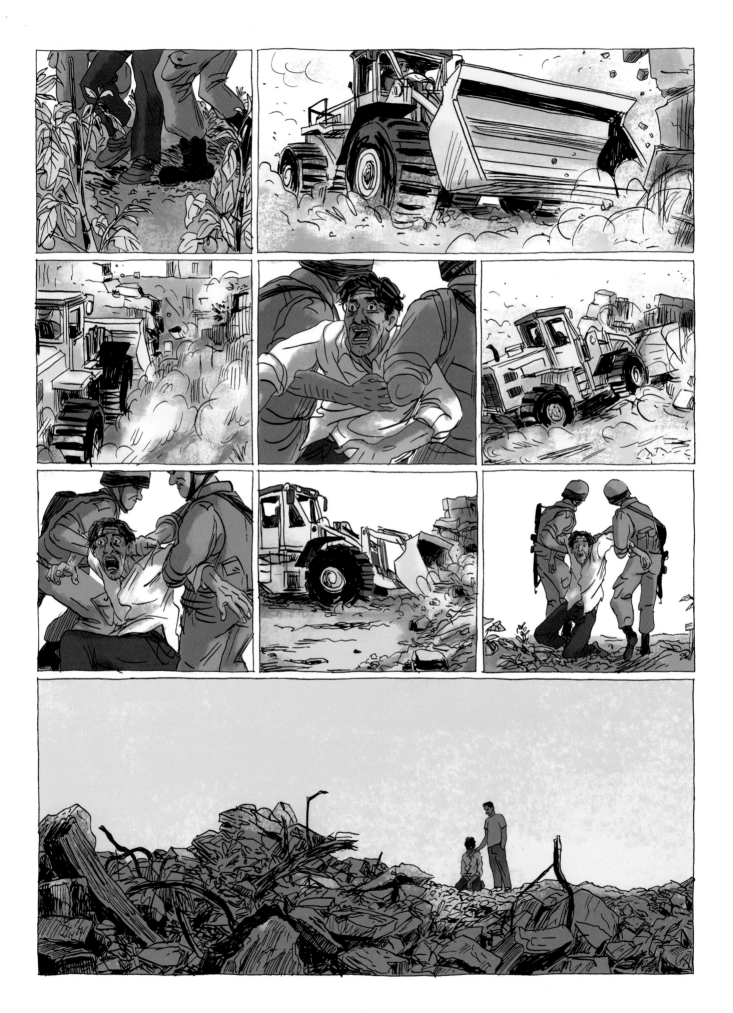

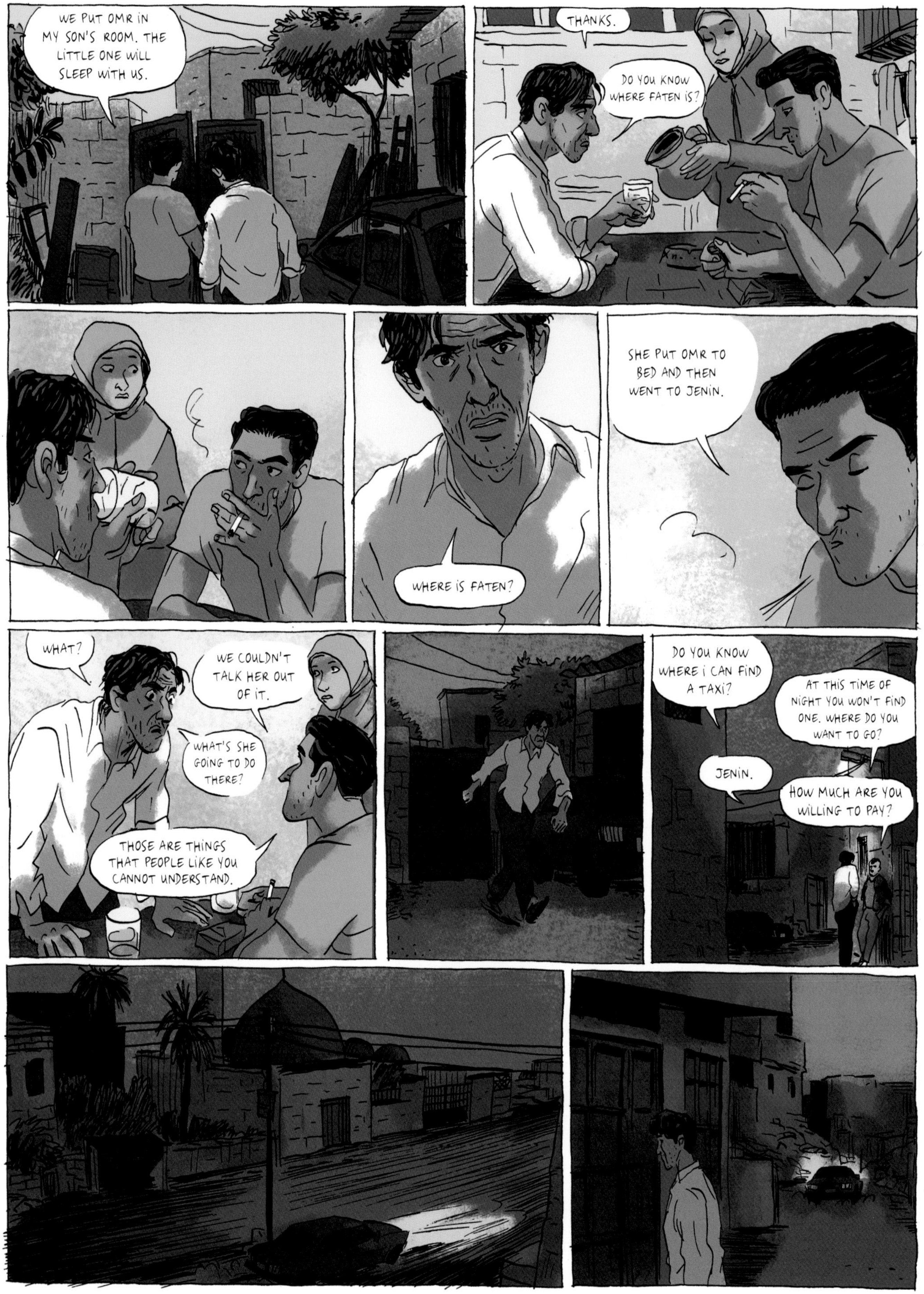
WE PUT OMR IN MY SON'S ROOM. THE LITTLE ONE WILL SLEEP WITH US.
THANKS.
DO YOU KNOW WHERE FATEN IS?
WHERE IS FATEN?
SHE PUT OMR TO BED AND THEN WENT TO JENIN.
WHAT?
WE COULDN'T TALK HER OUT OF IT.
WHAT'S SHE GOING TO DO THERE?
THOSE ARE THINGS THAT PEOPLE LIKE YOU CANNOT UNDERSTAND.
DO YOU KNOW WHERE I CAN FIND A TAXI?
AT THIS TIME OF NIGHT YOU WON'T FIND ONE. WHERE DO YOU WANT TO GO?
JENIN.
HOW MUCH ARE YOU WILLING TO PAY?

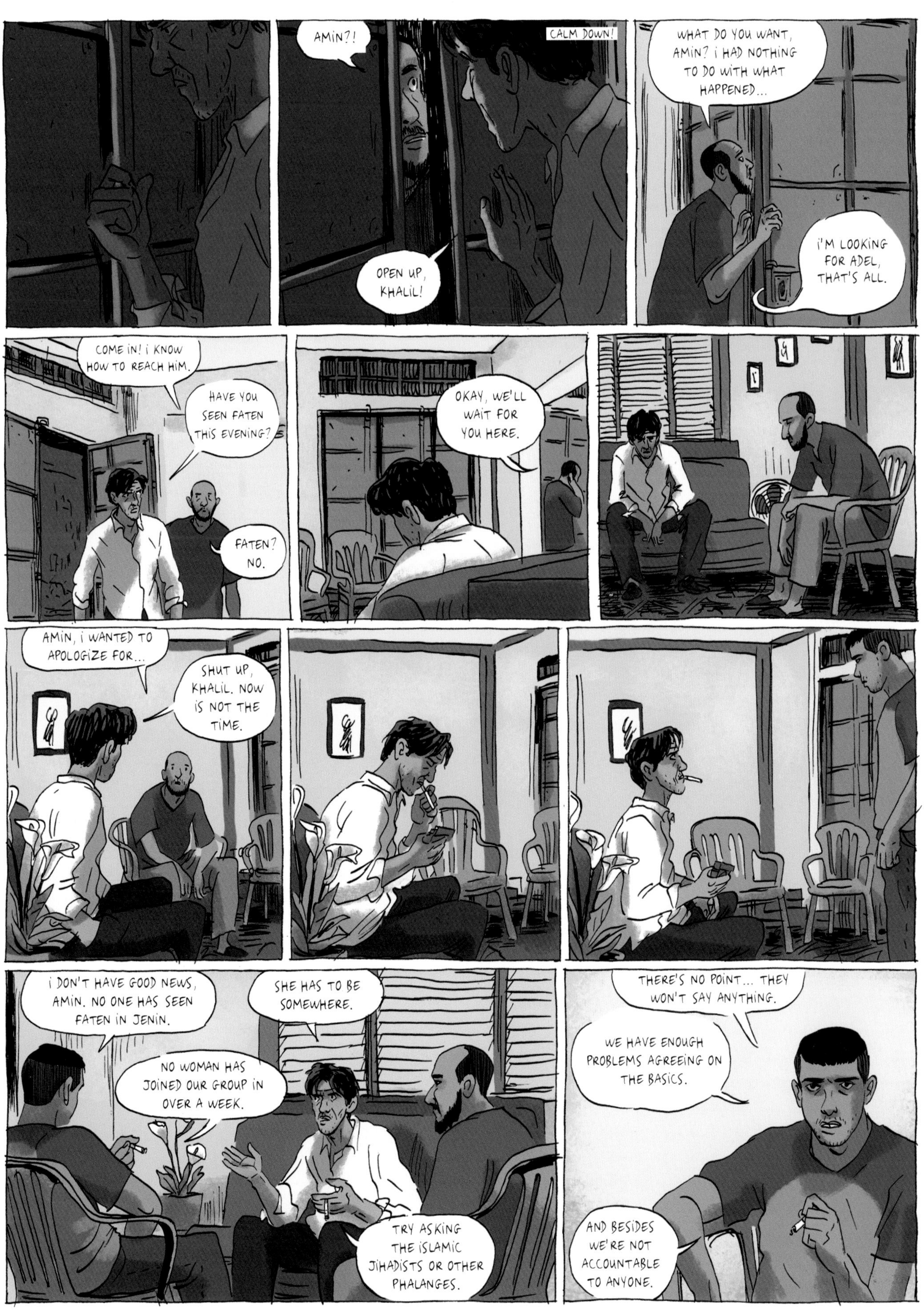
AMIN?!
CALM DOWN!
OPEN UP, KHALIL!
WHAT DO YOU WANT, AMIN? I HAD NOTHING TO DO WITH WHAT HAPPENED...
I'M LOOKING FOR ADEL, THAT'S ALL.
COME IN! I KNOW HOW TO REACH HIM.
HAVE YOU SEEN FATEN THIS EVENING?
FATEN? NO.
OKAY, WE'LL WAIT FOR YOU HERE.
AMIN, I WANTED TO APOLOGIZE FOR...
SHUT UP, KHALIL. NOW IS NOT THE TIME.
I DON'T HAVE GOOD NEWS, AMIN. NO ONE HAS SEEN FATEN IN JENIN.
SHE HAS TO BE SOMEWHERE.
NO WOMAN HAS JOINED OUR GROUP IN OVER A WEEK.
TRY ASKING THE ISLAMIC JIHADISTS OR OTHER PHALANGES.
THERE'S NO POINT... THEY WON'T SAY ANYTHING.
WE HAVE ENOUGH PROBLEMS AGREEING ON THE BASICS.
AND BESIDES WE'RE NOT ACCOUNTABLE TO ANYONE.

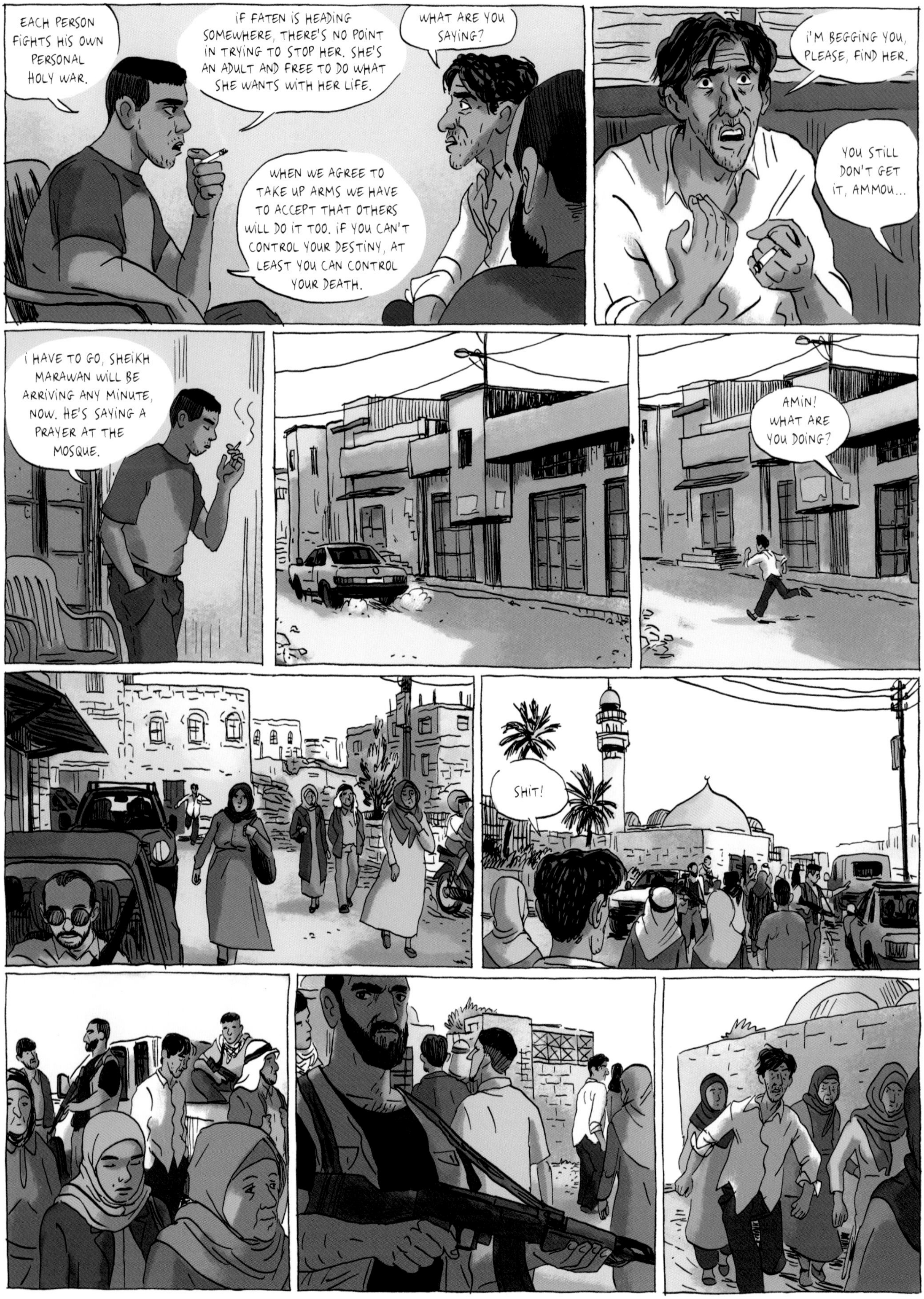
EACH PERSON FIGHTS HIS OWN PERSONAL HOLY WAR.
IF FATEN IS HEADING SOMEWHERE, THERE'S NO POINT IN TRYING TO STOP HER. SHE'S AN ADULT AND FREE TO DO WHAT SHE WANTS WITH HER LIFE.
WHAT ARE YOU SAYING?
WHEN WE AGREE TO TAKE UP ARMS WE HAVE TO ACCEPT THAT OTHERS WILL DO IT TOO. IF YOU CAN'T CONTROL YOUR DESTINY, AT LEAST YOU CAN CONTROL YOUR DEATH.
I'M BEGGING YOU, PLEASE, FIND HER.
YOU STILL DON'T GET IT, AMMOU...
I HAVE TO GO, SHEIKH MARAWAN WILL BE ARRIVING ANY MINUTE, NOW. HE'S SAYING A PRAYER AT THE MOSQUE.
AMIN! WHAT ARE YOU DOING?
SHIT!

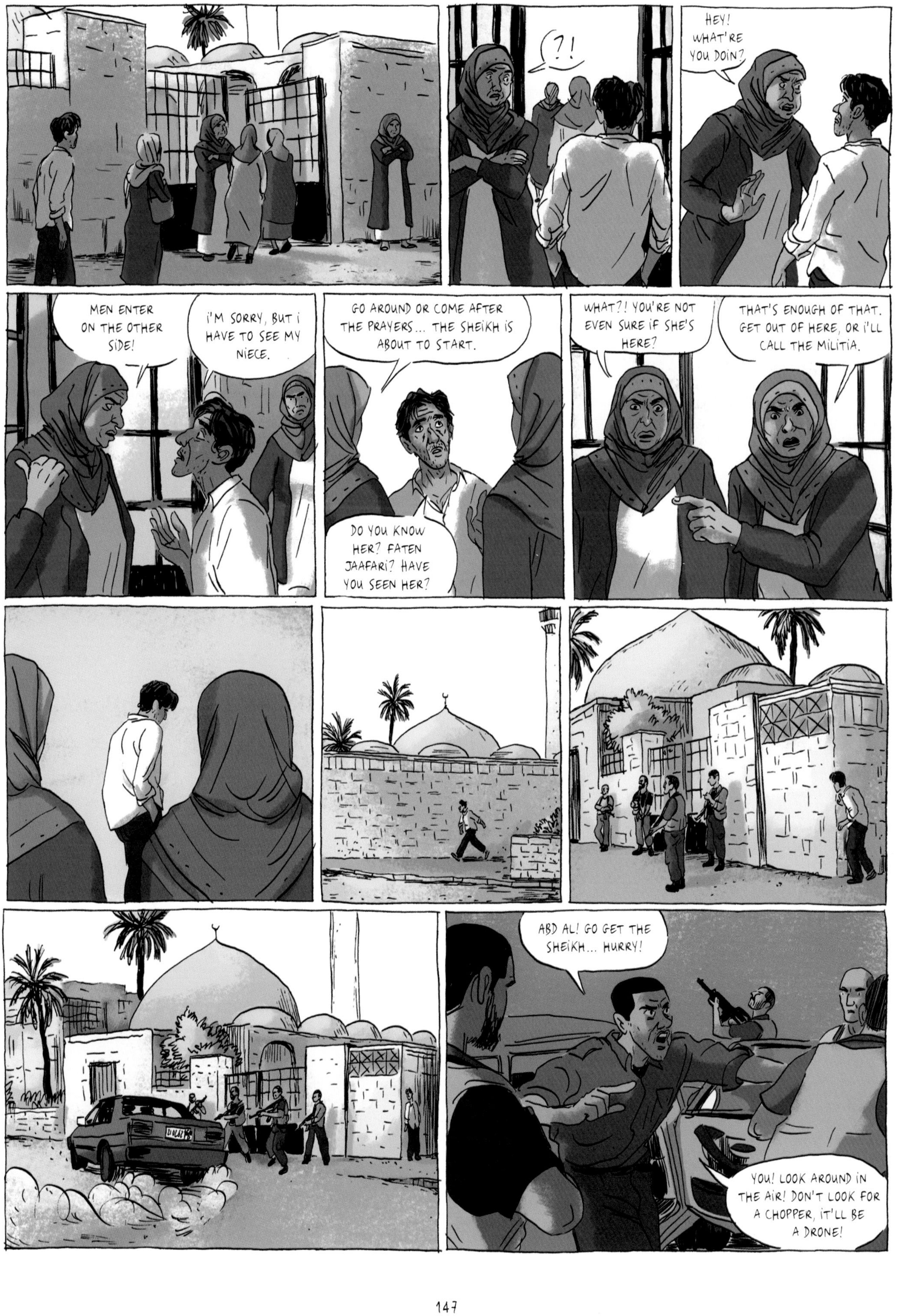
(?!)
HEY! WHAT'RE YOU DOIN?
MEN ENTER ON THE OTHER SIDE!
I'M SORRY, BUT I HAVE TO SEE MY NIECE.
GO AROUND OR COME AFTER THE PRAYERS... THE SHEIKH IS ABOUT TO START.
DO YOU KNOW HER? FATEN JAAFARI? HAVE YOU SEEN HER?
WHAT?! YOU'RE NOT EVEN SURE IF SHE'S HERE?
THAT'S ENOUGH OF THAT. GET OUT OF HERE, OR I'LL CALL THE MILITIA.
ABD AL! GO GET THE SHEIKH... HURRY!
YOU! LOOK AROUND IN THE AIR! DON'T LOOK FOR A CHOPPER, IT'LL BE A DRONE!

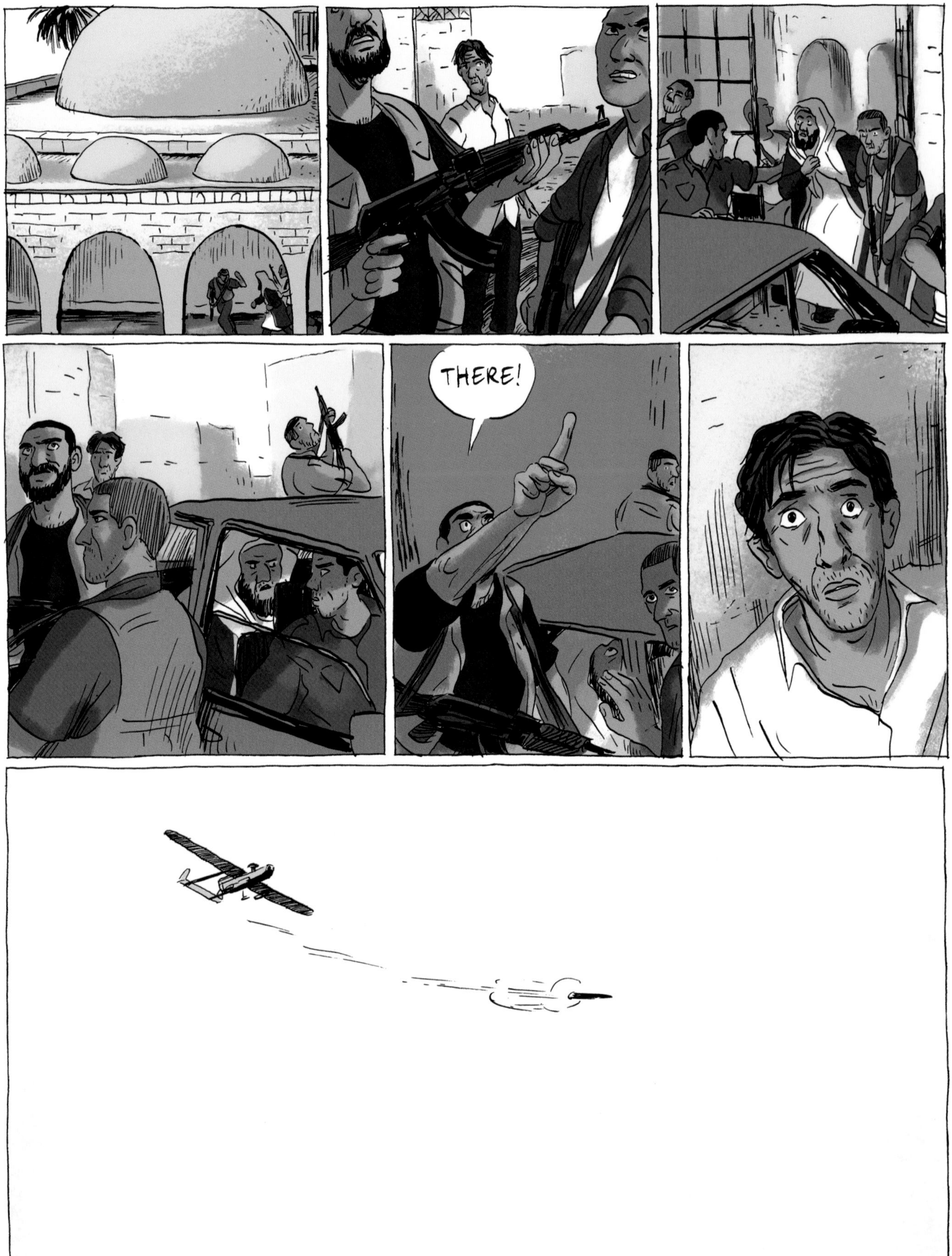
THERE!

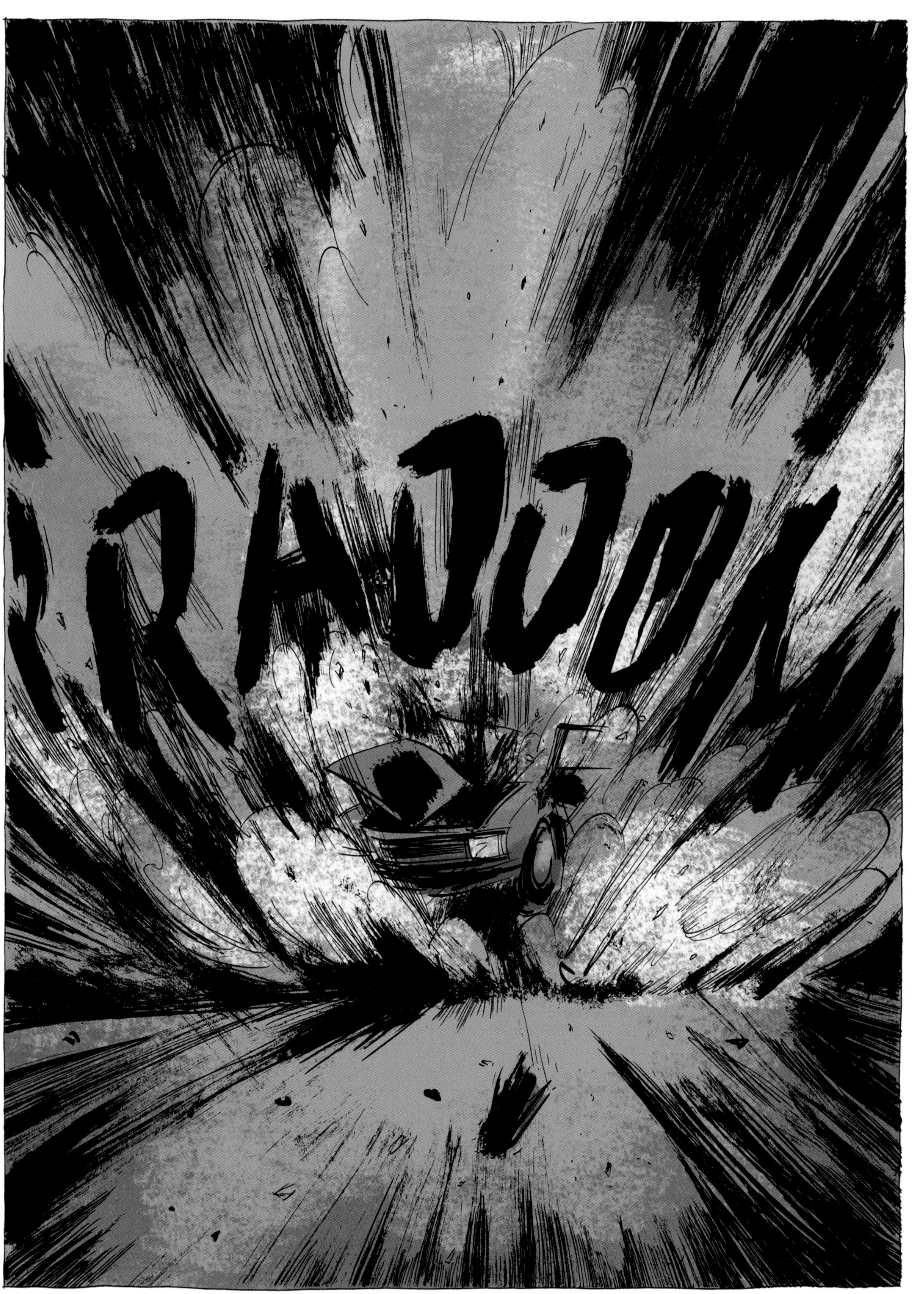

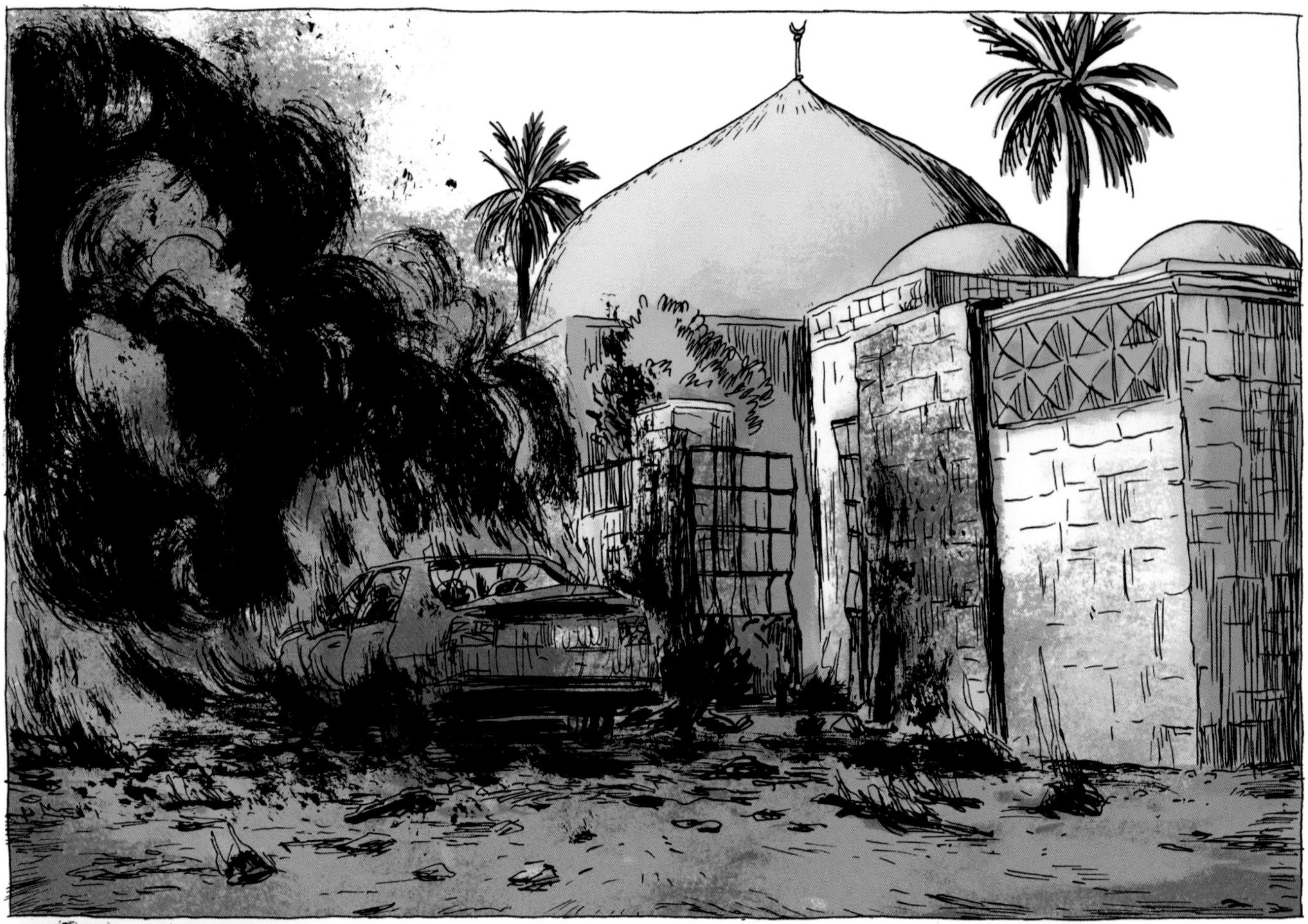

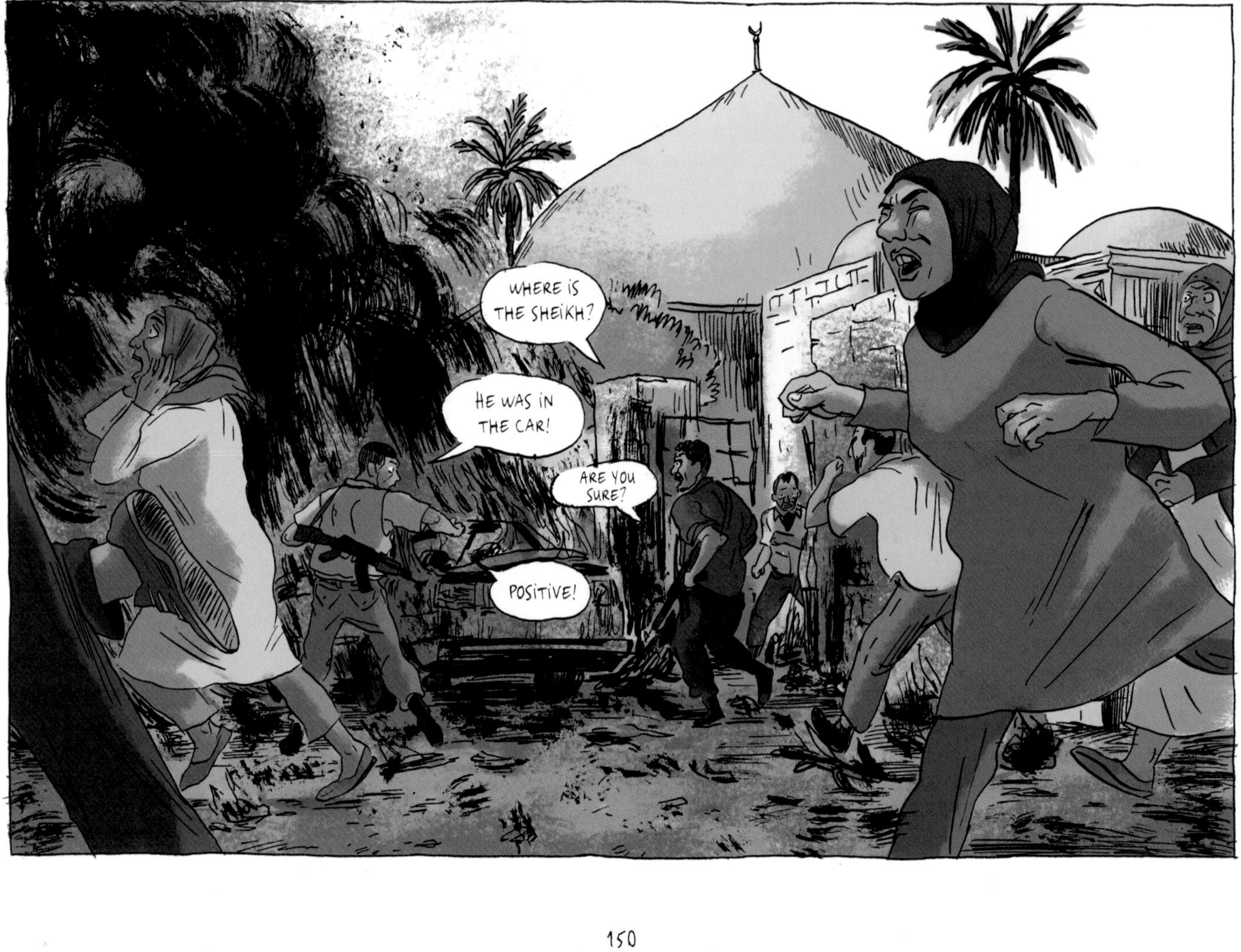
WHERE IS THE SHEIKH?
HE WAS IN THE CAR!
ARE YOU SURE?
POSITIVE!

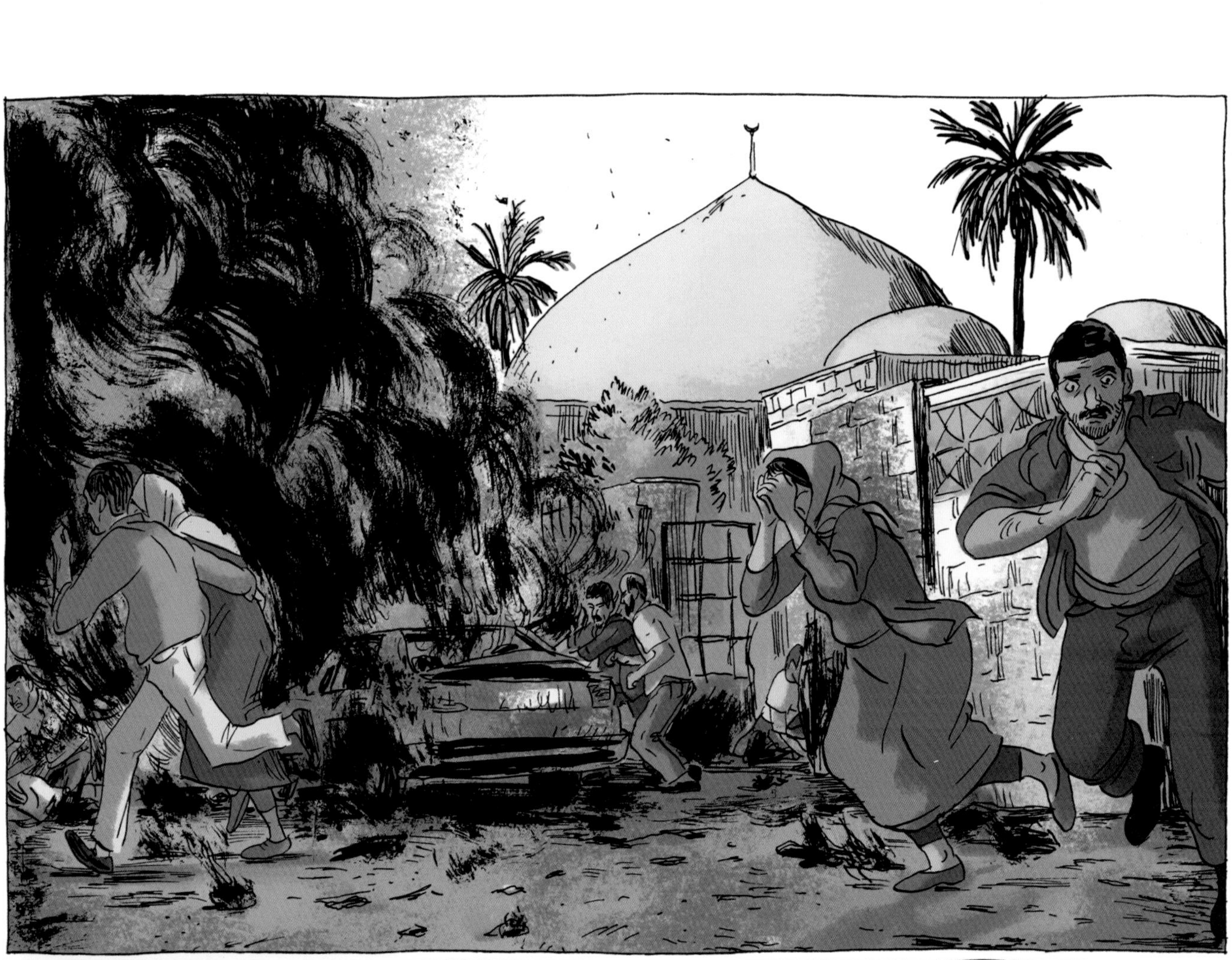

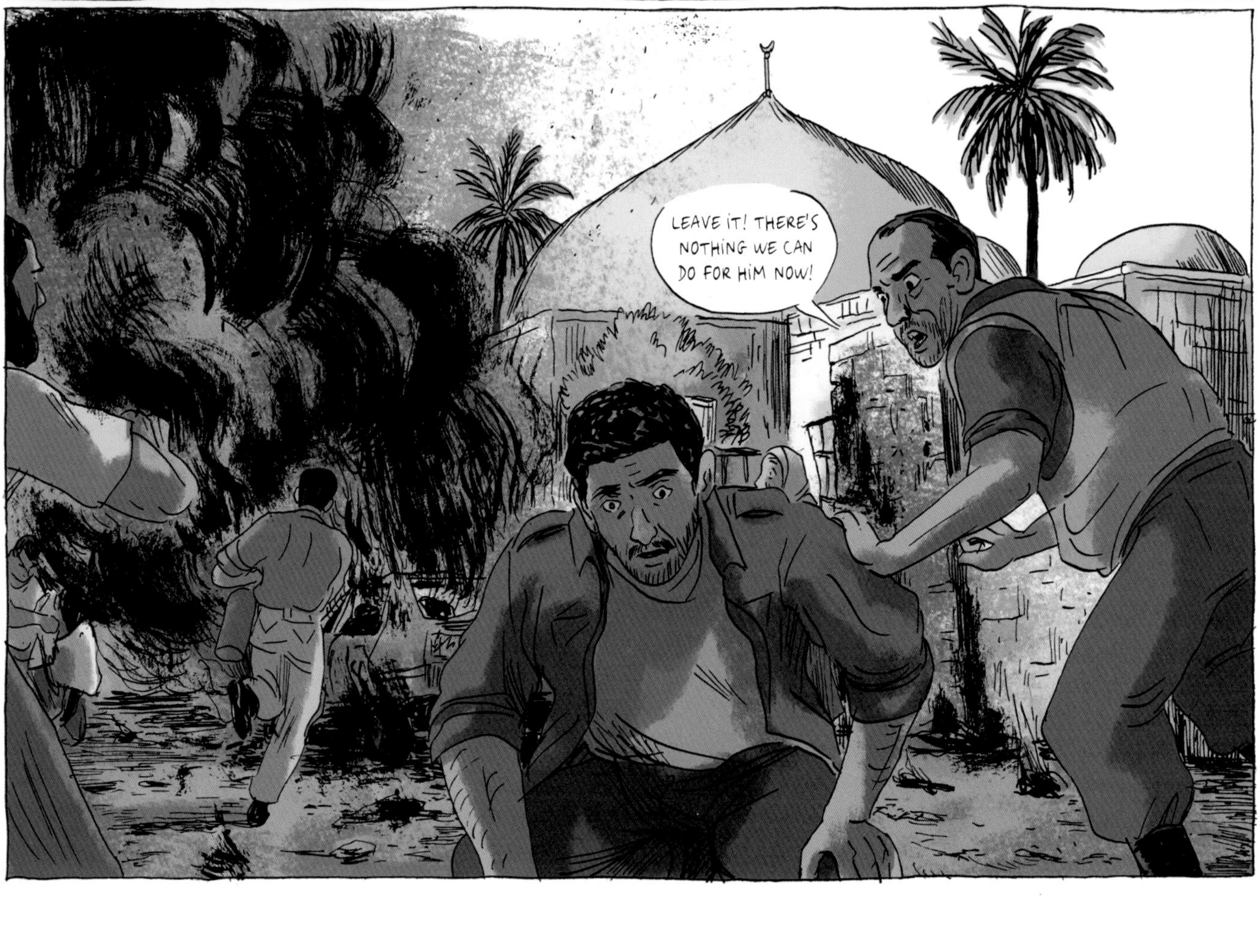
LEAVE IT! THERE'S NOTHING WE CAN DO FOR HIM NOW!

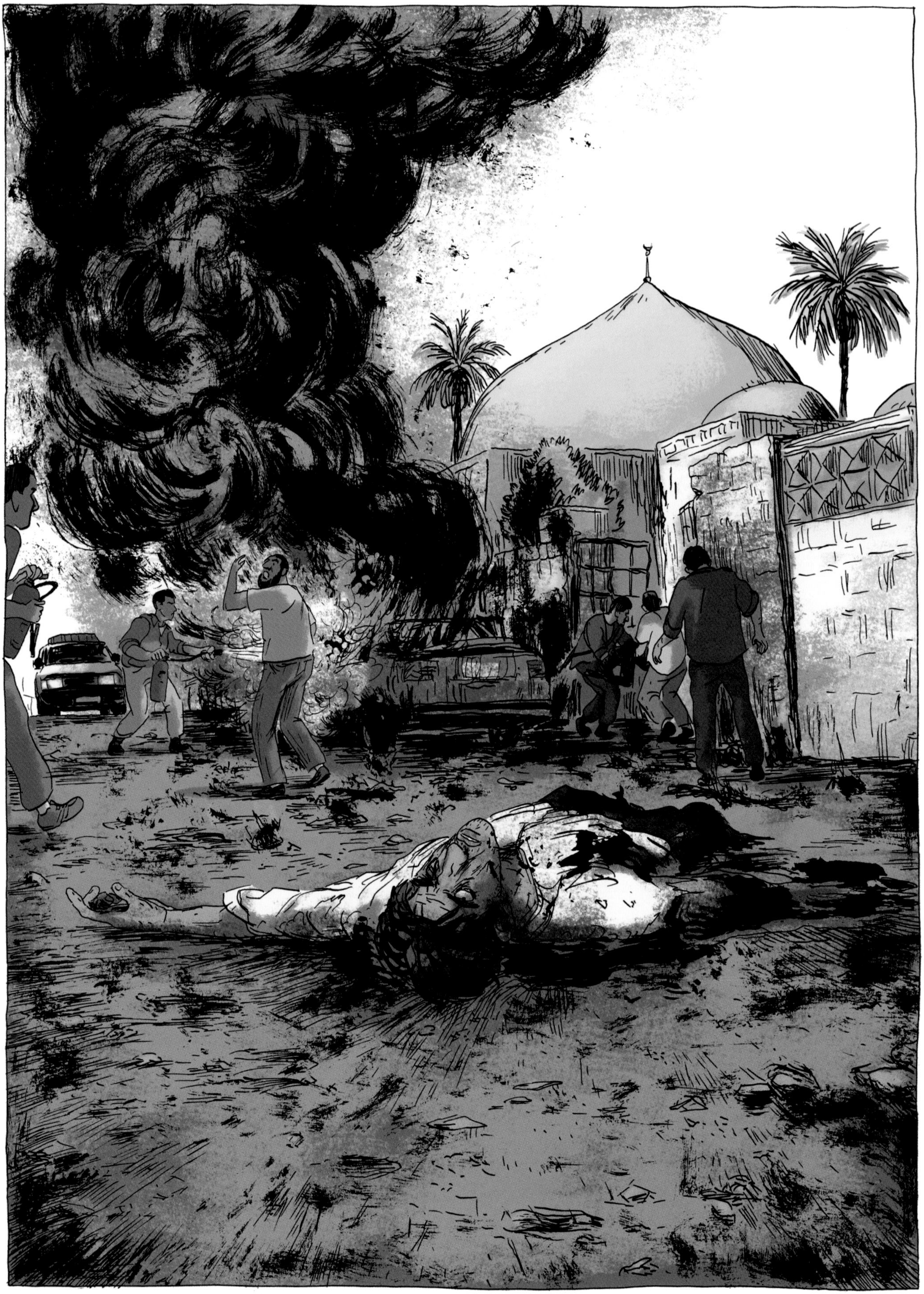